MARY LINCOLN

Mary Lincoln

WIFE AND WIDOW

PART I

BY

Carl Sandburg

PART II

LETTERS, DOCUMENTS & APPENDIX

BY

Paul M. Angle

HARCOURT, BRACE & WORLD, INC.

NEW YORK

Acknowledgments and Sources

Three letters written by Mary Todd before she was married, the earliest known letters written by her, and not hitherto published, are used in this work. These were a loan from Oliver R. Barrett of Chicago. Mrs. Annie Bryan of Peoria, Illinois, gave the use of other letters which help interpret the Mary Todd letters and give sidelights on the relationships of Abraham Lincoln, Mary Todd, and their gossiping friends.

OLIVER R. BARRETT gave the use of many original and unpublished letters, much documentary and pictorial material, besides giving time and keen, helpful criticism. It is many years now since Dr. William E. Barton instigated a search into forgotten corners of the Probate Court files of Cook County. Judge Henry Horner of that court personally conducted this search which brought to light the dusty and never published records of the testimony and the jury verdict regarding the insanity of Mrs. Lincoln. M. Llewellyn Raney, librarian of the University of Chicago, assisted in the delving for material in the late Dr. William E. Barton's Library of Lincolniana, now at the University of Chicago.

ACKNOWLEDGMENTS

Files of Springfield newspapers in the Illinois State Historical Library have been consulted besides files of newspapers and periodicals in Chicago and New York, and numerous scrap-books in various libraries and collections. The letters and manuscripts of Charles Sumner in the Harvard University Library have been consulted. References to Mrs. Lincoln in many Civil War letters and diaries were of service; the diary of Orville Hickman Browning, published by the Illinois State Historical Society, one of the most frequent visitors at the Lincoln home who was socially approved of by Mrs. Lincoln, was of extraordinary value. For one graphic scene in which Mrs. Lincoln violently upbraided her husband in the presence of Richard M. Oglesby the evidence rests on the personal statement of a friend of Oglesby, a responsible Illinois citizen now living; his reminiscences bearing on the Lincoln family are yet to be published. Scores of personality sketches of Mrs. Lincoln in magazine and newspaper articles were scrutinized. A dozen or more books on the wives of presidents or on social life in Washington, were consulted, the most notable of these proving to be Mary Clemmer Ames's "Ten Years in Washington." Other contemporaries of the Lincolns whose writings have strict value though their personal prejudices must be discounted, are Jesse Weik whose book "The Real Lincoln" contained items not used by him and William H. Herndon in their notable biography published some forty years earlier. That picturesque volume "Behind the Scenes" by the mulatto dressmaker, Elizabeth Keckley, who happened to be Mrs. Lincoln's helper and steadfast companion in her darkest hours, is not to be taken lightly as testimony. She sketches herself as well as Mrs. Lincoln in her book, is at moments lackadaisical, and again has the vivid solemnity of the negro spiritual. A chapter in Adam Badeau's "Grant in Peace" coincides in evidence with a personal statement, not as yet published, given by Oswald Garrison Villard based on conversations with his father, Henry Villard, New York *Herald* correspondent at Springfield and during the trip of Lincoln to Washington for inauguration. Among books by writers in our own time Katherine Helm's "Mary, Wife of Lincoln" and William H. Townsend's "Lincoln and His Wife's Home Town" have charm and intimacy, deliver a unique and essential quality of the Blue Grass region of Kentucky. In the writings of Ida M. Tarbell is a human approach that could not be neglected. Dr. William E. Barton's contribution in "The Women Lincoln Loved" represents long pondering over well-ascertained facts and is a living portrait. Julia Taft Bayne when a sixteen-year-old girl had playdays in the White House; her memories, gathered in the little volume "Tad Lincoln's Father," convey living moments from days long passed. The most valuable and extensive discussion and appraisal which has thus far appeared, is "Mrs. Abraham Lincoln" by Dr. William A. Evans, published at the time the manuscript of this volume was being sent to the printers. Dr. Evans is southern born, an Alabama man, whose career as a physician of high repute has lain entirely in the North. Without glossing over Mrs. Lincoln's defects, Dr. Evans assembles the known and the controverted facts, gives his own carefully reasoned conclusions representing keen personality analysis filtered through the wide charity of modern science at its best; fine human values flow from his work.

Contents

ix

Contents

Illustrations

xi

ILLUSTRATIONS

PART I

Prologue

TRAGEDY works in shadows, often dealing with a borderland of dark fate where neither the doctors nor the lawyers can tell just what is happening. Violence, money cares, tongues of malice, minds gone wrong, death on death—this is the stuff of tragedy.

In the year of 1882 there was a woman in Springfield, Illinois, who sat in widow's mourning dress, who sat in a room of shadows where a single candle burned. Outside the sun was shining and spring winds roamed the blue sky. For her that outside world was something else again—it was a world she had turned her back on.

Her habit now was day on day to go to this room of shadows lighted by a single candle. The doctor called it a habit by now; she had done this so often; the shadow room was part of her life. "No urging would induce her to go out into the fresh air," said the doctor.

For her the outside world was a lost world. She had seen enough of it. Her sixty-four years had covered a wide span of turmoil, bloody fighting, wild words, bitter wrangling of brothers. Of four sons born to her three were dead and to the fourth and eldest she had given her scorn, shut the door to him, and then taken him back into her arms. In the house where she sits in candlelight and shadows she had her wedding and put on a gold wedding ring inscribed "Love is eternal." From this town her husband went away—and she with him—through tumult, heavy years, anguish—and in the babel of tongues as to whether she loved her husband and was loyal to him there stood out for her one shining page of the record—where a United States senator from Massachusetts had told his colleagues: "Surely the honorable members of the Senate must be weary of casting mud on the garments of the wife of Lincoln; those same garments on which one terrible night, five years ago, gushed out the blood and brains of Abraham Lincoln. She sat beside him in the theatre, and she received that pitiful, that holy deluge on her hands and skirts, because she was the chosen companion of his heart. She loved him. I speak of that which I know. He had all her love."

The talking about her now had let down somewhat. Yet there was enough of it lingering. She would stay with her candlelight and the shadows. It was her way of adding to her words that she was weary—ready for the silence to which the boys, Taddie and Willie and Eddy, and her husband had gone.

Yet memories would come back. As a girl and a young woman she had said that some day she would be a Great Lady. This wish of her heart she had achieved. She had been the First Lady of the Land.

And yet was she sure of this? Could memory be tricking her about it? Had she really driven in an open carriage behind six milk-white horses while crowds made a pathway and flung roses at her and her husband? Had she led promenades in the White House, attended dinners, balls, cotillions where the Cabinet, members of Congress, and the foreign diplomatic corps paid attention to the wife of the President? Had it actually happened?

No, her memory was not tricking her. She had a store room of evidence, piled high with trunks, boxes, cases. These had been brought in by cart-loads until, said the doctor, "It was really feared that the floor of the store room would give way."

Here was a roomful of apparel: gowns of silk, rich and sweeping crinolines, shawls of rare lace, hats, gloves, shoes, ribbons, personal decorations that had pleased her; each in its time was vouched for as the most modish of the moment.

5

She lifts trunk covers and takes out garments, costly fabrics, handles them, lets her eyes rove over them, gathers the feel of them once more.

Though she now wears widow's mourning garb she had in her day been set in brilliance. Her dress for the 1865 inaugural of her husband brought a bill of $2,000 from a New York merchant. She had been lavish as to gloves, one dealer in Washington sending a bill for 300 pairs which she had purchased across four months. Then there was the tin box of jewels, valued at $5,000 in court proceedings. Her keepsakes of the bygone days were a resource to her now. What was said of these mementoes—that certain of them were stolen— they were saying it in the outside world from which she was now gone. The sun world was no longer hers. She lived in the candlelight and shadow.

Even though it had become an issue in a senatorial committee as to whether she had pilfered traditional belongings of the White House—wasn't that all of the past? Wasn't it over and done with? Was she not ready to move out into the final shadows? Who should care?

It was the closing year, the end of a woman whose life since maturity seldom had a pleasure not mixed with pain and fear. The headaches, the hot tongue lashings, the babblings and accusations—it was good-by to them all and—the summer of that year—good-by, proud world!

"Her memory remained singularly good up to the very close of her life," said the good doctor, Thomas W. Dresser. "She was bright and sparkling in conversation. Her face was animated and pleasing; and to me she was always an interesting woman; and while the whole world was finding fault with her temper and disposition, it was clear to me that the trouble was really a cerebral disease." He performed a post-mortem examination. The evidence was there in his opinion that she was a racked and driven woman—that her sudden tempests and her troublesome vagaries were written in the tissues of the brain early in her life, perhaps before she was born.

So all the babblings about her are only a vain exercise of the tongues of those who misunderstand. One may go to the facts. One may say this or that happened. On such a day she did so and so. The epithets, however, all the names people called her, can be written off, forgotten. They don't count. She lived, suffered, laughed, wept, sat in candlelight and shadows, and passed out from the light of the living sun.

They carried a burial casket out over the threshold her feet touched as a bride—and that was all.

Baby Days

DAVID TODD of Providence Township, Montgomery County, Pennsylvania, was Scotch Irish, of the Covenanters who made bloody war against the Established Church of England, fled to Ireland and emigrated to America.

In 1773 this David Todd sold his land in Pennsylvania for $12,000 and moved to Kentucky so as to be nearer the homes of his three sons.

These three, John, Levi and Robert, after educations at the Virginia school of their uncle, Reverend John Todd, had taken to the Wilderness Road and gone to Kentucky.

Among the first settlers of Lexington, the blue grass town which became a university seat and a center of culture, was Levi Todd. He took a hand in the fighting that was necessary for white people to hold the new country against the red men who once owned it and for long had fought wars among each other for the hunting and fishing rights.

Lieut. Levi Todd marched under General George Rogers Clark in campaigns to hold the West against Indian tribes and British troops. When Daniel Boone gave over command of the Kentucky state militia the office was assumed by Levi Todd ranking as Major-General. His uncle, Reverend John Todd, got from the

Kentucky legislature the charter for Transylvania Seminary, later a university of which General Levi Todd was a trustee. On the Richmond Pike near Lexington and neighbor to Henry Clay's home was the large and elegant country estate of Levi Todd, named "Ellerslie."

The seventh of Levi Todd's eleven children, born in 1791, was Robert Smith Todd, who at fourteen entered Transylvania University, studied mathematics, Latin, astronomy, logic, Greek, history, and according to the university president, James Blythe, "conducted himself in a becoming and praiseworthy manner." Leaving the university he studied law and was admitted to the bar in 1811. The twenty-year-old lawyer didn't begin practice; he held on to his job in the Fayette Circuit Court clerk's office. And he paid attentions to a seventeen-year-old girl, Eliza Parker. She was the daughter of Major Robert Parker, a Revolutionary War officer, and a first cousin of Levi Todd. The Parker home, it was said, was the first brick residence in Lexington. When Eliza's father died in 1800, the *Kentucky Gazette* noted him as "an early adventurer to Kentucky—of extensive acquaintance—and universally esteemed." His will leaving farms, slaves, town lots and personal property to his widow, enjoined, "It is my sincere will and desire that all my children shall be carefully brought up and well educated."

Then came the War of 1812. Robert S. Todd, as captain of a company of raw militiamen, disbanded his men and enlisted with them in the Lexington Light Infantry. Early in the field service Todd went down with pneumonia, was brought back to Lexington, recovered his health, and decided again to go to the fields of battle. Young Eliza Parker was willing he should go. She was also willing to marry him before he should go. On November 26, 1812, they were married. On the next day he kissed her good-by and with a brother rode off to join Kentucky soldiers camped in sleet and snow on the Maumee River. They marched to Fort Defiance through snow drifts and across icy streams. They marched with an expedition against Frenchtown on the River Raisin and in a battle with Proctor and his Indians the rifles and tomahawks of the red men killed half of the boys of the company from Lexington. The *Kentucky Gazette* noted with the news, "Never have the people of this town and its neighborhood met with a stroke so afflicting as that produced by the late battle of Raisin . . . We have all lost a relation or friend." Two of the Todd brothers, Sam and John, were wounded and taken prisoner. John ran the gauntlet and made an escape; Sam was adopted into a tribe and lived with the copper faces for a year, when his liberty was bought for a barrel of whiskey. Robert S. Todd was in the thick of the fighting, came through alive, and before the end of 1813 was at home in Lexington housekeeping with the young cousin he had married.

The couple were opposites in temperament. It was recorded of them, "Eliza was a sprightly, attractive girl, with a placid, sunny disposition, in sharp contrast to her impetuous, high-strung, sensitive cousin, Robert S. Todd."

A properous grocer, a partner in Smith & Todd's "Extensive Grocery Establishment," Clerk of the Kentucky House of Representatives, member of the Fayette County Court, and still later president of the Lexington Branch Bank of Kentucky, also a cotton manufacturer, Robert S. Todd was a solid and leading citizen. The growing family that came was served by negro slaves: Jane Saunders, the housekeeper; Chaney, the cook; Nelson, the body servant and coachman; old "Mammy Sally" and young Judy, who took care of the little ones.

Two daughters, Elizabeth and Frances, were born, then a son, Levi, then on December 13, 1818, Mary Ann Todd. Like the others Mary seemed to be one of the well born. If she was a cripple at birth no one knew it. If in the soft folds and convolutions underneath the bone frames of her head there was a disorder of structure and function marked for pitiless progressions, no one saw it or spoke of it. No one could. She was born as one more beautiful baby in the world, flawless and full of promise.

A baby brother came, died in his second summer. Then a girl who was named Ann Maria and thereafter Mary Ann dropped the Ann from her name, except in signing certain legal documents.

Another baby brother came. And the house was dark. And the one-horse gigs of doctors stood in front of the house. And the children were taken next door to their grandmother.

It was the Fourth of July; artillery cadets firing cannon; church bells ringing; famous generals visiting Henry Clay at a barbecue dinner, toasts to Washington, the Union and "The Ladies of the Western Country— the rose is not less lovely, nor its fragrance less delightful because it blooms in the Wilderness."

And the one-horse gigs of the doctors waited in front of the home of Robert S. Todd. The new child, the baby brother, came. But Eliza Parker Todd didn't live through it. It was the next day that old Nelson, the

15

black slave, hitched up the family carriage and delivered to friends of his master little cards with black borders, "funeral tickets," reading:

"Yourself and family are respectfully invited to attend the funeral of Mrs. Eliza P., Consort of Robert S. Todd, Esq., from his residence on Short Street, this Evening at four o'clock, July 6, 1825."

They buried the thirty-one-year-old wife and mother. And Robert S. Todd's younger sister, Ann Maria, came to help take care of the six children.

Seven months later Robert S. Todd had plans under way to marry Miss Elizabeth ("Betsy") Humphreys. She was the daughter of Dr. Alexander Humphreys of Staunton, Virginia. She had uncles distinguished in medicine and politics, and was herself mentioned as having "charm and culture." She quoted a First Family saying of the time: it takes seven generations to make a Lady. The talk of her possible marriage to Robert S. Todd was unpleasant to Mrs. Robert Parker, mother of Todd's first wife. She and others let it be known they did not approve. And on February 15, 1826, Robert S. Todd wrote to Miss Humphreys, then visiting in New Orleans, a letter which contained viewpoints, and embodied manners of address peculiar to that time.

"You have no doubt observed," he wrote to his intended wife, "with what avidity and eagerness an occasion of this kind is seized hold of for the purpose of detraction and to gratify personal feelings of ill-will and indeed how oftentimes mischief is done without any bad motive. May I be permitted to put you on your guard against persons of this description. Not that I wish to stifle fair enquiry, for I feel in the review of my past life a consciousness that such would not materially affect me in your estimation, although there are many things which I have done and said, I wish had never been done—and such I presume is the case of every one disposed to be honest with himself."

Eight months pass. They are engaged. He salutes her as "Dear Betsy," and is writing to her: "I hope you will not consider me importunate in again urging upon your consideration the subject of my last letter. I am sure if you knew my situation, you would not hesitate to comply with my wishes in fixing on a day for our marriage in this or the early part of the ensuing week."

The wedding came off at the bride's home in Frankfort, Kentucky, on November 1, 1826. The best man was John J. Crittenden, a United States senator.

By this second marriage Robert S. Todd had nine children. The first, a boy, named Robert Smith Todd, died a few days after birth. The others, three boys and five girls, grew into manhood and womanhood. Their father for nearly a quarter of a century was elected Clerk of the House of Representatives, held various public offices, conducted a bank which never failed, and in T. M. Green's volume, "Historic Families of Kentucky," was noted as "not a man of brilliant talents, but one of clear, strong mind, sound judgment, exemplary life and conduct, dignified and manly bearing, an influential and useful citizen."

The Daughter Grows Up

A<small>ND WHAT</small> was the childhood and the growing-up
of Mary Todd—having a father who was a
fighter, an old-school gentleman, a lawyer, a grocer, a
cotton manufacturer, a politician—having a mother
such as Eliza Parker Todd but only till she was eight
years old—having a stepmother in Elizabeth Humphreys Todd who was reported to be in earnest as to
the theory that seven generations are required to make
a Lady?

Certain it is that Mary Todd had the advantages of
the well-to-do class. As a baby there was a large house
with clean floors to crawl on, with wide rooms for
learning to walk. Outside the house was a big yard,
and next door the big yard of her grandmother, Widow
Parker. Grass, bushes, flowers, tall trees, birds, were
theirs for friends, with clean air and sky. Cooking, the
preparation and serving of food, was considered an art
among her people. Physically she had the comforts and
was well nourished. She ran, played tag, climbed trees,
invented mischief and was something of a tomboy, her
playmate sisters said. Once on his return from New
Orleans the father brought Mary and each of her sisters the stuff for new frocks, "lovely, sheer, embroidered pink muslin brought from France." Also for each
one a doll that squeaked when its little stomach was

pushed in. "The squeak sounded like 'Mama' and we hugged our babies," said one of the sisters. There were picnics in summer, barefoot wading in creeks, nutting parties in the fall, sleigh rides in winter, apple roastings at the chimney fireplace, a wide variety of games and sports.

She rode horseback and once raced a white pony of hers up the gravel driveway of Ashland where, it was said, Henry Clay himself came out to see her mount, a new possession. "He can dance—look!" shouted Mary, touching him with the whip—and the white pony went up on his white legs, forepaws curved in the air, with salutations to Henry Clay.

"What do you think about the pony?" she asked him, so the story goes. And he answered like a United States senator, "He seems as spirited as his present diminutive jockey. I am sure nothing in the State can outdistance him."

In their further talk Mary said, according to this tradition in the family, "Mr. Clay, my father says you will be the next President of the United States. I wish I could go to Washington and live in the White House." And Clay gave her the laughing promise, "If I am ever President I shall expect Mary Todd to be one of my first guests."

22

She early absorbed politics, it was said. While in short dresses with ribbons fluttering from her curly head she was allowed to come into the dining-room for dessert at her father's table, where she heard politicians of state and national reputation talk of the battles between Whigs and Democrats. "At fourteen she knew why she was a Whig and not a Democrat," it was said.

When she was ten years old General Andrew Jackson came to Lexington and troops, brass bands, horsemen, societies, gave him a grand turnout. Mary was for her Whig friend, Henry Clay, and told a Democrat she couldn't cheer for Jackson. "But," she added, having looked at Jackson, "he is not as ugly as I heard he was."

In the course of her quarrel with the Democrat, he said, "Andrew Jackson with his long face is better looking than Henry Clay and your father rolled into one." Mary declared, "We are going to snow General Jackson under and freeze his long face so that he will never smile again." After their words that day Mary and the Democrat didn't speak to each other for years. Thus her sister Emilie told it.

Until she was fourteen her schooling was in Dr. John Ward's Academy. He was strict with his pupils.

Recitations were held before breakfast. Classes assembled at five o'clock in the morning. In the winter Mary and her sister Elizabeth often walked in the dark before dawn several blocks to their school to recite their lessons, studied by candlelight the night before.

Of course, there were other lessons besides those at school. One spring morning Mary and Elizabeth ran out to the garden to have a look at a young wild turkey they heard cooing, "Peep! Peep!" The bird sound came from a thicket of honeysuckle vines over a summer house. It changed to a jay bird's rough call. And suddenly a mocking bird flew out. "The little rascal," said Elizabeth, "never tired of pretending to be some other creature, now a field lark, now a cardinal, now the gentle peep of a little turkey. We had hunted half an hour for that little turkey." Still another lesson, outside of school, came on the night a crowd of friends gathered to see the budding of a night-blooming cereus, supposed to bloom only once in a hundred years. It was a special occasion; the children were allowed to be up till midnight watching the slowly opening white petals of a strange flower.

She memorized classical poetry and recited it on so many occasions that friends joked her about it. She learned to sew, was the only one of the sisters who developed skill with the needle. So the sisters acknowledged.

She lived through the year cholera came; the house was heavy with smoke of burning tar; no fruits or vegetables could be eaten, only biscuits, eggs, boiled milk and boiled water. Coffin supplies ran out and Robert S. Todd had trunks and boxes hauled from the attic of his house for the dead.

And, of course, there were lessons in kindliness, humor, folk lore, from the negro slave, old Mammy Sally. She had imagination in telling of hell and the devil. The girls, listening, stopped their ears with their fingers. "We shivered," said Elizabeth. And once Mary's mischievous sense of humor rose and she asked about Satan's horns.

"Yes, honey," replied Mammy Sally, "ole man Satan bellers and shakes his head and sharpens up his horns on the ground, and paws up the dust with both his front feet at once." Mary inquired, "But what does he stand on when he is pawing with both feet? Has he four legs?" "No, honey, but he can stand on his tail and that makes him mo' fearsome like."

And Mary would argue that the devil's tail was black while Mammy insisted there was a Bible verse which settled the truth of the matter. "Neat but not gaudy

25

as the debil said when he painted his tail pea green."

She gave them her lore, did Mammy. She told them that the jay birds go to hell every Friday night and tell the devil all wrongdoings they have seen the week just passed. Elizabeth said Mary once sprang at a jay and chanted:

"Howdy, Mr. Jay. You are a tell-tale-tell.
You play the spy each day, then carry tales to hell."

From the windows of the Todd house on Main Street could be seen gangs of marching men, women and children—the black people—the slaves—handcuffed two by two—held by long chains that ran from the lead couple to the end—shambling on to the market, the auction block. The slave traders drove their human livestock by this route—marching them toward cotton and rice fields farther south.

Downtown at a public square, in the southwest corner, was an auction block where the children of Lexington saw men, women and children, sometimes a family, put up for sale to the highest bidder. In the opposite corner of the public square was a whipping post, a black locust log ten feet high and a foot thick, where negroes found guilty of violation of the white man's law, were flogged. One visitor wrote, "I saw this punishment inflicted on two of these wretches. Their screams soon collected a numerous crowd."

Mary's father was one of the twelve men called as a jury "to inquire into the state of mind of Caroline A. Turner," a woman of strong muscle and fierce temper, who had thrown a small negro boy from a second-story window onto a stone flagging below, bruising the backbone and crippling an arm and a leg for life. Another case much discussed in the Todd neighborhood was that of Mr. and Mrs. Maxwell, charged with "atrocious brutality" to a young female slave. Witnesses testified that Mrs. Maxwell and her son had beaten this barefooted, thinly-clad girl with a cowhide whip, lacerating the back, bruising the face, leaving scars on the nose and cheeks. Doctors found scars indicating she had been seared with a red-hot iron.

An emancipation society was formed in Lexington. A bill came before the legislature in 1828 aimed to stop importation of slaves into Kentucky. Among spokesmen for this bill were Robert J. Breckinridge and Cassius M. Clay, both personal and political friends of Robert S. Todd. Leading the opposition was Robert Wickliffe, father of two girlhood chums of Mary Todd. So it is clear that the slavery question as a human cause and a political issue was vividly alive and tangled for

Mary as she was a growing child and young woman.

One quiet night a knocking, knocking, went on somewhere outside the house. Mary was reading. The knocking kept on. She could not read while that knocking kept on. She cried out, "Mammy, what is that knocking?" The answer came in a whisper, "That might be a runaway nigger. We have a mark on the fence—I made it myself—to show that if any runaway is hungry he can get vittles right here. All of 'em knows the sign. I have fed many a one." It was a secret Mammy tried to keep—that any negro fugitive could have cornbread and bacon from her hands.

Over at Frankfort, twenty-eight miles away, was their grandmother, Mary Humphreys, owner of eight slaves. When she died her will gave freedom to all these slaves. One clause read:

"10th. I devise my negro girl, Jane, to my daughter, Elizabeth Todd, until the twenty-fifth day of December, Eighteen Hundred and Fourty-two, on which said date the said Jane is to be free of all kinds of servitude and should the said Jane have any children before the day on which she is to be free, the said child or children if boys are hereby devised to the said Elizabeth Todd until they respectively attain the age of twenty-eight years, whereby they are to be free and emancipate from all manner of servitude, if girls they are hereby devised to the said Elizabeth L. Todd until they respectively attain the age of twenty-one years, when they and any increase they may have are to be free and emancipate from all manner of servitude."

She was a decisive character, this Mary Humphreys, whom Mary Todd heard much of, and visited a number of times. She read Voltaire and Volney. She took Mary and Elizabeth to a ball in Frankfort. And they witnessed their grandmother at the age of seventy-three, in a satin gown and a lace cap imported from France, lead the grand march. She had exquisitry, for a venerable woman. The girl, Mary Todd, once remarked to a sister, "If I can only be, when I am grown up, just like Grandmother Humphreys, I will be perfectly satisfied with myself."

At fourteen Mary Todd entered the boarding-school of Madame Victorie Charlotte LeClere Mentelle. The madame was a scholar, musician, dancer. Her husband, Monsieur Augustus Waldemare Mentelle, had been "Histographer" to the French king whose head was lost in the Revolution which had made the Mentelles fugitives from the Paris where they were born. Their school was advertised in the Lexington *Intelligencer:* "Mrs. Mentelle wants a few more Young Ladies as

Scholars. She has hitherto endeavored to give them a truly useful & 'Solid' English Education in all its branches. French taught if desired. Boarding, Washing & Tuition $120 per year, paid quarterly in advance. 1½ miles from Lexington on the Richmond Turnpike road."

At this place Mary Todd had four years' training. It was her home except when on Friday evening Nelson, the coachman, called for her and took her to her father's house in Lexington where she stayed till early Monday morning. She made French a special study and gave her sisters the impression that was the only language Madame Mentelle permitted on the school premises. At sixteen Mary took the leading rôle in a French play. "She was the star actress of the school," noted a sister.

The Mentelle school was entirely aristocratic in tone. The atmosphere sought by Madame and Monsieur Mentelle was that of the royal court of France where they had once had entrée and office. They lived on memories of King Louis XVI and Queen Marie Antoinette. They spoke of these two "martyrs" with tears. The American democracy meant nothing in particular to them except that it gave them refuge and a home.

They taught class, breeding, manners, from the feudal European viewpoint rather than the Jeffersonian. The purpose was to bring up ladies of charm, culture, accomplishments.

Madame Mentelle admitted she "spared no pains with the graces and manners of the young Ladies submitted to her care." The dances taught were "the latest and most fashionable Cotillions, Round & Hop Waltzes, Hornpipes, Galopades, Mohawks, Spanish, Scottish, Polish, Tyrolienne dances and the Beautiful Circassian Circle."

Mary Todd had a good time at the Mentelle school, happy days, even though much of what she practiced at learning was a useless preparation for the years to come.

"She was a merry, companionable girl with a smile for everybody," said one fellow student at the Mentelle school. "She was really the life of the school, always ready for a good time." Besides, "she was one of the brightest girls in the school, always had the highest marks and took the biggest prizes." Thus the recollection of a Louisville woman many years after.

And Mary Todd had a good time in Lexington after she left the Mentelle school. There were homes in which girls gathered, played the piano, sang songs, and learned to waltz if their parents were Episcopalians like the Todds and if they could find young men to teach them. There were lectures on week nights, and twice on Sunday services at the churches, where every one who was any one went in what the Mentelle girls called one "grande toilette." There was a public ball when the legislature came from Frankfort in a body. And there were always parties, gala occasions when supper was served at midnight and when dawn broke before heavy-eyed coachmen handed the ladies into their carriages.

Life to Mary Todd was fresh, brimming with excitement. One of her most intimate friends, Margaret Stuart Woodrow, pictured her as abundantly alive, vibrant to sensations. They rode horseback together many a time, balanced on side-saddles, wearing long plumed hats and long skirts. Said Mrs. Woodrow: "She was very highly strung, nervous, impulsive, excitable, having an emotional temperament much like an April day, sunning all over with laughter one moment, the next crying as though her heart would break."

And her sister, Elizabeth, telling of Mary and the impressions men made on her in these early Lexington days, wrote: "Among them were many scholarly, intellectual men; but Mary never at any time showed the least partiality for any one of them. Indeed, at times, her face indicated a decided lack of interest and she accepted their attention without enthusiasm. Without meaning to wound, she now and then could not restrain a witty, sarcastic speech that cut deeper than she intended, for there was no malice in her heart. She was impulsive and made no attempt to conceal her feeling; indeed, that would have been impossible, for her face was an index to every passing emotion."

William H. Townsend, a Lexington man who sought for all existing records and interviews that would testify regarding the Mary Todd who grew up in Lexington, wrote the impression: "Brilliant, vivacious, impulsive, she possessed a charming personality marred only by a transient hauteur of manner and a caustic, devastating wit that cut like the sting of a hornet."

Winding Paths to Marriage

ONE OF THE EARLIEST KNOWN PHOTOGRAPHS
OF ABRAHAM LINCOLN

(Original in the Library of Congress)

"SHE IS THE VERY CREATURE OF EXCITEMENT,"
WROTE JAMES CONKLING TO MERCY LEVERING
OF THEIR GIRL FRIEND, MARY TODD, IN 1840

Unique proof from an unfinished engraving
(In the collection of Oliver R. Barrett)

Young women ready to consider marriage are not so common in a pioneer region. They are usually taken for better or worse early after arrival. And in the period in which Mary Todd came to southern Illinois, a former Kentuckian, John J. Hardin, who later defeated an important rival in a campaign for Congress, told of the scarcity of young women in an odd paragraph of a letter to a friend back in Kentucky. Hardin wrote, "Concerning the great and important matter of girls, it is not in my power to boast much. We have some sprightly ladies in town though they are few and indeed when this state is compared with yours in that respect it falls short indeed. I think it would improve if it were not for one reason, the girls get married so soon there is no time for improvement. Enterprising young men are numerous and when they have entered their land they want wives and will have them. It has occurred to me that a considerable speculation might be made by a qualified person who would bring out a cargo of the ladies. You recollect in the first settlement of Virginia a cargo of that description was brought in and sold for 150 pounds of tobacco per head. If they should be landed here shortly they might command in market at least several head of cattle apiece. Besides it would be a very great accommodation to many young ladies of my acquaintance who have been a long time trying to make an equal swap but as yet have not succeeded."

Up into this region to Springfield had come three Todd sisters. Elizabeth at fourteen was engaged to Ninian W. Edwards and at sixteen married him. Frances in 1839 had married William Wallace, a practicing physician, who kept a drug store in Springfield. And it may be that Mary Todd felt she might come across luck—or fate—where her sisters had.

When Mary Todd, twenty-one years old, came in 1839 to live with her sister, Mrs. Ninian W. Edwards [Elizabeth Todd], she was counted an addition to the social flourish of the town. They spoke in those days of "belles." And Mary was one. Her sister told how she looked. "Mary had clear blue eyes, long lashes, light brown hair with a glint of bronze, and a lovely complexion. Her figure was beautiful and no Old Master ever modeled a more perfect arm and hand." Whatever of excess there may be in this sisterly sketch it seems certain that Mary Todd had gifts, attractions, and was among those always invited to the dances and parties of the dominant social circle. Her sister's husband once remarked as to her style, audacity or wit, "Mary could make a bishop forget his prayers."

A niece of Mary Todd wrote her impression of how her aunt looked at twenty-two in the year 1840, when her eyes first lighted on Abraham Lincoln. As an impression it has its value, serving as the viewpoint and testimony of some of those who found adorable phases in Mary Todd. In this presentation she is a rare and cherished personage with "faint wild rose in her cheeks," tintings that came and went in the flow of her emotions. "Mary although not strictly beautiful, was more than pretty. She had a broad white forehead, eyebrows sharply but delicately marked, a straight nose, short upper lip and expressive mouth curling into an adorable slow coming smile that brought dimples into her cheeks and glinted in her long-lashed, blue eyes. Those eyes, shaded by their long, silky fringe, gave an impression of dewy violet shyness contradicted fascinatingly by the spirited carriage of her head. She was vital, brilliant, witty and well trained in all the social graces from earliest childhood. She could now without rebuke, wear the coveted hoop skirts of her childish desire, and with skirts frosted with lace and ruffles she ballooned and curtsied in the lovely French embroidered swisses and muslins brought up to her from New Orleans by her father. In stockings and slippers to match the color of her gown, all pink and white, she danced and swayed as lightly and gayly as a branch of fragrant apple blossoms in a gentle spring breeze. From her pink dimpled cheeks to her sophisticated pink satin slippers, she was a fascinating alluring creature." Such, in one viewpoint, was the woman Lincoln gathered in his arms some time in 1840 when they spoke pledges to marry and take each other for weal or woe through life.

For two years Mary Todd haunted Lincoln, racked him, drove him to despair and philosophy, sent him searching deep into himself as to what manner of man he was. In those two years he first became acquainted with a malady of melancholy designated as hypochondriasis, or "hypo," an affliction which so depressed him that he consulted physicians. What happened in those two years?

Some time in 1840, probably toward the end of the year, Lincoln promised to marry Miss Todd and she was pledged to take him. It was a betrothal. They were engaged to stand up and take vows at a wedding. She was to be a bride; he was to be a groom. It was explicit.

Whether a wedding date was fixed, either definitely or approximately, does not appear in Mary Todd's letter to Mercy Levering in December of 1840. Whether in that month they were engaged at all or not also fails

to appear. In this letter, however, we learn of Mary
Todd, her moods and ways, at that time. She writes
from Springfield, giving the news to her friend, mentioning Harriet Campbell who "appears to be enjoying
all the sweets of married life." She refers to another
acquaintance as ready to perpetrate "the crime of matrimony." This is light humor, banter, for the surmise
is offered, "I think she will be much happier."

Certain newly married couples, she observes, have
lost their "silver tones."

She raises the question, "Why is it that married folks
always become so serious?"

She is puzzled, perplexed, about marriage; it is one
of life's gambles; there seem to be winners and losers.
Her moods shift. Her head is full of many events and
people that may affect her fate. She sees time plowing
on working changes. She reports what the marching
months have done to a prairie stream. "The icy hand
of winter has set its seal upon the waters, the winds of
Heaven visit the spot but roughly, the same stars shine
down, yet not with the same liquid, mellow light as in
the olden time, some forms and memories that enhanced the place have passed by."

Reading along in this December letter of Mary Todd
one may gather an impressionistic portrait of her, a

ATTENTION!
THE
PEOPLE!!

A. LINCOLN, ESQ'R.,

OF *Sangamon County*, **one of the** *Electoral Candidates*, **will ADDRESS the PEOPLE**

This Evening !!

At Early Candlelighting, at the OLD COURT ROOM, (Riley's Building.)
By request of
MANY CITIZENS.

Thursday, April 9th, 1840.

HANDBILL ADVERTISING THE RISING YOUNG POLITICIAN, A. LINCOLN, AS YET UNMARRIED, TO SPEAK AT "EARLY CANDLELIGHTING"

little mezzotint. She can speak with grace. "Pass my imperfections lightly as usual," she writes Mercy. "I throw myself on your amiable nature, knowing that my shortcomings will be forgiven." She is aware of her tendency to be chubby. "I still am the same ruddy *pine-knot,* only not quite so great an exuberance of flesh, as it once was my lot to contend with, although quite a sufficiency."

Mary Todd made a little forecast in this letter. "We expect a very gay winter," she wrote. "Evening before last my sister gave a most agreeable party; upwards of one hundred graced the festive scene." Matilda Edwards, a cousin of Ninian Edwards, had come on from Alton. The party was for her. "A lovelier girl I never saw," writes Mary Todd.

It wasn't so gay a winter, however, either for one or the other of the engaged couple. Lincoln was uneasy, worried. Months of campaigning, traveling in bad weather, eating poorly cooked food and sleeping in rough taverns had made his nerves jumpy. He saw reasons why marriage would not be good for him or for Mary Todd. He wrote a letter to her, begging off. Then he showed the letter to Speed, whose reputation was lively for falling in love and falling out again. Speed threw the letter into the fire, saying in effect that

43

such feelings of the heart shouldn't be put onto paper and made a record that could be brought up later. It was New Year's Day, 1841. Lincoln went to the Edwards house and came back to Speed. He explained that he had told Mary all that was in the letter. And Mary broke into tears, Lincoln took her into his arms, kissed her, and the engagement was on again.

But Lincoln was wretched. He had yielded to tears, had sacrificed a reasoned resolve because he couldn't resist the appeal of a woman's grief. Mary Todd saw his condition, saw that he was not himself, saw further that anything between them was impossible until he should recover. And so, regretfully but without bitterness, she released him from the engagement.

Over Springfield in the circles of these two principal persons the word spread that Mary Todd had jilted Lincoln. After leading him on, encouraging him, she suddenly had decided it was not for the best. So there would be no wedding. And both were content to let the bald fact stand without explanation.

Then Lincoln broke down completely. Two weeks after the night he had tried to tell Mary Todd how he felt and had failed, he took to his bed, miserably sick. Only Speed and Doctor Henry saw him. Six days later he was up and around, due, it was said, to the strong brandy which the doctor had prescribed in large quantities. But he was not the old-time Lincoln. How he looked to others was told by James C. Conkling in a letter to his fiancée, Mercy Levering, Mary Todd's close friend. "Poor Lincoln! How are the mighty fallen!" wrote Conkling. "He was confined about a week but though he now appears again he is reduced and emaciated in appearance and seems scarcely to possess strength enough to speak above a whisper. His case is at present truly deplorable but what prospect there may be for ultimate relief I cannot pretend to say." No keen or quick sympathy for Lincoln stands forth from Conkling's letter. He writes as though he and others of a limited circle were watching a man recovering from punishment received in the tangles of an ancient trap, suffering of a sort all men and women must know in the pilgrimage of life. As one of Bobby Burns's poems declares none has the right to expect sympathy for toothache, thus also there is a sort of unwritten law that those smitten with love, and rejected by the ones loved, must expect kindly laughter rather than tears from their friends. Howsoever that may be we have Conkling's letter saying of Lincoln, "I doubt not but he can declare 'That loving is a painful thrill. And not to love more painful still,' but would not like

45

to intimate that he has experienced 'That surely 'tis the worst of pain To love and not be loved again.' "

Lincoln wrote two letters to his law partner, Congressman John T. Stuart at Washington, D. C. In one letter he notes, "I have within the last few days, been making a most discreditable exhibition of myself in the way of hypochondriasm." In the second letter: "I am now the most miserable man living. If what I feel were equally distributed to the whole human family, there would not be one cheerful face on the earth. Whether I shall ever be better I cannot tell; I awfully forbode I shall not. To remain as I am is impossible; I must die or be better, it appears to me."

His doctor, A. G. Henry, advised a change of scene, a complete break from his present surroundings. He would go to Bogota, Columbia, if Stuart could get him the consulate at that South American port. He wrote, referring to the effort Stuart was making to have him appointed consul, "The matter you spoke of on my account you may attend to as you say, unless you shall hear of my condition forbidding it. I say this because I fear I shall be unable to attend to any business here, and a change of scene might help me. If I could be myself, I would rather remain at home with Judge Logan. I can write no more."

Stuart failed to land the consulate. And Lincoln never saw the shores of South America.

In weeks and months that followed, the limited circle of insiders who believed they knew "what was going on," whispered, spoke and wrote to each other about Lincoln's being jilted by Mary Todd. "Poor A—," wrote Mercy Levering in February. "I fear his is a blighted heart! perhaps if he was as persevering as Mr. W— he might be finally successful." And Conkling replied, "And L. poor hapless swain who loved most true but was not loved again—I suppose he will now endeavor to drown his cares among the intricacies and perplexities of the law."

The memory of Lincoln, the story teller, the gay one, remained fresh, and Conkling recalled it. "No more will the merry peal of laughter ascend *high in the air,* to greet his listening and delighted ears. He used to remind me sometimes of the pictures I formerly saw of old Father Jupiter, bending down from the clouds, to see what was going on below. And as an agreeable smile of satisfaction graced the countenance of the old heathen god, as he perceived the incense rising up—so the face of L. was occasionally distorted into a grin as he succeeded in eliciting applause from some of the fair votaries by whom he was surrounded.

47

But alas! I fear his shrine will now be deserted and that he will withdraw himself from the society of us inferior mortals."

Mary Todd meantime moved gayly and serenely through the little social whirl of Springfield. "Miss Todd and her cousin, Miss Edwards," Conkling wrote to Mercy Levering, "seemed to form the grand centre of attraction. Swarms of strangers who had little else to engage their attention hovered around them, to catch a passing smile." And with what he meant to be humor of some sort Conkling added, "By the way, I do not think they were received, with even ordinary attention, if they did not obtain a broad grin or an obstreperous laugh."

A letter of Mary's written to Mercy Levering in June of the summer of 1841 shows that her heart was not so gay after all. And furthermore, she didn't believe that everything was over and the past all sealed so far as she and Lincoln were concerned.

"The last three months have been of *interminable* length," she confesses. "After my gay companions of last winter departed, I was left much to the solitude of my own thoughts, and some *lingering regrets* over the past, which time can alone overshadow with its healing balm. Thus has my *spring time* passed. Summer in all its beauty has come again. The prairie land looks as beautiful as it did in the olden time, when we strolled together and derived so much of happiness from each other's society—this is past and more than this."

Meantime also rumors traveled that Mary Todd was seriously interested in Edwin B. Webb, a widower. Mary assures her friend Mercy these rumors are mistaken. She writes in this June letter that many visitors are in Springfield for the court sessions. "But in their midst the *winning widower* is not. Rumor says he with some others will attend the supreme court next month."

Mercy Levering in her last letter to Mary Todd had intimated that Mary and the widower were "dearer to each other than friends." Now Mary proceeds to put herself on record as to this. "The idea was neither new nor strange, dear Merce. The knowing world, have coupled our names for months past, merely through the folly and belief of another, who strangely imagined we were attached to each other. In your friendly and confiding ear allow me to whisper that my *heart can never be his*. I have deeply regretted that his constant visits, attention &c should have given room for remarks, which were to me unpleasant. There being a slight difference of some eighteen or twenty summers in our years, would preclude all possibility of congeneality of feeling, without which I would never feel justifiable in resigning my happiness into the safe keeping of another, even should that other be, far too worthy for me, with his two *sweet little objections.*"

Was she at this time keeping Lincoln in mind and heart for marriage? We can only guess and surmise. It is reasonably certain that Lincoln used with Mary Todd the same words, the same point, he made with Mary Owens three years previous when he wrote Miss Owens to whom he was sort of tentatively engaged. "There is a great deal of flourishing about in carriages here, which it would be your doom to see without sharing it. You would have to be poor, without the means of hiding your poverty. Do you believe you can bear that patiently?"

Lincoln took marriage as a bargain between two persons and he wished the terms of the bargain to be crystal clear, if possible. With Mary Owens, before they went their separate ways, he had been crystal clear. And he probably spoke to Mary Todd the same sort of words he put on paper for Mary Owens. Not often does the pre-nuptial writer of love letters make himself quite so lucid as did Lincoln in writing Mary Owens: "Whatever woman may cast her lot with mine, should any ever do so, it is my intention to do all in my power

to make her happy and contented; and there is nothing
I can imagine that would make me more unhappy
than to fail in the effort. I know I should be much
happier with you than the way I am, provided I saw
no signs of discontent in you. What you have said to
me may have been in the way of jest, or I may have
misunderstood it. If so, then let it be forgotten; if
otherwise, I much wish you would think seriously before you decide. What I have said I will most positively
abide by, provided you wish it. My opinion is that you
had better not do it."

On this presentation Mary Owens had released him.
Perhaps on the same sort of presentation on "the fatal
first of January" Mary Todd had on second thought
released him.

Was it possible also that Lincoln knew well it was
true, as others said, and as he himself said, that he was
no ladies' man, that he was, as Mary Owens declared
"deficient in the little links that make for woman's
happiness"? Would that explain why his words to
Mary Owens in a letter, seemed rather to smack of
justice than of passion and affection? Perhaps Lincoln
knew that love which has not yet been tested by the
stress and storm of life is a bewildering and tangled
mesh to those who have their feet in it. Perhaps he

was uncannily aware of, and did not care to join in with, the flaming folly of those lovers who out of wild embraces cry, "Love like ours can never die!" Perhaps he was suspicious that the fiercest loves soon burn out; he would rather have plain affection than consuming passion. Possibly he saw eye to eye with Henrik Ibsen declaring, "There is no word that has been soiled with lies like that word love."

Something like this was in his heart and head when he wrote Mary Owens words of a sort that he may have repeated to Mary Todd. "You must know that I cannot see you or think of you with entire indifference; and yet it may be that you are mistaken in regard to what my real feelings toward you are. If I knew you were not, I should not trouble you with this letter. Perhaps any other man would know enough without further information; but I consider it my peculiar right to plead ignorance, and your bounden duty to allow the plea. I want in all cases to do right, and most particularly so in all cases with women. I want at this particular time, more than anything else, to do right with you; and if I knew it would be doing right, as I rather suspect it would, to let you alone, I would do it."

Something like this, in viewpoint and theory as to relationships between man and woman before mar-

A LETTER FROM MARY TODD TO MERCY LEVERING IN 1841 BEFORE "TIME HAS WROUGHT ITS CHANGES." IN AN ECONOMICAL POSTSCRIPT SHE WRITES OF HER REFUSAL TO ACCOMPANY A FRIEND ON HER BRIDAL TOUR "AS FAR AS PEORIA"

MARY LINCOLN
GOWNED IN A DOLLY
VARDEN PATTERN
OF THE
VICTORIAN PERIOD

riage, may have been in his heart and head when he spoke with Mary Todd. Farther back would be viewpoints of life and the laughing philosopher's contemplations involved in Lincoln's Rabelaisian letter to Mrs. Orville H. Browning on how and why Mary Owens released him from their tentative engagement.

And now though Mary Todd had sent him a letter releasing him from their engagement, Mary in her June letter of 1841 to Mercy Levering is referring to Joshua Speed, Lincoln's friend and roommate. She has had a letter from Speed who is visiting his old home in Kentucky. Speed brings to mind Lincoln and she writes of him. *"His* worthy friend [Lincoln], deems me unworthy of notice, as I have not met *him* in the gay world for months. With the usual comfort of misery, [I] imagine that others were as seldom gladdened by his presence as my humble self, yet I would that the case were different, that he would once more resume his station in Society, that 'Richard should be himself again.' Much, much happiness would it afford me."

The implication was there in her letter that time would bring her and Lincoln together again. Though she had been in the social whirl, danced with other men, had her name linked with suitors for marriage, Lincoln was talked of as solitary. Her hope was, so she wrote Mercy Levering, that "Richard should be himself again," that Lincoln would recover from the bad health, the nervous exhaustion, which marked him in the winter of 1840.

Now that his roommate, Speed, had gone to Kentucky, Lincoln began rooming at the house where he had boarded, taking his meals, since coming to Springfield. There also had lived Sarah Rickard, dark-haired and seventeen, disconsolate at the departure of Speed of the "ever-changing heart." Lincoln and Sarah went places together. They saw a melodrama, "Babes in the Wood," wherein the babes died in the forest and little birds came and covered them over with leaves. Once Lincoln joked of marriage. There was Biblical precedent for a union between Sarah and Abraham, he said with raillery in his voice and eyes. Sarah moved into the country, and there, at intervals, Lincoln visited her, reporting the state of her feelings to his friend in Kentucky. Under his ministrations the girl forgot the hurt that had been in her heart since Speed had gone, so that Lincoln wrote to him: "One thing I can tell you which I know you will be glad to hear, and that is that I have seen Sarah and scrutinized her feelings as well as I could, and am fully convinced she is far happier now than she has been for the last fifteen months past."

And of these things biographers, innocently misled by the mysterious deletion of a name in letters and by statements not quite frank from elderly men and women, have made a tale of Lincoln and a love he never felt.[1]

Early in 1841 Speed sold his store in Springfield and went to Kentucky. In August Lincoln went to visit him, to rest for weeks in the big Speed home near Louisville. There he met Fanny Henning, the young woman Speed was planning to marry. The wedding date was set. Lincoln went back to Springfield but for months he and Speed were haunted by the approaching wedding. Speed was as shaken and worried about it as Lincoln had been about his affair with Mary Todd. Speed returned to Springfield for a long visit but on leaving for Kentucky again Lincoln handed him a letter to read on the stage to St. Louis and the steamboat for Louisville. The letter was an argument fortifying Speed and giving him reasons and courage for going through with his wedding as planned. "I know what the painful point is with you at all times when you are unhappy: it is an apprehension that you do not love her as you should. What nonsense!"

[1] A more detailed presentation of the Sarah Rickard episode is on page 344.

Speed reached home, found his intended bride sick, the doctors worried. He wrote Lincoln he was in the depths of misery. Lincoln replied, "Why, Speed, if you did not love her, although you might not wish her death, you would most certainly be resigned to it." He asked pardon if he was getting too familiar. "You know the hell I have suffered on that point, and how tender I am upon it."

Speed married Fanny Henning in February of 1842, and Lincoln's letter of congratulation declared, "I tell you, Speed, our forebodings (for which you and I are peculiar) are all the worst sort of nonsense." Speed had written that something indescribably horrible and alarming still haunted him. He implied marriage was no good to him. Lincoln predicted, "You will not say *that* three months from now, I will venture. When your nerves get steady now, the whole trouble will be over forever. Nor should you become impatient at their being very slow in becoming steady." Thus the recovering victim of "nerves" assured one struggling.

Also in this advice to Speed, Lincoln includes a little argument that both he and Speed had been dreaming fool dreams about marriage bringing an impossible paradise. They had overrated the benefits and romance of matrimony. "You say you much fear that the

Elysium of which you and I dreamed so much is never to be realized. Well, if it shall not, I dare swear it will not be the fault of her who is now your wife. I now have no doubt, that it is the peculiar misfortune of both you and me to dream dreams of Elysium far exceeding all that anything earthly can realize."

When, a month later, Speed wrote that he was happy and Lincoln's predictions had come true, Lincoln replied, "Your last letter gave me more pleasure than the sum total of all I have enjoyed since that fatal first of January, 1841." Again he refers to Mary Todd. She still haunts him. "Since then it seems to me that I should have been entirely happy, but for the never absent idea that there is *one* still unhappy whom I have contributed to make so. That still kills my soul. I cannot but reproach myself for even wishing to be happy while she is otherwise. She accompanied a large party on the railroad cars to Jacksonville last Monday, and on her return spoke, so that I heard of it, of having enjoyed the trip exceedingly. God be praised for that!"

Speed now sent a warning that Lincoln must either soon make up his mind to marry Miss Todd or put her out of his thoughts completely, forget her. This was correct advice, Lincoln wrote back. "But, before I resolve to do one thing or the other, I must gain my confidence in my own ability to keep my resolves when they are made. In that ability, you know I once prided myself, as the only or chief gem of my character; that gem I lost, how and where you know too well. I have not yet regained it; and, until I do, I cannot trust myself in any matter of much importance."

Perhaps Lincoln used some of these very words to Mary Todd when later in 1842 they were brought together at the home of Mrs. Simeon Francis, wife of Lincoln's friend, the editor of the Sangamo *Journal*. Neither Lincoln nor Mary Todd knew beforehand they were to be brought face to face by Mrs. Francis, so it was said. It was a pleasant surprise. The first meeting was followed by many others. Among the very few who knew of these meetings was Julia Jayne, a close friend of Mary Todd. With these two young women Lincoln joined in the fall of 1842 in writing pieces for the Sangamo *Journal* satirizing James Shields, state auditor, who challenged Lincoln to a duel which at the finish dissolved into apologies that meant nothing in particular. Yet it was an adventure with fresh excitements daily; it drew the couple closer.

Early in October Lincoln wrote Speed he knew well that Speed was happier than when first married. He could see in Speed's letters "the returning elasticity of spirits" resulting from marriage. "But," he wrote, "I want to ask you a close question. 'Are you now in *feeling*, as well as *judgment*, glad you are married as

---

MARRIAGES.

Abraham Lincoln and Mary Todd, married, November 4. 1842—

Robert Todd Lincoln and Mary Harlan, married September 24th 1868.

PAGE HEADED "FAMILY RECORD" IN THE LINCOLN FAMILY BIBLE. THE FIRST ENTRY IS IN THE HANDWRITING OF ABRAHAM LINCOLN; THE SECOND IN THAT OF ROBERT TODD LINCOLN

you are?' From anybody but me this would be an impudent question, not to be tolerated; but I know you will pardon it in me. Please answer it quickly, as I am impatient to know."

Speed's answer to Lincoln, it seemed, was yes, he was

glad both in feeling and judgment that he had married as he did.

A few weeks later, on November 4, 1842, Lincoln and Mary Todd were married at the Ninian W. Edwards home. The Reverend Charles Dresser in canonical robes performed the ring ceremony for the groom, thirty-three years old, and the bride, twenty-three years old.

Mary Todd was now to have fresh light on why newly married couples lose their "silver tones," if they do. She was to know more clearly the reply to her query of two years previous, "Why is it that married folks always become so serious?"

In one of his letters advising Speed to marry, Lincoln had written that his old father used to say, "If you make a bad bargain, hug it all the tighter."

In a letter five days after his wedding to a Shawneetown lawyer regarding two law cases, Lincoln closed with writing, "Nothing new here, except my marrying, which, to me, is a matter of profound wonder."

Twenty-four years later Joshua Speed wrote Herndon, "If I had not been married and happy—far more happy than I ever expected to be—Lincoln would not have married."

Twenty-two Years of Marriage

THIS was the beginning of the twenty-two years of married life for this oddly-matched couple. They were "the long and the short of it," as Lincoln said more than once. The wife was sensitive about the picture they made standing alongside each other; she never allowed a photograph to be made of them as a couple. They were opposites in more than height. She was chubby; he was lean. She was swift of tongue and vehement in phrase; he was reserved and drawling. While he was rated as coming from the lower working class, "scrubs," she considered herself as indubitably of the well-bred upper class, patrician, and according to one of her sisters, she was in a vexed mood for a moment on the night of her wedding and made a reference to the difficulties in being involved with "plebeians."

The contrast between them which grew in the years was in temper or control. She grew more explosive; her outbursts came at more frequent intervals, were more desperate exhibitions, enacted in the presence of more important persons. Her physical resources and mental ability took on such added pathos from year to year that in a wide variety of ways many who met her referred to her as "a sad case." This while her husband's patience developed, his self-discipline deepened, and in the matter of self-control, knowing what he was doing while he was doing it, he was increasingly noted as a marvel.

The houses they lived in marked their pilgrimage together, (1) the Globe Tavern in Springfield where they lived cheaply and made plans, (2) the one-and-a-half story Eighth Street house where they set up housekeeping, (3) Mrs. Spriggs' modest boarding house in Washington, D. C., (4) the Eighth Street house in Springfield with a full second story added, (5) the White House in Washington, D. C., also known as the Executive Mansion.

Nearly always between these two there was a moving undertow of their mutual ambitions. Though his hope of achievement and performance was sometimes smothered and obliterated in melancholy, it was there, burning and questing, most of the time. And with Mary Todd Lincoln the deep desire for high place, eminence, distinction, seemed never to leave her. And between these mutual ambitions of theirs might be the difference that while he cared much for what History would say of him, her anxiety was occupied with what Society, the approved social leaders of the upper classes, would let her have.

As a newly elected Congressman's wife in 1846, she

had gay pulses; she had predicted her husband would go up the ladder and she with him. On his trip to Washington to sit in Congress, she took him by a detour to Lexington, Kentucky, to meet her relatives and the playmates of her youth. She joined him later in Washington where they lived at the plain boarding house of Mrs. Spriggs—and where he saved enough of his salary to pay off the last of the store-keeping debts he got loaded with about twelve years earlier when he learned that as a merchant he was a total loss.

Then her gay pulses as a Congressman's wife went down as her husband lost his seat in the national body. The hope then came that he would be appointed Land Office Commissioner of the United States by the newly elected Whig President, Zachary Taylor. They would live in Washington. Lincoln wrote letters, pulled wires, used connections, traveled to Washington, went the limit as an office seeker. It is not known whether he naturally felt he would enjoy the work of running a federal bureau in the national capital, and that it would be an experience worth his while—or whether his wife spurred him on in the only audacious effort he ever put forth for an appointive office. The job was landed by another man. It was not cheerful news at the Lincoln home in Springfield. Lincoln took up mathematics for its mental discipline and sunk himself deep in law study and practice.

Four babies were borne by Mary Todd Lincoln in ten years, all boys, Robert Todd (1843), Edward Baker (1846), William Wallace (1850), Thomas (1853). They made a houseful. Their mother had maids for housework but until the family went to the White House to live, she usually sewed her own dresses, did much of the sewing for the children, and took on herself many of the thousand and one little cares and daily chores that accompany the feeding and clothing of babies, and upbringing of lusty and mischievous boys. She had hours, days, years of washing and nursing these little ones, tending their garments, overseeing their school studies, watching their behavior, instructing them as to the manners of gentlemen, keeping an eye on their health, working and worrying over them when they were sick. Even those who could not see her as pleasant company, even the ones who believed her a vixen and a shrew, gave testimony that she was an exceptional mother, brooding over her offspring with a touch of the tigress.

Her little Eddy died in 1850, not quite four years old; that was a grief. Thomas, nicknamed Tad, had a misshapen palate and lisped; he had brightness, whim-

66

sical bold humor; he was a precious burden to his mother and father.

Mrs. Lincoln knew that her husband understood her faults. She believed she knew his failings and instructed him. Across their twenty-two years of married life there were times when she was a help. Often too she knew she presumed on his patience and good nature, knowing that when calm settled down on the household he would regard it as "a little explosion" that had done her good. In the matter of faults she may have heard him tell of meeting a farmer who wanted Lincoln to bring suit against a next-door neighbor. And Lincoln suggested that the farmer should forget it; neighbors are like horses; they all have faults and there is a way of accommodating yourself to the faults you know and expect; trading a horse whose faults you are used to for one who has a new and a different set of faults may be a mistake. Undoubtedly Lincoln had a theory that a turbulent woman and an unruly horse must be met with a patience much the same for either the woman or the horse.

She terrorized housemaids, icemen, storekeepers, delivery boys, with her tongue lashings. He knew these tempers of hers connected directly with the violent headaches of which she complained for many years.

67

He knew they traced back to a deep-seated physical disorder, sudden disturbances that arose and shook her controls till she raved and was as helpless as a child that has spent itself in a tantrum. Sentences of letters she wrote show that she felt guilty and ashamed over her outbreaks of hysteria; she wished they had never happened, felt deeply that she had made a fool of herself. If Lincoln ever suspected that these habitual brainstorms were the result of a cerebral disease eating deeper into the tissues from year to year, it is not revealed in any letter or spoken comment in the known record.

In the courting days and in the earlier years of marriage his nickname for her was "Molly." After the children came he called her "Mother." When complaints were raised against her he tried to smooth out the trouble, telling one man who had been tongue-lashed that he ought to be able to stand for fifteen minutes what he [Lincoln] had stood for fifteen years. Much can be inferred from a letter he wrote to the editor of a new Republican newspaper which Mrs. Lincoln had thrown out of the house in a huff. "When the paper was brought to my house," he explained, "my wife said to me, 'Now are you going to take another worthless little paper?' I said to her *evasively,* 'I have not directed

"HOW MUCH, I WISH INSTEAD OF WRITING WE WERE TOGETHER THIS EVENING. I FEEL VERY SAD AWAY FROM YOU"

(In the collection of Oliver R. Barrett)

From an affectionate, domestic letter written by Mrs. Lincoln to her husband when he was a Congressman in 1848.

RARELY DID THE
CAMERA FIND MRS.
LINCOLN WITHOUT
HER FAVORITE
FLOWERS

the paper to be left.' From this, in my absence, she sent the message to the carrier."

Did she on one occasion chase him out of the house with a broomstick? One woman told of it years afterward. It may have been so, though no other witness has come forward to tell about it, and the next-door neighbors, the Gourleys, recalled no affair of the broomstick. "I think the Lincolns agreed moderately well," said James Gourley. "As a rule Mr. Lincoln yielded to his wife—in fact, almost any other man, had he known the woman as I did, would have done the same thing. She was gifted with an unusually high temper and that usually got the better of her. She was very excitable and when wrought up had hallucinations." Once she was afraid of rough characters doing violence to her and the maid. Her wailing brought Gourley over and he spent the night guarding the house. "The whole thing was imaginary," said Gourley. Though others living farther away emphasized her bad peculiarities, Gourley declared, "I never thought Mrs. Lincoln was as bad as some people here in Springfield represented her." When one of her spells of temper came on, Lincoln at first seemed to pay no attention. "Frequently he would laugh at her, which is a risky thing to do in the face of an infuriated wife;

69

but generally, if her impatience continued, he would pick up one of the children and deliberately leave home as if to take a walk. After he had gone, the storm usually subsided, but sometimes it would break out again when he returned."

Did she throw a bucket of water on his head from a second-story window as he stood at the front door asking to be let in? Such a tale has been told and was once published in a foreign language newspaper—printed as fun for the readers who for years laughed at one stage jester asking another, "Who was that lady I seen you with last night?" "That wasn't no lady; that was my wife." There are legends which grow by what they feed on. Possibly once during the eighteen or nineteen years of the married life of the Lincolns in Springfield she threw a bucket of water on him at the front door—possibly once—though Herndon and others never heard of it.

Though the talk and the testimony blame the woman chiefly there seems to have been one time that the man too lost his control. Lincoln was at the office one morning before Herndon arrived. His hat over his eyes he gave a short answer to Herndon's "Good morning," sat slumped till noon, and then made a meal of crackers and cheese. On the day before, on a Sunday morning, Mrs. Lincoln was in a bad mood, one thing led to another and after repeated naggings Lincoln took hold of her and pushed her toward an open door facing Jackson Street, calling in his peculiar high-pitched voice, "You make the house intolerable, damn you, get out of it!" Churchgoers coming up Jackson Street might have seen and heard all. How would they know it was the first and only time in his life he had laid rough hands on his wife and cursed her? Even letting it pass that people had seen and heard what happened how could he blame himself enough for letting himself go in such cheap behavior? So Sunday had been a day of shameful thoughts. The night had brought no sleep. And at daybreak he had come to the law office, without breakfast, without hope.

The marriage contract is complex. "Live and let live," is one of its terms. It travels on a series of readjustments to the changes of life recurring in the party of the first part and the party of the second part. Geared to incessant ecstasy of passion, the arrangement goes smash. Mutual ambitions, a round of simple and necessary duties, occasional or frequent separations as the case may be, relieved by interludes of warm affection—these are the conditions on which many a long-time marriage has been negotiated. The mood and color of this normal married life permeate the letters that passed between Lincoln and his wife when he was in Congress. Their household talk across the twenty-two years must have run along many a day and hour in the mood of these letters; exchanges of news, little anxieties about the children and the home, the journeyings of each reported to the other. When he hurried home from the law office during a thunderstorm, knowing that she was a terror-struck and sick woman during a thunderstorm, it was an act of accommodation by one partner for another. Likewise when a man appeared at the office saying the wife wanted a tree in their home yard cut down, it was accommodation again in his saying, "Then for God's sake let it be cut down!"

All romance is interrupted by the practical. The most passionate of lovers must either go to a hotel or set up housekeeping. And either is a humdrum piece of business in a sheer romance. Many a woman has said, "I love you, but the roast is burning and we must leave our kisses till after dinner." Managing a family and household is the work and care of a husband and wife as distinguished from two lovers. The husband must attend to the "husbandry," the bread-and-butter supply, while his wife loves, cherishes and obeys him; that is the theory; an ancient Saxon verb has it that she "wifes" him. We know from the 1848 letters of Lincoln and his wife that he was husbanding their resources and that she "wifed" him.

We can be sure, too, that for much of the time Lincoln and his wife went about their concerns peacefully and with quiet affection for each other. Domestic flareups, nerve-snappings, come to all couples; perhaps to these two they simply came more frequently and more violently. Authentic records—letters written without any thought of future readers—contain many glimpses of placid relations. One can read nothing but calm contentment into Lincoln's sentence about a novel he had received from a friend: "My wife got hold of the volume I took home, read it half through last night, and is greatly interested in it." Only the comradeship that comes to those who understand each other can be inferred from Mrs. Lincoln's comment on a trip east: "When I saw the large steamers at the New York landings I felt in my heart inclined to sigh that poverty was my portion. How I long to go to Europe. I often laugh and tell Mr. Lincoln that I am determined my next husband shall be rich."

Together the two shared in the social life of Springfield, entertained and went to parties. The diary of

73

Orville H. Browning, who spent weeks every year in the capital, refers often to parties which Mr. and Mrs. Lincoln gave or attended. Mrs. Lincoln's letters show the extent of these diversions. "Within the last three weeks," she wrote in 1857, "there has been a party almost every night and some two or three grand fetes are coming off this week." Most pretentious of these, but typical of many others, was Governor Bissell's reception where "a fine brass and string band discoursed most delicious music, and the dancers kept the cotillions filled until a late hour."

As the years passed and Lincoln's fame grew, there came occasional happy outings, brief escapes for Mrs. Lincoln from the routine of keeping house and managing children. There was a trip, with other lawyers, state officers and their wives, over the lines of the Illinois Central Railroad in the summer of 1859. The Springfield newspapers announced the party's departure and the Chicago papers noted the arrival of the travelers, among them the "Hon. A. Lincoln and family," at the Tremont House. Upon their return to Springfield the men bought a gold-headed cane at Chatterton's jewelry store, had their names inscribed upon it, and presented it to the conductor of the train as a token of appreciation.

There was another trip the same year when Lincoln went to Ohio to make Republican speeches, taking Mrs. Lincoln and one of the boys with him. The first audience, at Columbus, was small, but as the trip progressed enthusiasm mounted and ever-larger crowds were present to warm Mrs. Lincoln's pride in her husband's reputation. At Cincinnati marchers with bands met them at the station and escorted them to the Burnet house with cannon booming a salute. They stayed two days, spending several pleasant hours with one of Mrs. Lincoln's cousins.

Lincoln's health, his work, his political aims, are told about in a letter which he wrote to his wife in 1860 on the eastern trip that took him to New York for the Cooper Union speech and nine other speeches. This platform work came hard for him and he made clear to Mrs. Lincoln that he was a troubled man and why. While visiting their son Robert, at Exeter, New Hampshire, he wrote her a letter on March 4, saying, "I have been unable to escape this toil. If I had foreseen it, I think I would not have come east at all. The speech at New York, being within my calculation before I started, went off passably well and gave me no trouble whatever. The difficulty was to make nine others, before audiences who had already seen all my ideas in

75

print." Thus he let her know that if his nine other speeches seemed rather poor there was a reason. Neither he nor she knew at that hour how powerful a factor the Cooper Union address would prove in bringing him the nomination for President a few months later. Nor could they guess that a year from the day he wrote this letter he would be taking oath as President at Washington, and again he would be saying in but slightly different words, "I have been unable to escape this toil."

Communications like this have a color not found in the progress of a man and wife whose days are a succession of uninterrupted quarrels. Nevertheless, we know there were terrible interludes. Under the progression of her malady, the hammering wear and tear of the repeated periods of hysteria and hallucinations, there was a fading of a brightness seen in her younger years. Compliments came less often. She lost her "silver tones." More than twenty years after her query, "Why is it that married folks always become so serious?" she wrote querulously, "The weather is so beautiful, why is it, that we cannot feel well?" The days in which she was neither feeling well nor looking well increased. Her sudden angers interrupting a smoothly moving breakfast, her swift wailings in the dark quiet of night time when fears came to possess her—these brought long thoughts to her husband. Did she become to him a manner of symbol—a miniature of the Sea of Life, smooth and shining with promises and then suddenly treacherous and hateful with devastation? We do not know. It may be so. We cannot be sure in such a realm of the deeper undertows that move people into words and acts.

We do know that from year to year there was a growing control in her husband, a strange and more mystic tinting of his spirit. Under the bonds and leashes that wove and tied his life with that of Mary Todd he saw a self-development that became a mystery to his friends. The outstanding trait of him, according to Herndon, was that he was a "learner," raising the question whether he was indeed such a learner that he could apply to the benefit of his own growth the maxim he quoted to Speed from his father, "If you make a bad bargain, hug it all the tighter."

He was a man in whom the stream of motive ran sluggish. Herndon's theory was that Mary Todd often roused him out of sluggishness, out of vague dreams, into definite actions. When his melancholy weighed down and overslaughed his ambition, Mary Todd with her tongue, arguments, reminders, was a "whiplash."

This, of course, is speculation, an attempt to read secrets in development of human personality. Under the patient exterior of Abraham Lincoln lay a turmoil, a vast criss-cross of volcanic currents of which he himself might have had difficulty to tell had he ever tried to unbosom and make clear the play of motives that operated between him and Mary Todd in their twenty-two years of married life.

Pride ran deep in Mary Todd Lincoln, pride of a depth and consuming intensity that might ally it with the pride which the Puritans named as the first of the seven deadly sins.

When Lincoln was defeated for United States Senator from Illinois in 1855, his wife was in the gallery watching the balloting. Lyman Trumbull, a rival of the same party, won. And though Julia Jayne, the wife of Trumbull, had been a bridesmaid at Mary Todd's wedding, and they had joined in writing poetry and letters to the Sangamo *Journal,* it is said that always after Trumbull's election there was coolness between her and her old-time chum.

Her anxiety matched that of her husband when he ran for the United States Senate against Douglas in 1858. She was not one of those wives who wish their husbands to quit the troublous arena of politics. She had a belief in her own skill at politics and found the rôle of adviser fascinating.

Months of exaltation, of life intensified, followed Lincoln's nomination at Chicago. Mary Lincoln was no longer the wife of a small-town lawyer; like her husband, she was a public character. The transformation thrilled her. The newspaper correspondents who thronged to Springfield gave her space in their dispatches. There was keen delight in reading in the New York *Herald* that she was "especially gracious and entertaining," and able to inject "brilliant flashes of wit and good nature" into a political conversation. There was keen delight, too, in meeting men who sought out her husband at the frame house on the corner of Eighth and Jackson streets—men whose names were household words, Salmon P. Chase, Thurlow Weed, Cameron, Carl Schurz, Horace Greeley.

With the election, life for Mary Lincoln was pitched to an even higher key. "She is in fine spirits!" wrote one of her friends a few days after the result was known.

Still and all, it was not so pleasant for her. Western democracy had its own ways, was not always considerate of feelings. On one of the nights of Republican celebration crowds swarmed through the Lincoln resi-

79

dence. They wanted a look at the President-elect and his lady. Sweat-stained shirts crushed elaborate gowns; muddy boots trampled satin slippers. And more than once Mary Lincoln's cheeks flushed as she found herself the object of a stare and overheard the ill-concealed words: "Is that the old woman?"

With Lincoln's inauguration as President of the United States in 1861 she hugged to her heart the gratification of being the First Lady of the Land. Her fond dream had come true, yet for her it was not merely a signal that she was to wife, comfort, cherish the new President and help him carry the load. She took it she was also an adviser, an ex-officio cabinet officer, an auxiliary First Magistrate. From the first she suggested appointments and was vehement as to who should fill this or that place.

Was there need for her to blaze forth with hot comments on important men whom Lincoln had chosen for heavy work? Why in the presence of visitors refer to William H. Seward, named to be Secretary of State, as a "dirty abolition sneak"?

Henry Villard, correspondent of the New York *Herald,* told of a story he had from a man who went to bring Lincoln to the railroad train which was waiting to carry the President-elect to Washington for inauguration. And the man said Lincoln's wife was lying on the floor of their room in the Chenery House raging and convulsive, her apparel disordered, moaning she would not go to Washington until her husband promised to make a certain federal appointment. It was a story—possibly nothing to it and possibly true. In any case it was told by Villard as probably true. That Villard at this time was writing little character sketches of Lincoln and his wife for the New York *Herald,* entirely favorable, filled with well-measured praise and affection, lends color to the story. That Mrs. Lincoln changed her plans and itinerary, and did not leave Springfield on the same train with her husband, may or may not be a circumstance in the incident. That Lincoln made one of the most poignantly moving and melancholy speeches of his career that morning just before the train carried him away from Springfield forever may also be no circumstance at all.

Was it a woman's jealousy of her husband or a selfish personal pride or both that brought her decree regarding White House promenades? The established custom followed by Presidents and Presidents' wives up till her time was that the President should lead the grand march with another woman on his arm while the next

couple would be the President's wife on the arm of
another man. Mary Todd Lincoln decreed that she and
she only should be the woman on the President's arm
when he led the promenade. No other woman but her

INAUGURATION BALL COSTUMES, EVENING OF MARCH 4, 1861

should be in the First Couple. And it was so ordered
and maintained from then on.

She is credited with pluck for staying at the White
House with her husband and children through the
Spring days of 1861 when it seemed as though Wash-
ington would be captured, when the Confederates
could easily have taken the Capitol and White House.
She refused to travel north to Philadelphia and safety.

She had resources of courage; not stamina particularly but a steady audacity.

The Washington tumult wore heavily on her in the Summer of 1861. She went to Long Branch, the ocean resort near New York City. There she conducted herself quietly, trying to rest, keeping away from the social whirl. The New York *Herald,* however, had sent a clever special writer to the scene; he scribbled columns of gush as though the President's wife were an American Queen, maintaining a royal seclusion, wearing a haughty manner. The keen thrusts and malicious manipulations of this writer were reprinted in newspapers fighting the administration. The ridicule went beyond her and struck at her husband in the White House. She learned what curious twists of viewpoint can be put upon a lonely distracted woman seeking a place to look at the wide ocean in peace and meditation; it couldn't be done.

She became a topic. "Mrs. Lincoln held a brilliant levee at the White House on Saturday evening. She was superbly dressed." Thus *Leslie's Weekly* in February of 1863. The same periodical in its number of October 10 that year gave its readers a brief item: "The reports that Mrs. Lincoln was in an interesting condition are untrue."

A bold agitator for abolition and woman's rights, Jane Grey Swisshelm, editor of a paper at St. Cloud, Minnesota, and later a war nurse, gave out words of high admiration and deep affection for Mrs. Lincoln. The words were seized on. *Leslie's Weekly* quoted them: "Her complexion is fair as that of a young girl, her cheeks soft, plump and blooming, and her expression tender and kindly. It was one of those faces I feel like stopping on the street to kiss, because it recalls one that was dearest of all in childhood's days. I think the features are not classical, but I forget them. It was a pleasant face to look on." To this *Leslie's* added: "The Boston *Courier* spitefully reminds its readers that Mrs. Swisshelm is an office-holder. No one can doubt Mrs. Swisshelm's womanly earnestness who remembers the fierce war she waged with Harriet Prewett of the Yazoo *Gazette,* about the weight of their respective babies." Thus she met persiflage, bantering. Or again she was the topic of strict news information as when in July of 1863, journals carried the item: "Mrs. Lincoln nearly met with a fatal accident in consequence of her horses taking fright. She threw herself out of her carriage. Fortunately no bones were broken, and after some restorative she was taken to her residence."

I fancy the "blue room", will look dreary this evening, so if you & the Gov are disengaged, wander up & see us — I want to become accustomed to vast solitude by degrees The paper is ready for your notice — Bring the Gov — with you —

Truly your friend

Mary Lincoln

"I WANT TO BECOME ACCUSTOMED TO VAST SOLITUDE
BY DEGREES," WRITES MRS. LINCOLN EARLY IN 1861

(In the collection of Oliver R. Barrett)

MARY LINCOLN

From a painting by Frank B. Carpenter, White House resident in 1864
and author of "Six Months in the White House." An idealized portrait executed some time after the war. (Courtesy of The Milch Galleries, New York)

A steady parade of items about her three "brothers" in the Confederate armies was published in southern and northern newspapers. They were in fact half-brothers, sons of Mary Todd's father by his second wife.

"The Rebel officer who called the roll of our prisoners at Houston is Lieutenant Todd, a brother of the wife of President Lincoln," ran a newspaper line. "He is tall, fat, and savage against the 'Yankees.'" Journals for and against the Lincoln administration reprinted, in December of 1863, information from the Richmond *Enquirer* reading: "Mrs. Todd of Kentucky, the mother of Mrs. Lincoln, arrived in this city on the steamer *Schultz,* Thursday night, having come to City Point on the flag of truce boat. She goes South to visit her daughter, Mrs. Helm, widow of Surgeon-General Helm, who fell at Chickamauga. Mrs. Todd is about to take up her residence South, all her daughters being here, except the wife of Lincoln, and Mrs. Kellogg, who is at present in Paris."

The talk grew and spread that in the White House was a woman traitor and spy, the President's wife, sending information south. On one occasion the sad-faced President appeared of his own volition before a Congressional investigating committee to give them his solemn personal assurance that his wife was loyal to the Union cause.

One by one the Todd brothers in the Confederate army were killed. And little by little the talk died down that their half-sister in the White House was an informer in sympathy with the southern side.

It was war.

"Lizzie, I have just heard that one of my brothers has been killed," said Mrs. Lincoln one day to her negro dressmaker, Elizabeth Keckley. And she went on, "Of course, it is but natural that I should feel for one so nearly related to me, but not to the extent that you suppose. He made his choice long ago. He decided against my husband, and through him against me. He has been fighting against us; and since he chose to be our deadly enemy, I see no special reason why I should bitterly mourn his death."

The tension of being a Kentuckian at war with the South was in her plea, "Why should I sympathize with the rebels? They would hang my husband tomorrow if it was in their power, and perhaps gibbet me with him. How then can I sympathize with a people at war with me and mine?"

Broken aristocrats, southern sympathizers, disgruntled office seekers, gossips shaken with war brainstorms, employed their tongues on the new social leader of the capital, the new First Lady. And she gave them too many chances to strike at her. More than rumor and passing chatter lay back of Charles Francis Adams, Jr.'s recording of a function he attended at Mrs. Eames's: "If the President caught it at dinner, his wife caught it at the reception. All manner of stories about her were flying around; she wanted to do the right thing, but, not knowing how, was too weak and proud to ask; she was going to put the White House on an economic basis, and, to that end, was about to dismiss 'the help,' as she called the servants; some of whom, it was asserted, had already left because 'they must live with gentlefolks'; she had got hold of newspaper reporters and railroad conductors, as the best persons to go to for advice and direction. Numberless stories of this sort were current; and Mrs. Lincoln was in a stew."

In the White House she was sometimes designated as "Mrs. President." She took an interest in the case of a soldier who was sentenced to face a firing squad for going to sleep on picket duty. When Lincoln mentioned the case to General George B. McClellan, commanding, he said "the Lady President" was anxious the boy be pardoned. McClellan in writing to his wife told

. When I was a member of Congress a dozen years ago, I boarded with the lady who writes the within letter. She is a most worthy and deserving lady; and if what she desires can be conveniently done, I shall be much obliged. I say this sincerely and earnestly—

May 31. 1861

A. Lincoln

Hon Mr Smith:

We boarded some months, with Mrs Sprigg, & found her a most estimable lady & would esteem it a personal favor, if her request, could be granted.

Mrs A. Lincoln

UNUSUAL INSTANCE OF THE HANDWRITINGS OF MR. AND MRS. LINCOLN ON ONE PAGE

her it had pleased him to grant a request from "the Lady President."

In her own eyes she was more than "the Lady President"; she conceived of her position as carrying with it prerogatives and privileges akin to those of royalty. She was fond of referring to those who frequented the White House as the "Court," and at times she made requests, forced exactions, as one who ruled by monarchic decree and whim rather than as the wife of an elected President. There was the case of Mrs. Taft's bonnet, trivial but characteristic. After one of the Marine Band concerts Julia Taft and her mother went to the portico of the White House to pay their respects to Mrs. Lincoln. "I noticed Mrs. Lincoln looking intently at my mother's bonnet," the daughter recorded. "After a few words of greeting, she took my mother aside and talked with her for a moment. While I could not hear their conversation, I knew someway that they were talking about my mother's bonnet and I was a bit puzzled at the look of amazement on my mother's face. I did not see why my mother should look so surprised at a passing compliment from Mrs. Lincoln." That evening she overheard scraps of a guarded conversation between her mother and father: learned that the milliner who had made Mrs. Taft's bonnet had also made one for Mrs. Lincoln but had not had enough ribbon for the strings, and that Mrs. Lincoln had asked her mother for those from her own bonnet. The daughter concluded: "It was an outstanding characteristic of Mary Todd Lincoln that she wanted what she wanted when she wanted it and no substitute!"

Seward, whom Mrs. Lincoln disliked and sought to replace with Sumner, recognized the trait and bowed to it. When Mrs. Lincoln asked Attorney General Speed to go to City Point with her early in April, 1865, Speed, behind in his work, demurred and consulted Seward. Whereupon, in Speed's words, his colleague "arose and walked the floor, and said with great emphasis, the request of the President's wife was equivalent to a command, and you must obey." And Speed went.

She intervened constantly in the matter of offices—for postmasterships, West Point cadetships—even the reorganization of the Cabinet. She wrote from the Soldiers' Home, Washington, D. C., to James Gordon Bennett, publisher and editor of the New York *Herald* in the fall of 1862, telling him she favored cabinet changes and would do what she could to bring them about:

"From all parties the cry for a 'change of cabinet' comes. I hold a letter, just received from Governor Sprague, in my hand, who is quite as earnest as you have been on the subject. Doubtless if my good patient husband were here instead of being with the Army of the Potomac, both of these missives would be placed before him, accompanied by my womanly suggestions, proceeding from a heart so deeply interested for our distracted country. I have a great terror of strong-minded ladies, yet if a word fitly spoken and in due season can be urged in a time like this, we should not withhold it."

Her jealousies of other women who seemed in the slightest to be in favor with the President were noticeable. Mrs. Keckley recorded the conversation of one evening as Lincoln was pulling on his gloves in Mrs. Lincoln's room just before escorting her to a reception downstairs in the White House. With a twinkle in his eyes he remarked, "Well, mother, who must I talk with tonight—shall it be Mrs. D.?"

"That deceitful woman! No, you shall not listen to her flattery."

"Well, then, what do you say to Miss C.? She is too young and handsome to practice deceit."

"Young and handsome, you call her! You shall not

judge beauty for me. No, she is in league with Mrs. D., and you shall not talk with her."

"Well, mother, I must talk with some one. Is there any one that you do not object to?" And he fussed at buttoning a glove, a mock gravity on his face.

"I don't know as it is necessary you should talk to anybody in particular. You know well enough, Mr. Lincoln, that I do not approve of your flirtations with silly women, just as if you were a beardless boy, fresh from school."

"But, mother, I insist that I must talk with some. body. I can't stand around like a simpleton, and say nothing. If you will not tell me who I may talk with, please tell me who I may *not* talk with."

"There is Mrs. D. and Miss C. in particular, I detest them both. Mrs. B. also will come around you, but you need not listen to her flattery. These are the ones in particular."

"Very well, mother; now that we have settled the question to your satisfaction, we will go downstairs." And he gave her his arm.

One evening Mrs. Keckley had arranged Mrs. Lincoln's hair and helped her into a dress of white satin trimmed in black lace, with a surprise of a long trail in the height of daring fashion. She entered the Guest's

Room where Willie Lincoln lay abed with a cold and fever. And as Elizabeth Keckley wrote of it, "As she swept through the room, Mr. Lincoln was standing with his back to the fire, his hands behind him, and his eyes on the carpet. His face wore a thoughtful, solemn look. The rustling of the satin dress attracted his attention. He looked at it a few moments; then, in his quaint, quiet way remarked—

" 'Whew! Our cat has a long tail tonight!'

"Mrs. Lincoln did not reply. The President added:

" 'Mother, it is my opinion, if some of that tail was nearer the head, it would be in better style'; and he glanced at her bare arms and neck. She had a beautiful neck and arm and low dresses were becoming to her. She turned away with a look of offended dignity, and presently took the President's arm, and both went downstairs to their guests, leaving me alone with the sick boy."

The cup of happiness ran over for Mary Todd Lincoln at times when she realized to the full her ambition to be a Great Lady and publicly approved as such. Praise was showered on her and lavish compliments bestrewn over her after the White House party which she gave on February 5, 1862. *Leslie's Weekly* made this social function the topic of a leading article, elaborately illustrated. "There has been a social innovation at the White House," the article began, "and the experiment has been a brilliant success." Until this event came off there had been "a false deference to the false notion of democratic equality." Except for State dinners to foreign ministers and cabinet members the parties previously had consisted of public receptions where the Executive Mansion was thrown open, as *Leslie's Weekly* noted, "to every one, high or low, gentle or ungentle, washed or unwashed," resulting in a "horrible jam" endurable only "by people of sharp elbows, and destitute of corns, who don't object to a faint odor of whiskey." Now, however, Mrs. Lincoln had inaugurated the practice of "respectable people in private life" by inviting five hundred of the "distinguished, beautiful, brilliant" people representing "intellect, attainment, position, elegance." Whether the writer in *Leslie's* was lit up with genuine enthusiasm or was just a plain snob, he or she wrote as though conveying glad tidings. "Indeed, no European Court or capital can compare with the Presidential circle and the society at Washington this winter, in the freshness and beauty of its women. The North, while it has confessedly been possessed of even more than its numerical proportion of beautiful and accomplished women, has never before been in a social supremacy. The power which controlled the Government has been altogether Southern, and society has always taken the same hue. But all that is changed now, and the dingy, sprawling city on the Potomac is bright with the blue of Northern eyes, and the fresh, rosy glow of Northern complexions." Early in the evening the windows of the White House were lighted for gayety, and by half-past nine the entrances were crowded with guests and carriages lined the White House yard to the avenue. Invitation cards were presented at the door. The ladies in swishing, crinkling crinoline and their escorts in silk top hats and cutaway coats passed to the second-story dressing rooms. They returned to the grand entrance, were shown into the Blue Room, then conducted to the grand saloon or East Room where the President and his wife greeted them while the Marine Band played soft music from a side-room. At half-past eleven doors were thrown open to an apartment where sandwiches were served with drinks from a huge Japanese punchbowl. The regular supper came afterwards, served by Maillard of New York in the Dining Room. The reporter noted that Mrs. John J. Crittenden's jewels were diamonds, her gown of black velvet, richly trimmed with lace, while her head-dress was composed of crimson flowers. Also

the wife of Gen. George B. McClellan, "the observed
of all observers, leaning on the arm of her distinguished
husband, looked most regal in her dress of white, with
bands of cherry velvet, a tunic of white looped with
crimson, and a head-dress of white illusion, *a la vierge*."
Mrs. Commodore Levy was there, "most bewitchingly
piquante in a dress of white illusion and gold, with six
small flounces over a slip of white glace silk, a wreath
of white flowers mingled with golden ears of wheat,
and a necklace and earrings of Oriental pearls." It
was noted too: "The Hon. Mrs. Squier looked most
charming in a pink silk, exquisitely trimmed with
swansdown, which well accorded with her soft and
spirituelle beauty. A wreath of ivy with its long and
graceful tendrils, mingled most bewitchingly with her
blonde and waving hair. Her ornaments were opals and
diamonds." Also the reporter for *Leslie's Weekly* recorded: "Mrs. Griffin was simply but tastefully attired
in a corn-colored silk; head-dress of bright crimson
flowers. She was the observed of all, as she leaned on
the arm of the President."

Many were named as present and set off with distinction. But the lavish comment was reserved for Mrs.
Lincoln. "Primarily, we must remark the exquisite
taste with which the White House has been refitted

under Mrs. Lincoln's directions is in no respect more remarkable than in the character of the hangings of the various rooms, which relieve and set off the figures and dresses of lady guests to the greatest advantage. First, as hostess, and second in no respect, Mrs. Lincoln. She was attired in a lustrous white satin robe, with a train of a yard in length, trimmed with one deep flounce of the richest black chantilly lace, put on in festoons and surmounted by a quilling of white satin ribbon, edged with narrow black lace. The dress was, of course, décolleté and with short sleeves, displaying the exquisitely moulded shoulders and arms of our fair 'Republican Queen,' the whiteness of which were absolutely dazzling. Her head-dress was a coronet wreath of black and white crêpe myrtle, which was in perfect keeping with her regal style of beauty. Let us here add *en passant,* that Mrs. Lincoln possesses that rare beauty which has rendered the Empress of the French so celebrated as a handsome woman, and which our Transatlantic cousins call *la tête bien planté.* Her ornaments were pearls."

Such was the presentation of Mrs. Lincoln to the wide national audience of a popular illustrated weekly newspaper. She had wanted this recognition. It slaked a thirst she had. Later that same year, in November,

New York newspapers gave many paragraphs to her visit there. But it was not so pleasant a visit. For the Lincoln administration at Washington had been losing ground and the end of the war seemed far off. *Harper's Weekly* published a large engraving from a photograph portrait of Mrs. Lincoln, with the news: "Mrs. Lincoln has lately been spending some time in this city, and has been serenaded and visited by many of our leading citizens." Along with this was the information that one of her brothers, killed in battle, had been the jailer of Union prisoners at Richmond. "His brutality and cruelty were such, however, that Jefferson Davis finally removed him from the post, and sent him to join his regiment. Mrs. Lincoln's sisters are understood to sympathize rather with the rebels than with the Government. It is probably this division of sentiment which has given rise to the gossip and scandal respecting the views of the lady who presides over the White House."

At one time newspapers and common talk were filled with accusations and suspicions that she was getting military secrets from her husband and White House callers, and sending the information to Southern commanders. She told the White House clerk who handled mail, William O. Stoddard, that she would prefer he opened all her mail as it came. "Don't let a thing come to me that you've not read first yourself, and that you are not sure I would wish to see. I do not wish to open a letter, nor even a parcel of any kind,

To

Taddie Lincoln

from his loving

Mother

Dec 4ᵗʰ 63

MRS. LINCOLN INSCRIBES A GIFT TO HER SON
In the collection of Oliver R. Barrett

until after you have examined it. Never!" Stoddard took it on himself to throw into the waste basket and the fireplace many accusing and threatening letters addressed to her, written by persons Stoddard considered "insane and depraved."

In all the representations of the gossips, however, there was never an intimation during war time that she mistreated her children. A story that she had whipped Tad came later—and was on the face of it a malicious fabrication. She was fond of her young ones, and if anything, overindulged them. And something of this mother heart was stirred into action as the train-loads of broken and battered soldiers were unloaded at Washington fresh from the battlefields. Much that she did was worthy of her place and her own best impulses. Day after day she visited the wounded in the Washington hospitals, talked with them, took them fruit and delicacies, wine and liquors that admirers had sent for the use of the White House table. In her own way she tried to lighten the burden her husband was carrying. She invited old Illinois friends to breakfast at the White House so that he might forget himself for a few moments in talk of old times. She made him ride with her on bright afternoons in the hope that an hour or two of fresh air would blot some of the fatigue from his face.

A different reputation might have been built up for her, W. O. Stoddard, the mail clerk, believed, if she had taken pains now and then to have the newspaper correspondents know of her hospital visits, her donations of supplies, and other good works. Yet even to Stoddard, who wanted to overlook her faults, she was

MRS. LINCOLN
READY FOR THE
INAUGURAL BALL

THE LADY OF THE
WHITE HOUSE, SOME-
TIMES ALLUDED TO AS
"MRS. PRESIDENT"

War time card portraits of Mrs. Lincoln widely published in periodicals
and treasured in family albums throughout the north.
(Originals in Illinois State Historical Library)

FOUR PICTURES OF MRS. LINCOLN WIDELY CIRCULATED DURING
WAR TIME

difficult. "It was not easy, at first," he wrote, "to understand why a lady who could be one day so kindly, so considerate, so generous, so thoughtful and so hopeful, could, upon another day, appear so unreasonable, so irritable, so despondent, so even niggardly, and so prone to see the dark, the wrong side of men and women and events."

On a chilly day in February, 1862, Willie Lincoln had gone riding on his pony and taken a cold that passed into fever. He was twelve years old, a blue-eyed boy, not strong, liked his books, sometimes curled up in a chair with pencil and paper and tried his hand at writing poems. One verse of his piece titled "Lines on the Death of Colonel Edward Baker" read:

> "There was no patriot like Baker,
>   So noble and so true;
> He fell as a soldier on the field,
>   His face to the sky of blue."

As he lay that night breathing rather hard there drifted up to the room the fragments of music from the Marine Band playing in the Ball Room below. Though the doctor had said there was no reason for alarm about the patient the President had ordered no dancing for that evening. Several times Mrs. Lincoln left the party below and came upstairs to stand over Willie's bed and see how he was.

A few days later the mystic and inevitable messenger came for the boy. Elizabeth Keckley wrote: "The light faded from his eyes, and the death-dew gathered on his brow." She had been on watch but did not see the end, telling of it, "I was worn out with watching, and was not in the room when Willie died, but was immediately sent for. I assisted in washing him and dressing him, and then laid him on the bed, when Mr. Lincoln came in." He lifted the cover from the face of his child, gazed at it long, and murmured, "It is hard, hard to have him die."

The mother wept for hours, and at moments moaned in convulsions of grief.

They closed down the lids over the blue eyes of the boy, parted his brown hair, put flowers from his mother in his pale, crossed hands, and soldiers, senators, the cabinet officers, ambassadors, came to the funeral. The mother couldn't come. She was too far spent.

The body was sent west to Illinois for burial. And the mother clutched at his memory and if his name was mentioned her voice shook and the tears came. "She could not bear to look upon his picture," said Mrs. Keckley. "And after his death she never crossed the threshold of the Guest's Room in which he died, or the Green Room in which he was embalmed."

The death of Willie gave impetus to the malady gnawing at her brain. Noah Brooks told how a charlatan named Colchester posed as a spiritualistic medium, induced her to receive him at the Soldiers' Home and in a darkened room pretended to receive messages from the dead boy. Brooks revealed the fraud. She turned to others for revelations. In amazement Orville H. Browning recorded in his diary: "Mrs. Lincoln told me she had been, the night before, with old Isaac Newton, out to Georgetown, to see a Mrs. Laury, a spiritualist and she had made wonderful revelations to her about her little son Willie who died last winter, and also about things on the earth. Among other things she revealed that the cabinet were all enemies of the President, working for themselves, and that they would have to be dismissed, and others called to his aid before he had success."

Mary Lincoln was a woman who had never restrained her emotions, had all her life given way to gusts of anger and temper. When grief came, it shook her with irresistible force. Mrs. Keckley told of a scene. "In one of her paroxysms of grief the President bent kindly over his wife, took her by the arm, and gently

led her to the window. With a stately, solemn gesture, he pointed to the lunatic asylum. 'Mother, do you see that large white building on the hill yonder? Try and control your grief, or it will drive you mad, and we may have to send you there.'"

She was one of those who in their misery cannot realize that sympathy is a short-lived plant, that with the world at large pity shades quickly into resentment at sustained sorrow. In the summer of 1863 Gideon Welles found it necessary to speak to Lincoln about the weekly concerts of the Marine Band, which had been discontinued the previous summer after Mrs. Lincoln had protested. Lincoln said that his wife would not consent to a resumption of the concerts, certainly not until after the Fourth of July. Welles pressed the point: the people had grumbled last year, and would grumble more if the concerts were not resumed. He wrote in his diary: "The public will not sympathize in sorrows which are obtrusive and assigned as a reason for depriving them of enjoyments to which they have been accustomed, and it is a mistake to persist in it."

The war years pounded on. McClellan, whom Mrs. Lincoln epitomized as a "humbug," was eventually replaced by Ulysses S. Grant. "He is a butcher," she told her husband as Grant was moving slowly and at terrible cost toward Richmond. "But he has been very successful in the field," argued the President, as Mrs. Keckley heard it. Mrs. Lincoln responded, "Yes, he generally manages to claim a victory, but such a victory! He loses two men to the enemy's one. He has no management, no regard for life. If the war should continue four years longer, and he should remain in power, he would depopulate the North. I could fight an army as well myself. According to his tactics, there is nothing under the heavens to do but to march a new line of men up in front of the rebel breastworks to be shot down as fast as they take their position, and keep marching until the enemy grows tired of the slaughter. Grant, I repeat, is an obstinate fool and a butcher."

"Well, mother," came the President's slow and ironical voice, "supposing that we give you command of the army. No doubt you would do much better than any general that has been tried."

In the spring of 1864 the President and Mrs. Lincoln went to City Point for a visit with Grant's army. Adam Badeau of Grant's staff was riding in an ambulance with Mrs. Lincoln and Mrs. Grant and happened in the course of talk to say that the wives of army officers at the front had been ordered to the rear. This indicated that lively fighting was soon to begin, a sure sign,

Badeau remarked, for not a lady had been allowed to stay at the front except Mrs. Griffin, the wife of General Charles Griffin, who had a special permit from the President.

"What do you mean by that, sir?" came the cry from Mrs. Lincoln. "Do you mean to say that she saw the President alone? Do you know that I never allow the President to see any woman alone?"

Badeau tried to tone down what he had said. "I tried to palliate my remark," he noted later. And in doing so he smiled some sort of a smile which brought from the raging woman the reply, "That's a very equivocal smile, sir. Let me out of this carriage at once. I will ask the President if he saw that woman alone." She told Badeau in the front seat, to have the driver of the ambulance stop. He hesitated. She thrust her arms past Badeau and took hold of the driver. Mrs. Grant at that point managed to quiet Mrs. Lincoln enough to have the whole party set out on the ground. General George G. Meade now came up and paid his respects to the President's wife. She went off on the arm of the Gettysburg commander before Badeau could give Meade the word that he mustn't mention Mrs. Griffin getting a special permit from the President to stay at the front. Later, however, Badeau saluted Meade as a diplomat, for when Meade and Mrs. Lincoln returned she said to Badeau, "General Meade is a gentleman, sir. He says it was not the President who gave Mrs. Griffin the permit, but the Secretary of War." And when Badeau and Mrs. Grant talked over the day's events they agreed it was all so mixed-up and disgraceful they would neither of them ever mention to anybody what had happened, except that she would tell her husband.

The next day was worse. For it happened that the wife of General Ord, commander of the Army of the James, was not subject to the order retiring wives to the rear, and mounted on a horse suddenly found herself riding alongside President Lincoln, with Mrs. Lincoln and Mrs. Grant in an ambulance just behind them. Mrs. Lincoln caught sight of them and raged. "What does this woman mean by riding by the side of the President? and ahead of me? Does she suppose that *he* wants *her* by the side of him?"

Mrs. Grant did her best to quiet the frenzied woman. Then she came in for a tongue-lashing, in the midst of which Mrs. Lincoln flashed out, "I suppose you think you'll get to the White House yourself, don't you?" Mrs. Grant replied she was satisfied where she was; she had greater honor than she had ever expected to reach.

"Oh!" was the reply. "You had better take it if you can get it. 'Tis very nice."

Major Seward, a nephew of the Secretary of State, now came riding alongside the ambulance and tried for a joke. He didn't know what was going on. It seemed all in the day's gayety for him to call out: "The President's horse is very gallant, Mrs. Lincoln. He insists on riding by the side of Mrs. Ord." The wild cry came, "What do you mean by that, sir?" And the young major's horse began acting fractious and he dropped to the rear.

The trip ended. Mrs. Ord came to the ambulance and suddenly found herself facing a storm of insults, epithets and dirty names, before a crowd of army officers. What did she mean by following the President? And Badeau wrote, "The poor woman burst into tears and inquired what she had done, but Mrs. Lincoln refused to be appeased, and stormed till she was tired. Mrs. Grant still tried to stand by her friend, and everybody was shocked and horrified."

And the evening of that day was worse yet. On a steamer in the James River at a dinner given by President and Mrs. Lincoln to General and Mrs. Grant and the General's staff, Mrs. Lincoln openly and baldly before all suggested that General Ord should be removed from command. He was unfit for his place, to say nothing of his wife. General Grant, of course, had to reply that so far as he could see General Ord was a good commander.

During this City Point visit these outbreaks of Mary Todd Lincoln kept on. And according to Badeau, "Mrs. Lincoln repeatedly attacked her husband in the presence of officers because of Mrs. Griffin and Mrs. Ord . . . He bore it as Christ might have done; with an expression of pain and sadness that cut one to the heart, but with supreme calmness and dignity. He called her 'mother,' with his old-time plainness; he pleaded with eyes and tones, and endeavored to explain or palliate the offenses of others, till she turned on him like a tigress; and then he walked away, hiding that noble, ugly face that we might not catch the full expression of its misery."

One night toward the end of the war Richard J. Oglesby rode in a carriage with President and Mrs. Lincoln. As a brigadier at Corinth Oglesby received wounds it took him a year to recover from, and Lincoln had wired Grant saying Oglesby was an "intimate friend" and he wished news of his wounded associate in Illinois law and politics. And after the carriage ride that night in Washington, Oglesby told an Illinois crony, a responsible friend with whom he sometimes talked and drank all night, just what had happened. This friend gave Oglesby's version of what happened in these words:

"Oglesby went with a committee to get Lincoln to speak at a mass meeting in the interests of the sanitary fair commission. Lincoln said he was all tired out; he ought not to go; he needed rest. But they kept pressing him about how important it was till at last he said he would go if they would pledge him he wouldn't have to speak. They said the main point was that he should be present personally and he wouldn't be required to speak. So, that night Oglesby and the President and Mrs. Lincoln got into a carriage and rode to the meeting. A large crowd was on hand. The chairman introduced the main speaker, whose speech was well received though it was a prepared address. Then there were calls for Lincoln. The chairman told the crowd Lincoln had come with no expectation of delivering an address and they would have to excuse him. But the crowd wouldn't have it that way. They persisted. And at last Lincoln stood up and started to speak. Now Lincoln never was much on short speeches; he generally had some proposition to discuss up and down. And he delivered some remarks, the best he could; it wasn't much of a speech. But the crowd gave him a generous round of applause and were enthusiastic. Then a little later Lincoln and Mrs. Lincoln and Oglesby walked out to the front of the building to meet the carriage. It was a cold evening and the driver had taken the horses around the block to keep them warm. And as the carriage was about to arrive, Mrs. Lincoln broke out in a humiliated and exasperated way, in words like, 'That was the worst speech I ever listened to in my life. How any man could get up and deliver such remarks to an audience is more than I can understand. I wanted the earth to sink and let me go through.' And that was all that was said. The carriage came. The three of them, Lincoln, Mrs. Lincoln, and Oglesby got in and rode to the White House without a word spoken. There Lincoln and Mrs. Lincoln got out without a word, and the carriage drove off to take Oglesby to his quarters. It was a strange incident."

Her speech included frequent use of the word "Sir." Men recalled her overuse of "Sir." Mrs. Keckley several times noted the expression, "God, no!" when Mrs. Lincoln wished to be emphatic in denial.

She spoke to Mrs. Keckley of an "unprincipled set" of politicians with whom she was having dealings in 1864 toward the reëlection of the President in the coming campaign. "Does Mr. Lincoln know what your purpose is?" asked Mrs. Keckley.

"God, no! he would never sanction such proceedings, so I keep him in the dark, and will tell him of it when it is all over. He is too honest to take the proper care of his own interests, so I feel it my duty to electioneer for him."

Henry Villard made note of the "common set of men and women" in whose company she was too often seen. Out of them he singled, for an example of both type and method, the so-called "Chevalier" Wikoff, a handsome, well-mannered, well-educated pretender who was in reality merely a salaried social spy of the New York *Herald*. "Wikoff showed the utmost assurance in his appeals to the vanity of the mistress of the White House," Villard wrote. "I myself heard him compliment her upon her looks and dress in so fulsome a way that she ought to have blushed and banished the impertinent fellow from her presence. She accepted Wikoff as a majordomo in general and in special, as a guide in matters of social etiquette, domestic arrangements, and personal requirements, including her toilette, and as always welcome company for visitors in her salon and on her drives."

Mrs. Keckley told of her impression of the White

House couple. "I believe that he loved the mother of his children very tenderly. He asked nothing but affection from her, but did not always receive it. When in one of her wayward, impulsive moods, she was apt to do and say things that wounded him deeply. If he had not loved her, she would have been powerless to cloud his thoughtful face. She often wounded him in unguarded moments, but calm reflection never failed to bring regret." Thus ran the observation of this remarkable mulatto woman who as friend and helper of Mary Todd Lincoln was more notable than any other who tried to smooth her pathway.

One day in 1864 she told Mrs. Keckley that the re-election of Mr. Lincoln was important to her. "Somehow I have learned to fear that he will be defeated. If he should be defeated, I do not know what would become of us all. To me, to him, there is more at stake in this election than he dreams of."

"What can you mean, Mrs. Lincoln?"

"Simply this. I have contracted large debts, of which he knows nothing, and which he will be unable to pay if he is defeated."

"What are your debts, Mrs. Lincoln?"

"They consist chiefly of store bills. I owe altogether about twenty-seven thousand dollars, the principal por-

tion at Stewart's in New York. You understand, Liza-
beth, that Mr. Lincoln has but little idea of the expenses
of a woman's wardrobe. He glances at my rich dresses,
and is happy in the belief that the few hundred dollars I obtain from him supply all my wants. I must
dress in costly materials. The people scrutinize every
article that I wear with critical curiosity. The very fact
of having grown up in the West subjects me to more
searching observation. To keep up appearances I must
have money—more than Mr. Lincoln can spare for me.
I had, and still have, no alternative but to run in debt."

"And Mr. Lincoln does not even suspect how much
you owe?"

"God, no! and I would not have him suspect. The
knowledge would drive him mad. He does not know
a thing about my debt, and I value his happiness, not
to speak of my own, too much to allow him to know
anything. This is what troubles me so much. If he is re-
elected, I can keep him in ignorance of my affairs; but
if he is defeated, then the bills will be sent in, and he
will know all." And having told this, "something like
a hysterical sob escaped her."

Meantime, outside the White House and over the
country the discussion, the talk, the gossip, of four
years about the First Lady of the Land, had gathered

headway. Her reputation had become the sinister crea-
tion of thousands of personal impressions spoken by
people who had seen her or talked with her; of thousands of newspaper items about her coming and going
to Long Branch, Saratoga Springs, Boston, New York,
for rest, for parties and receptions, for shopping; of
hundreds of items about gifts presented to her, her
house, her boys; of hundreds of items of public prints
and private gossip about her gowns and coiffures, her
jewels and adornments; of private information held by
scores of persons in high office who knew of her capri-
ces, tempers, jealousies. The journalist, biographer and
novelist, Mary Clemmer Ames, set forth a viewpoint
common to a large and possibly overwhelming major-
ity of the men and women of the country who held
any definite viewpoint at all. "Wives, mothers and
daughters, in ten thousand homes, were looking into
the faces of husbands, sons and fathers, with trembling
and with tears, and yet with sacrificial patriotism. They
knew, they felt the best-beloved were to be slain on the
country's battlefields. It was the hour for self-forgetting.
Personal vanity and elation, excusable in a more peaceful time, seemed unpardonable in this. Yet, in review-
ing the character of Presidents' wives, we shall see that
there was never one who entered the White House with

A PHOTOGRAPH OF
LINCOLN IN 1865,
PROBABLY BY BRADY

(*From the collection of
Frederick H. Meserve*)

"SHE WON'T THINK
ANYTHING ABOUT IT,"
WERE LINCOLN'S
LAST WORDS

CHAIR IN WHICH THE
PRESIDENT SAT WHEN
SHOT BY ASSASSIN

(*From the
Illinois State Historical Library*)

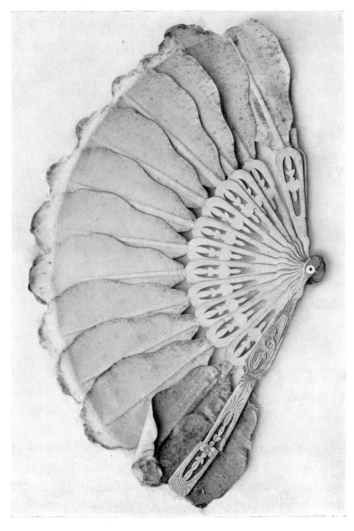

FAN CARRIED BY MRS. LINCOLN ON THE NIGHT OF THE ASSASSINATION—BLOOD-STAINED
AND SPOTTED

(In the collection of Oliver R. Barrett)

such a feeling of self-satisfaction, which amounted to personal exultation, as did Mary Lincoln. To her it was the fulfillment of a life-long ambition, and she made her journey to Washington a triumphal passage."

Mary Clemmer Ames wrote what was partly over-statement, partly and in degree a harsh judgment, yet she also reported what was in the heart of numbers of women. "In the distant farm house women waited, breathless, the latest story of battle. In the crowded cities they gathered by thousands, crying, only, 'Let me work for my brother; he dies for me!' With the record of the march and the fight, and of the unseemly defeat, the newspapers teemed with gossip concerning the lady in the White House. While her sister-women scraped lint, sewed bandages, and put on nurses' caps, and gave their all to country and to death, the wife of the President spent her time in rolling to and fro between Washington and New York, intent on extravagant purchases for herself and the White House. Mrs. Lincoln seemed to have nothing to do but to 'shop,' and the reports of her lavish bargains, in the newspapers, were vulgar and sensational in the extreme. The wives and daughters of other Presidents had managed to dress as elegant women, without the process of so doing becoming prominent or public. But not a new dress or jewel was bought by Mrs. Lincoln that did not find its way into the newspapers."

In the White House Mrs. Ames saw "a lonely man, sorrowful at heart, weighed down by mighty burdens"; toiling and suffering alone. Washington had become one vast hospital. "The reluctant river laid at the feet of the city its priceless freight of lacerated men. The wharves were lined with the dying and the dead. One ceaseless procession of ambulances moved to and fro . . . Our streets resounded with the shrieks of the sufferers. Churches, halls and houses were turned into hospitals . . . Through it all Mrs. Lincoln 'shopped.' . . . The nation seemed goaded at last to exasperation. Letters of rebuke, of expostulation, of anathema even, addressed to her, personally, came in to her from every direction. Not a day that did not bring her many such communications, denouncing her mode of life . . . To no other American woman had ever come an equal chance to set a lofty example of self-abnegation to her countrywomen. But just as if there were no national peril, no monstrous national debt, no rivers of blood flowing, she seemed chiefly intent upon pleasure, personal flattery and adulation; upon extravagant dress and ceaseless self-gratification."

The politicians with whom Mrs. Lincoln held interviews and had dealings regarding appointments and nominations, also her extreme household economy, were discussed by thousands in somewhat the words of Mary Clemmer Ames. "Vain, seeking admiration, the men who fed her weakness for their own political ends were sure of her favor. Thus, while daily disgracing the State by her own example, she still sought to meddle in its affairs. Woe to Mr. Lincoln if he did not appoint her favorites. Prodigal in personal expenditures, she brought shame upon the President's House by petty economies, which had never disgraced it before. Had the milk of its dairy been sent to the hospitals, she would have received golden praise. But the whole city felt scandalized to have it haggled over and peddled from the back door of the White House. State dinners could have been dispensed with, without a word of blame, had their cost been consecrated to the soldiers' service; but when it was made apparent that they were omitted from personal penuriousness and a desire to devote their cost to personal gratification, the public censure knew no bounds."

Mary Clemmer Ames reports what happened as a result of the letters that poured in on the Lady President. "From the moment Mrs. Lincoln began to receive recriminating letters, she considered herself an injured individual, the honored object of envy, jealousy and spite, and a martyr to her high position. No doubt some of them were unjust, and many more unkind; but it never dawned upon her consciousness that any part of the provocation was on her side, and after a few tastes of their bitter draughts she ceased to open them."

There came the reëlection of the President in the fall of 1864. There came the night of April 14, 1865, when she was alongside her husband in a box at Ford's Theatre. She sat close to him, leaned on him, as she afterward told it to her friend, Dr. Anson G. Henry. And she was a little afraid her behavior might be embarrassing to the daughter of Senator Harris of Rhode Island sitting near by. She said to the President, "What will Miss Harris think of my hanging on to you so?" "She won't think anything about it." And those were his last words. There came the assassin's bullet. And soon Abraham Lincoln lay on a bed in the back room of the Peterson house across from Ford's Theatre, breathing hard all night long and trying to struggle back to consciousness. His wife sat in the front room weeping, "uttering heartbroken exclamations all night long," leaving the house with the moan, "O my God, and I have given my husband to die!" There came to her such dumb despair as made all pain in her life

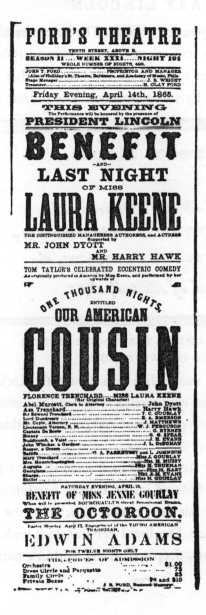

FORD'S THEATRE

TENTH STREET, ABOVE E.

SEASON II ..... WEEK XXXI ..... NIGHT 191
WHOLE NUMBER OF NIGHTS, 400.

JOHN T. FORD .... PROPRIETOR AND MANAGER
(Also of Holliday's St. Theatre, Baltimore, and Academy of Music, Phila
Stage Manager .... J. B. WRIGHT
Treasurer .... H. CLAY FORD

Friday Evening, April 14th, 1865.

THIS EVENING

The Performance will be honored by the presence of

PRESIDENT LINCOLN

BENEFIT

—AND—

LAST NIGHT

OF MISS

LAURA KEENE

THE DISTINGUISHED MANAGERESS AUTHORESS, and ACTRESS
Supported by

MR. JOHN DYOTT

AND

MR. HARRY HAWK

TOM TAYLOR'S CELEBRATED ECCENTRIC COMEDY
As originally produced in America by Miss Keene, and performed by her
upwards of

ONE THOUSAND NIGHTS,

ENTITLED

OUR AMERICAN

COUSIN

FLORENCE TRENCHARD...... MISS LAURA KEENE
(Her Original Character)

Abel Murcott, Clerk to Attorney .... John Dyott
Asa Trenchard .... Harry Hawk
Sir Edward Trenchard .... T. C. GOURLAY
Lord Dundreary .... E. A. EMERSON
Mr. Coyle, Attorney .... J. MATTHEWS
Lieutenant Vernon, R. N. .... W. J. FERGUSON
Captain De Boots .... C. BYRNES
Binney .... J. G. SPEAR
Buddicomb, a Valet .... E. B. EVANS
John Whicker, a Gardner .... J. L. DeBONAY
Rasper, a Groom ....
Bailiff .... G. A. PARKHURST and L. JOHNSON
Mary Trenchard .... Miss J. GOURLAY
Mrs. Mountchessington .... Mrs. M. MUZZY
Augusta .... Miss H. TRUEMAN
Georgiana .... Miss M. HART
Sharpe .... Mrs. A.M. EVANS
Skillet .... Miss M. GOURLAY

SATURDAY EVENING, APRIL 15.

BENEFIT OF MISS JENNIE GOURLAY
When will be presented BOURCICAULT'S Great Sensational Drama,

THE OCTOROON.

Easter Monday, April 17. Engagement of the YOUNG AMERICAN
TRAGEDIAN,

EDWIN ADAMS

FOR TWELVE NIGHTS ONLY

THE PRICES OF ADMISSION

Orchestra $1.00
Dress Circle and Parquette 75
Family Circle 25
Private Boxes .... $6 and $10

J. R. FORD, Business Manager.

PLAY BILL FOR
FORD'S THEATRE,
NIGHT OF
APRIL 14, 1865

till then seem easy in comparison. The bitterness of the hour was that so few friends could come to speak a word or touch her hand or sit in quiet with her and give her comfort by silent presence. The nearest to a

Green Room.

Admit the Bearer to the
EXECUTIVE MANSION,
On **WEDNESDAY,** *the*
19th of April, 1865.

ADMISSION CARD TO THE FUNERAL SERVICES
AT THE WHITE HOUSE

great friend that came then was Elizabeth Keckley, the mulatto woman who carried solace and ministering hands, and who was given trust and confidence that no others received.

Mary Clemmer Ames fathomed some of the bitterness of the hour. "Mrs. Lincoln bewept her husband. There is no doubt but that, in that black hour, she suffered great injustice. She loved her husband, with the intensity of a nature, deep and strong, within a narrow channel. The shock of his untimely taking-off, might have excused a woman of loftier nature than hers for any accompanying paralysis."

This was nearly the word, "paralysis." She lay physically helpless for days and wandered mentally and called for death to take her, crying she had lost all worth living for. It was five weeks before she was able to leave the White House. "It was not strange she stayed five weeks," wrote Mary Clemmer Ames. "It would have been stranger had she been able to have left it sooner. It was her misfortune that she had so armed public sympathy against her, by years of indifference to the sorrow of others, that when her own hour of supreme anguish came, there were few to comfort her, and many to assail. She had made many unpopular innovations upon the old serene and stately régime of the President's house. Never a reign of concord in her best day, in her hour of affliction it degenerated into absolute anarchy. The long-time steward [overseer and caretaker] had been dethroned, that Mrs. Lincoln might manage according to her own will. While she was shut in with her woe, the White House was left without a responsible protector. The rabble ranged through it at will. Silver and dining-ware were carried off, and have never been recovered. It was plundered, not only of ornaments, but of heavy articles of furniture. Costly sofas and chairs were cut and injured. Exquisite lace curtains were torn into rags, and carried off in pieces."

While all of this was going on downstairs, Mrs. Lincoln in her apartments upstairs refused to see any one but servants, while day after day immense boxes containing her personal effects were leaving the White House for the West. "The size and number of these boxes," noted Mrs. Ames, "with the fact of the pillaged aspect of the White House, led to the accusation, which so roused public feeling against her, that she was robbing the National House, and carrying the national property with her into retirement. This accusation, which clings to her to this day [1871], was probably unjust. Her personal effects, in all likeliness, amounted to as much as that of nearly all other Presidents' wives together, and the vandals who roamed at large through the length and breadth of the White House, were quite sufficient to account for all its missing treasures."

Broken Woman

THE TEN years between 1865 and 1875 were desperate for poor Mary Todd Lincoln. When the tongues of many begin wagging with a war-time hate there are reputations created, impressions spread, which are true only in the sense that the apparitions in concave or convex mirrors are in proportion. Mary Clemmer Ames in her book, "Ten Years in Washington," issued eight years after Mrs. Lincoln left the White House, recognized that the pictures of Mrs. Lincoln had run into riotous caricatures and wrote, "The public did Mrs. Lincoln injustice, in considering her an ignorant, illiterate woman. She was well born, gently reared, and her education above the average standard given to girls in her youth. She is a fair mistress of the French language, and in English can write a more graceful letter than one educated woman in fifty. She has quick perceptions, and an almost unrivalled power of mimicry. The only amusement of her desolate days, while shut in from the world in Chicago, when she refused to see her dearest friends and took comfort in the thought that she had been chosen as the object of preëminent affliction, was to repeat in tone, gesture, and expression, the words, looks and actions of men and women who, in the splendor of her life in Washington, had happened to offend her. Her lack was not a lack of keen faculties, or of fair culture, but a constitutional inability to rise to the action of high motive in a time when every true soul in the nation seemed to be impelled to unselfish deeds for its rescue. She was incapable of lofty, impersonal impulse. She was self-centered, and never in any experience rose above herself. According to circumstances, her own ambitions, her own pleasures, her own sufferings, made the sensation which absorbed and consumed every other. As a President's wife she could not rise above the level of her nature, and it was her misfortune that she never even approached the bound of her opportunity."

This is almost equivalent to saying that Mary Todd Lincoln never grew up, that she kept a child mind in the body of a matured woman, that she could not learn responsibility and meet it, that in her later years she had her mind fixed on the same shows and baubles of life that please a girl at a tea party for dolls. This would be too easy and offhand an explanation of the tumults that drove Mary Todd Lincoln through life. If she is to be compared with other Presidents' wives, other White House ladies whose performances rate higher in history for conduct and sacrifice, it may be she has an alibi, apology so perfect that her ghost could answer, "Did God in His infinite wisdom ever weigh down any

White House woman with a devastating curse such as rode in my blood and brain?"

There are crippled brains on which it is no more wise to visit impatience or excoriation or ordinary verdicts of guilty, than upon crippled bodies. We do not kick the physically clumsy for being what they are. Neither can we deal with the mentally thwarted in a vocabulary of blame. They are in a world outside the realm of sanity, balance, respectability, serenity, sweetness and light.

Letter after letter poured from her in which she cried life was too heavy for her, the burning too fierce. Part of it was the acting of a frustrated and furious woman trying to impose her will on a United States Congress which for years resisted her efforts towards a pension. Most of her crying out loud, publicly and privately, however, ran back to the pressure of tongs of fate that clamped tighter and tighter in the lobes of her brain. She was, as her physician and friend later declared, the victim of a cerebral disease. When she hurled petty and spiteful accusations in a way to lead few people or none to believe what she was saying, she was speaking with the tongue of an irresponsible woman. When she tried to dramatize herself as a pauper, "seeking lodging from one place to another" it was the impulse of a disordered brain. When the administrator of her husband's estate made the public record, as required by law, that the property for equal sharing among Abraham Lincoln's three heirs was valued at $110,000.00, her mind was so far gone that she could not realize it was time for her to drop the rôle of a woman wronged in money matters. During many years of her life she had overridden obstacles, she had exercised a stubborn and commanding power that brought her things she wanted. The old Covenanter blood ran deep in her; she was a fighter; and she would fight on now against simple circumstances impossible to surmount. Her waning mind could no longer grasp obstacles in the face of which an intelligent woman would know her cue was complete silence.

She still had vitality, sometimes furious in its rush at her enemies, and again frantic and futile, lacking direction, not knowing how or when to hit. It may even be that the pathos of her fate was known to her. She may have suspected that her mind and temperament were too imperfect for adjustment to the human equation into which life had thrust her. And what flickers of suspicion she had were overcome by her pride, by her abiding belief that destiny had set her for a Great Lady and she would enact that rôle to the last breath of her

combative spirit. Yet it seems also that even though
she did believe she could surmount this or that barrier,
that she could win in this or that contest against indi-
viduals, there was nevertheless a whole of life—a vast
brutal phantasmagoria which had her conquered in
middle age and in her youth. She was writing in 1865
that "life is indeed a heavy burden and I do not care
how soon I am called hence." Also: "My heart is indeed broken, and without my beloved husband, I do
not care to live."

When her letters printed in the New York *World*
announced a public auction of her personal wardrobe
for the purpose of getting funds for herself and family
to live on, she had rushed into it on an impulse with no
forethought as to the misery such an action would give
to the few who were loyal to her for what she had been
in the past. She sent a letter to Elizabeth Keckley. "I am
writing this morning with a broken heart after a sleepless night of great mental suffering. R. [Robert] came
up last evening like a maniac, and almost threatening
his life, looking like death, because the letters of the
World were published in yesterday's [Chicago] papers. I could not refrain from weeping when I saw him
so miserable. But yet, my dear good Lizzie, was it not
to protect myself and help others—and was not my

motive and action of the purest kind? Pray for me that this cup of affliction may pass from me, or be sanctified to me. I weep whilst I am writing." She ended the letter: "I am nearly losing my reason."

She could fight the outside world and fling back spite for spite but the wild reproaches of her eldest son, "looking like death," gave her a night of tears. Robert, just two years out of Harvard and looking forward to a career as a lawyer, with his inclinations and prospects associated with the respectable and wealthy classes, had been shocked at the sudden news that his mother was publicly selling to the highest bidder one lace dress, one flounced dress, five lace shawls, three camel-hair shawls, one lace parasol cover, one sable boa, one white boa, one set of furs, two Paisley shawls, two gold bracelets, sixteen dresses, two opera cloaks, one feather cape, one diamond ring, one child's shawl, twenty-eight yards of silk, and other articles. From the way Robert behaved his mother knew that he and others were ashamed of her and afraid of what she would do next. The "old clothes speculation," as her sale was designated, was the farthest she had ever drifted from being in public a Great Lady. Before her time more than one First Lady of the Land had been accused of taking away White House belongings. Yet

MRS. LINCOLN IN PARTY
GARB AND AGAIN IN
MOURNING COSTUME,
WITH THE CURIOUS
IMMOBILITY OF LINE AND
FEATURE SHOWN IN ALL
HER PHOTOGRAPHS

THE IRREPRES-
SIBLE TAD

A LATER LIKE-
NESS OF TAD

Taken in Frank-
furt, Germany

MRS. LINCOLN IN DARK ATTIRE

(Photographs from the collection of Oliver R. Barrett)

none of the mistresses of the Executive Mansion had ever invited the public to an auction of her personal apparel, jewels, keepsakes.

After a night of tears Mary Lincoln wrote, "I pray for death this morning. Only my darling Taddie prevents my taking my life. I shall have to endure a round of abuse from the Republicans because I dared to relieve a few of my wants." And it came to her that her face, her looks, were changing for the worse, and she wrote, "What a world of anguish this is—and how I have been made to suffer! You would not recognize me now. The glass shows me a pale, wretched, haggard face, and my dresses are like bags on me." She was becoming more of a stranger, an alien to some who had known her for years. Robert was writing to a young woman he was to marry soon, "I have no doubt that a great many good and amiable people wonder why I do not take charge of her affairs and keep them straight but it is very hard to deal with one who is sane on all subjects but one. You would hardly believe it possible, but my mother protests to me that she is in actual want and nothing I can do or say will convince her to the contrary. Do you see that I am likely to have a good deal of trouble in the future, do what I can to prevent it."

The troubled woman wrote of "debts staring me in

the face," of lacking "the simplest daily necessities," of pressing unpaid bills. "I wish I could forget myself." She recalled her "angel boy in Heaven"—Willie Lincoln whose death in 1862 had been a shock to her. "He was too pure for Earth and God recalled His own."

She mentioned suffering with "fearful" headaches. She wrote of "friends," of "false-hearted villains" trying to ruin her. "The agitation of mind has very much impaired my health." She apologized for an explosion of behavior. "Never, dear Lizzie think of my great nervousness the night before we parted; I had been so harassed with my fears." She went deep in pity for herself: "If I had committed murder in every city in this blessed Union, I could not be more traduced." She wrote in October, 1867, "A piece in the morning *Tribune,* signed 'B,' pretending to be a lady, says there is no doubt Mrs. L. *is* deranged—has been for years past and will end her years in a lunatic asylum. They would doubtless like me to begin it *now*." She wrote the same month, "The Springfield *Journal* had an editorial a few days since, with the important information that Mrs. Lincoln had been known to be *deranged* for years, and should be pitied for all her *strange acts*." Her immediate thought in that connection was that "in the comfortable stealings by contracts from the Government, these low creatures are allowed to hurl their malicious wrath at me, with no one to defend me or protect me, if I should starve." And while she wrote and spoke of starving, of economy, of being clothed shabbily, Judge David Davis filed a statement of the assets of the estate of her husband, amounting to $110,000.00.

The impression was definite now in many circles that Mary Todd Lincoln was mentally unsound, was a pathological case requiring attention, treatment, at least retirement from affairs which would bring her in any way before the public. She met these requirements for a time by going to London and continental Europe, taking Tad with her. They lived quietly. Tad studied with a tutor who came daily in London. His mother was anxious about his education. They went together among wonderful mountains and valleys. She read French novels. She saw few of her homeland people. She wrote one letter reporting foggy weather and rain, rain, rain, beating on the window. "The loneliness of this winter words could not express, nor pen write its horrors."

She wrote long letters to Mary Harlan Lincoln, who had married Robert. Some of these were brimming

135

with vitality and affection. She was better for living in strange lands and among strangers. So it seemed at moments. Yet the old headaches still visited her; she told of attacks of neuralgia in the head. It almost seemed she knew the storms of life were over for her, that her strength was gone for any more of the bitter contests into which she had flung herself. "I am well aware without my physician so frequently repeating to me—that quiet is necessary for my life."

Now she had fairly well stepped out of the public gaze. The reports and rumors of her in the public prints had nearly died down. They flared up, however, in connection with the bill of Senator Charles Sumner to award her a pension of $5,000 a year, the amount of interest due her on her husband's salary if he had lived to serve out his term. In the end the bill passed with the pension fixed at $3,000 a year. While the bill was under consideration Mrs. Lincoln heard of the sister of a United States congressman being in Paris. And she wrote an eight-page letter on black-bordered paper, pleas and arguments for her pension, asking help of the congressman's sister. The letter was "confidential." She wished it burned. She made personal allusions to the wife of President Grant, to the wife of E. B. Washburne, French ambassador. These personal allusions were uncalled for. Once more the public prints in America dealt with her griefs and ways.

There could be little doubt hot wires were being drawn through her eyes. There were steel springs in her head. The tongs of an iron fate pressed between her aching temples.

She went home—to America—to Chicago. Tad Lincoln, now eighteen years old, a whimsical and promising boy, was stricken with typhoid and died. And no one could say of the mother and widow mourning at the grave of the third of her four sons that her life had been laid in pleasant paths.

She made mistakes and was blamed. A friend inquired why she was blamed with "her brain on fire with pain."

Bitter Cups

Is EACH of our lives a book? And when it is done
and over, having a first and last chapter, can we
turn the pages backward or forward and read what the
years did to this or that one of us? Perhaps this is so
and we can turn to the year 1875 and see what happened to Mary Todd Lincoln.

She had left Chicago where her one living son Robert had married and begun law practice. And from
Florida where she was spending the winter she suddenly sent a telegram in March to Dr. Ralph N. Isham,
their family physician. The life of her boy was in danger; she called on the doctor to save her boy. She was
taking a train for Chicago.

When she arrived in Chicago her boy, in very good
health, and Dr. Isham met her at the railroad depot.
And talking with her boy and seeing his face smoothed
out her fears and she seemed to be a sensible and lively
woman again.

The long trip from Florida had been nice and pleasant, she told them—except that in Jacksonville, where
she bought a cup of coffee, some enemy had put poison
in the coffee; she refused to drink the coffee believing
it would mean her death. Thus there were people lying
in wait seeking her death. So her talk implied.

Would she go with her son to his home and stay?

141

No, she couldn't, she must go to the Grand Pacific Hotel, in the center of the turmoil of Chicago. And the son must go with her to the hotel and stay with her.

So that night and following nights Robert Lincoln slept in a room next to his mother—though his sleep was interrupted. His mother would knock on the door of his room calling that she was in danger. To ease her mind he slept on a lounge in her room. Or again she came into his room and he gave her his bed while he took a couch.

She screamed, "You are going to murder me," when Robert intercepted her in a downgoing elevator. A fire would destroy Chicago and Robert's house would be the only one left standing, she told him. She brought forth from a pocket and showed to Robert $57,000 worth of stocks and bonds she was carrying on her person. She told him that a man had taken her pocketbook, promising to return it at a certain hour; the man was a Wandering Jew she had met in Florida; she seated herself next to a wall and pretended to be repeating what the man was saying to her through the wall.

The joy she had shown at first on her return from Florida passed away. She spoke of physical torments inflicted on her. Needles of flame were being drawn through her head. A watch must be kept for persons hiding near by waiting to murder her. An Indian was pulling wires out of her eyes. There were steel springs in her head which doctors were taking out.

In two days shopping in April she bought $772.03 worth of sashes, ribbons, ties, pointe lace, silk handkerchiefs, gloves, hose, pointe collars. She bought two Shetland *coiffures,* two parasols, three dozen handkerchiefs, seventeen pairs of gloves. She bought three watches for $450, jewelry costing $700, a bolt of silk, $200 worth of soaps and perfumes. Though having no house of her own and refusing to live at her son's house, she bought lace curtains, $213.00 worth at Ellen & Mackey, $336.83 worth at Hollister & Phelps.

Naturally by now there was town talk about her. The chambermaids and bellboys at the hotel said nothing they could do pleased her. The hotel manager was worrying and suggested some other place would make a better residence for her.

On May 18, 1874, Dr. Ralph N. Isham dated a document of that day and wrote:

"I hereby certify that I have examined Mrs. Mary Lincoln—widow—and that I am of the opinion that she is insane and a fit subject for hospital treatment."

On the next day attorneys for Robert T. Lincoln
(Ayer & Koles, and Leonard Swett) entered in the
county court of Cook County, before Judge M. R. M.
Wallace an application to try the question of sanity. It
read to begin with: "The petition of Robert T. Lincoln
would respectfully represent that his mother, Mary
Lincoln, widow of Abraham Lincoln, deceased, a resident of Cook County is insane, and that it would be
for her benefit and for the safety of the community
that she should be confined." It named seventeen witnesses who should be summoned, estimated her estate
to be valued not exceeding $75,000.00 and prayed for a
conservator to be appointed to manage and control her
estate.

On the same day the county court clerk signed a
writ to the sheriff stating in part: "You are therefore
hereby commanded to arrest said Mary Lincoln, widow
of Abraham Lincoln, deceased, to have her on the 19th
day of May, A. D. 1875, at 2 o'clock P. M. before our
County Court, and then and there to await and abide
the result of the trial."

On the same day of May 19th a jury of twelve men
heard the witnesses and brought a verdict, "We . . .
are satisfied that the said Mary Lincoln is insane and
is a fit person to be sent to a State Hospital." Her age

was fifty-six years, it was set forth. "The disease is of unknown duration; the cause is unknown."

Besides retail storekeepers, and the son Robert, five physicians testified. Dr. Willis Danforth said he had treated Mrs. Lincoln several weeks in 1873 for fever and nervous derangement of the head. She had imaginings that "some one was at work on her head, an Indian was removing the bones from her face and pulling wires out of her eyes." He visited her again in 1874 when she was suffering from nervous debility. "She complained that some one was taking steel springs from her head and would not let her rest. She was going to die within a few days, had been admonished to that effect by her husband. She imagined that she heard raps on a table conveying the time of her death, and would sit and ask questions and repeat the supposed answer the table would give." On general topics her conversation was rational. Her derangement did not arise from bodily condition nor physical disease. "I . . . am of the opinion that she is insane."

Robert T. Lincoln closed his difficult session as a witness with saying, "I have had a conference with her cousin and Major Stuart of Springfield, and Judge Davis of the Supreme Court, all of whom advised me in the course I have taken. I do not regard it safe to

I hereby certify that I have examined Mrs Mary Lincoln - I know - and that I am of the opinion that she is insane and a fit subject for Hospital treatment

Ralph N. Isham M.D.

THE CERTIFICATE OF MRS. LINCOLN'S PHYSICIAN ON HER MENTAL CONDITION

To the Hon. M. R. M. WALLACE, Judge of said Court:

The petition of......Robert T. Lincoln

would respectfully represent that his mother Mary Lincoln, widow of Abraham Lincoln, deceased, a resident of Cook County is insane, and that it would be for her benefit and for the safety of the community that she should be confined in the Cook County Hospital or the Illinois State Hospital for the insane. The facts in her case can be proven by......Ralph N. Isham

a regular practicing physician, and by......Willis Danforth, Samuel M. Turner, Charles Gossage, E. S. Isham, Jerome O. Stagg, E. H. Groh, S. Handstock, James B. Stone, C. J. Holmes, J. P. Arnold, Jno. A. Frank, R. L. Patterson, J. S. Jewell, F. S. Smith, and others intimate acquaintances of the said Mrs. Patterson who reside in said County

all whom are residents of this County, and that the said Mary Lincoln

has property and effects consisting of......Negotiable securities and other personal property

the value of which does not exceed the sum of......Seventy-five thousand Dollars.

THE PETITION OF ROBERT LINCOLN TO THE COUNTY COURT OF COOK COUNTY allow her to remain longer unrestrained. She has long been a source of great anxiety. . . . She has no home, and does not visit my house because of a misunderstanding with my wife. She has always been kind to me. She has been of unsound mind since the death of her husband, and has been irresponsible for the last ten years. I regard her as eccentric and unmanageable. There was no cause for her recent purchases, as her trunks are filled with dresses she never wears. She never wears jewelry."

The hearing was conducted quietly, decently. The jurors were business and professional men chosen to do a difficult and responsible task of citizenship with delicacy and honor. On June 14th Robert T. Lincoln was issued letters of conservatorship by the county court, "duly appointed Conservator for Mary Lincoln, widow of Abraham Lincoln, diseased." The usual form was observed by the county court and a statement of the trial and its results, with the names of the jurors, was entered on a large sheet titled "Lunatic Record. County Court of Cook County." The Court Clerk, H. Lieb, filed papers marked "Mary Lincoln, Lunatic."

It was a heavy day's work, done by men with heavy hearts. The color of death was in the air. The proceedings had a touch of burial service in them. Something

148

And our last resort — a plain yet
genteel boarding, does not exempt,
us, from charges, that I shall
have to exert myself, in the
future, to meet. I will write
no more to day. for I became
so thoroughly chilled on yesterday
that my limbs — ache with pain
and I am sure, the terrible trial
we are passing through — will
only pain your gentle heart,
by the recapitulation —
— With much love, I remain
always truly
Mary Lincoln,

MARY LINCOLN WRITES MRS. J. H. ORNE
JAN. 4, 1866
(In the collection of Oliver R. Barrett)

ROBERT TODD LINCOLN
IN MANHOOD

ROBERT TODD LINCOLN
IN YOUTH AS A
HARVARD GRADUATE

(Both in the collection
of Oliver R. Barrett)

that had been alive, with control and direction, was gone. Something that once had vitality and bloom had become victim to rot and dissolution while yet partly alive. Death itself with the complete paralysis of the mind and the laying away of the cold remains of the physical structure in the ground—this is easy to gaze on as compared with looking from day to day and month to month at a mind in ruins, being eaten away by a slow destroyer. The test of living next to this personal tragedy came hard on Robert T. Lincoln. For fifty years after it he was a shy man. His shyness was spoken of. It could be traced back to any one of several tragedies to which his eyes and ears were witness.

Mary Lincoln was taken now to Batavia, Illinois, a place set on hills overlooking long slopes of the Fox River Valley. In a private sanitarium under the care of a distinguished specialist she was better off than she had been for years. Robert T. Lincoln wrote a letter to Mrs. J. H. Orne, a long-time friend of his mother and himself. "Six physicians informed me that by longer delay I was making myself morally responsible for some very probable tragedy, which might occur at any moment. Some of my Eastern friends have criticized the public proceedings in court, which seemed to them unnecessary. Against this there was no help, for we have a statute in this State which imposes a very heavy penalty on any one depriving an insane person of his liberty without the verdict of a jury. My mother is, I think, under as good care and as happily situated as is possible under the circumstances. She is in the private part of the house of Dr. Patterson and her associates are the members of his family only. With them she walks and drives whenever she likes and takes her meals with them or in her own room as she chooses, and she tells me she likes them all very much. The [her] expression of surprise at my action which was telegraphed East, and which you doubtless saw, was the first and last expression of the kind she has uttered and we are on the best of terms. Indeed my consolation in this sad affair is in thinking that she herself is happier in every way, than she has been in ten years. So far as I can see she does not realize her situation at all. I can tell you nothing as to the probability of her restoration. It must be the work of some time if it occurs."

It was a letter more like his father than any we know of that ever came from Robert T. Lincoln. He ended it: "The responsibility that has been and is now on me is one that I would gladly share if it was possible to do so, but being alone as I am, I can only do my duty as it is given me to see it."

State of Illinois, } ss.
COUNTY OF COOK.

In the County Court of Cook County:

THE PEOPLE OF THE STATE OF ILLINOIS,

To the Sheriff of said County:—*GREETING:*

Whereas, it has been represented to the Honorable M. R. M. WALLACE, Judge of this Court, by *Robert T. Lincoln* in a petition duly verified, that *Mary Lincoln widow of Abraham Lincoln deceased* is believed to be insane, and whereas said Judge has appointed the hearing of said petition for the *Nineteenth* day of *May* A. D. 1875 at 2 o'clock P. M.

UPPER HALF OF THE WARRANT FOR THE ARREST OF MARY LINCOLN, WIDOW OF ABRAHAM LINCOLN

After three months in the Batavia sanitarium Mary Lincoln was taken for a visit with her sister Elizabeth (Mrs. Ninian W. Edwards) in Springfield, Illinois. From September 13, 1875, to June 7, 1876, Robert T. Lincoln paid checks to Ninian W. Edwards ranging from $100 to $875. The total of $4,599.28 was itemized in the report of the conservator to the Cook County court as being "for expenses of Mrs. Lincoln during her visit and sojourn at Springfield, Illinois, being money sent Hon. N. W. Edwards, and by him given to Mrs. Lincoln, to be expended by her for her comfort and support." Every service and attention advised by skilled physicians, besides anything of help that money could buy, was hers. Her sister Elizabeth, whom she called "Lizzie," was a cheerful presence, was thoughtful. So Mary Lincoln grew better.

Her jewels had been taken away from her. And she wanted them. Also there were nine trunks of dresses and other personal belongings of old days which she wanted. And on December 15, 1875, Robert T. Lincoln appeared before Judge Wallace of the Cook County court and set forth that "Mrs. Lincoln is exceedingly anxious and desirous to have the custody and use of the articles of personal jewelry contained in a Tin Box mentioned by the undersigned in the inventory filed

You are therefore hereby commanded to arrest said *Mary Lincoln*

Widow of Abraham Lincoln deceased to have her on the 19th

day of *May* ... A.D. 1875 at 2 o'clock P.M., before our County

court, and then and there to await and abide the result of the trial,

And have you then and there this Writ, and make due service as the law directs.

Witness, HERMANN LIEB, Clerk of our said Court, and

the Seal of said Court at Chicago, in said County, this 19th

day of *May* ... A.D. 1875

Hermann Lieb Clerk.

LOWER HALF OF THE WARRANT FOR THE ARREST OF MARY LINCOLN

by him. The Box is now in the Fidelity Safe Depository for safe keeping and Mrs. Lincoln has its key." Judge David Davis and Leonard Swett had been consulted as friends, "familiar with the facts of Mrs. Lincoln's case" and they advised compliance with her request; she ought to be allowed her jewels and gowns of old days if she wanted them. The conservator "does not think Mrs. Lincoln will make any improper disposition of the articles contained in the box"; possession would benefit her. So she regained her jewels. Also, three days later the court gave leave for her to again have nine trunks "containing wearing apparel principally," the conservator believed. "She needs for her use a great part thereof."

When Mary Lincoln had been one year and nearly a month in classification and under treatment as insane, her attorney, Isaac Arnold, petitioned the Cook County Court for removal of her conservator and a restoration of all rights, privileges, and property. On June 15 a sworn statement of Ninian W. Edwards was filed with the court testifying, "Mrs. Lincoln has been with me for nine or ten months, and her friends all think she is a proper person to take charge of her own affairs." The statement thus opened and then went on to repeat, "She has been with me about nine months,

Personal property of which the value is not estimated,

A tin box containing personal jewelry, and also nine

trunks containing wearing apparel and other articles,
in care of Knowner
All stored for safe Keeping in the "Fidelity-Safety-
Depository" in Chicago, having been locked and the Keys
retained by Mrs. Lincoln. Mrs. Lincoln.

Summary.

Cash	$ 1,029.35
United State Bonds and Stocks	58,070.00
Personal Bond	8,876.00
Personal property of which value is given	5,549.83
Total	$73,454.18

$5,000.00

PART OF A DOCUMENT TITLED: INVENTORY OF THE REAL AND PERSONAL ESTATE
OF MRS. ABRAHAM LINCOLN

and her friends all of them recognize that she is a fit person to take care of and manage her own affairs. That she is in such condition that she can manage her own affairs." One circumstance was detailed: "She has not spent all that she was allowed to spend during the past year, and we all think she is in a condition to take charge of her own affairs."

And on the same day of June 15, 1876, the court removed the conservator, Robert T. Lincoln, restored Mary Lincoln to her rights and property, and she received from Robert T. Lincoln an elaborate, scrupulous and thoroughly detailed accounting of her money, estate, pension papers, bonds, leases, expenses for physicians, attendants, nurses, railroad fare, telegrams, storage and express charges, including $6.00 for repair of a music box and $151.00 for hack hire and shadowing by Pinkerton detectives.

And now as a free woman again, free to come and go, free to make her own decisions, what would Mary Todd Lincoln do? She told her sister she couldn't stand it to meet old friends. "Lizzie, they will never cease to regard me a lunatic, I feel it in their soothing manner. If I should say the moon is made of green cheese they would heartily and smilingly agree with me. I love you, but I cannot stay. I would be much less unhappy in the midst of strangers." And to strangers she went. She put the Atlantic Ocean between herself and her old friends. In Germany, France, Italy, she lived—mostly alone, often without servant or companion, and sometimes with no letters passing between her and Robert so that for periods of time he did not know where she was—a worn struggler having only memories to live with— letting it be known as little as possible who she was— hiding her name as a fugitive. She wrote few letters. One told of her pleasure at being far from "the border ruffian west."

She was in her sixtieth year in Pau, France, in December of 1879, living cheaply, doing without a servant. And mounting a stepladder one day to fix a picture over a mantelpiece, she fell to the floor. She was kept to her bed with inflammation of the spinal cord and a partial crippling of the legs. She got up and managed to travel to Nice where again she had to go to bed for rest. She improved enough to board a ship for the homeland. Something told her it was time now to go home.

Aboard the ship was the world-famous actress Madam Sarah Bernhardt. Arriving at the Port of New York a crowd of people and a group of newspaper reporters were at the dock—and there were cheers and

excitement—over the arrival of Bernhardt. The New
York *Sun* told of how it was necessary for a policeman
to put his hand on the shoulder of a little old woman
with a wrinkling face and streaks of white in her hair;
she must stand back while a path was made for the
footlight queen to her carriage.

Mary Lincoln stayed a little time in New York for
consultation and medical treatment. Then Springfield,
Illinois, again—home with sister Lizzie. There she hid
herself as best she could; weather permitting, the windows were shut and the shades pulled down. Her talk
among the few friends who saw her was of her husband, of her poverty, of ingratitude and misunderstanding. It was a brief interlude of joy when her son, Robert, and his wife arrived and set in her lap their girl
child named Mary for her grandmother.

More and more she shrank from the outside world.
When invited for a drive she might or might not go.
If she did the carriage curtains must be drawn. She was
weary of faces. In earlier years she wanted everybody,
the whole world, to see her. That was past. Now she
wanted to be alone with what was so deeply past. She
wrote in a letter, "Ah, my dear friend, you will rejoice
when you know that I have gone to my husband and
children."

She lingered on, muttering of shadows that waited for her beyond this world. She sought healing in a trip to New York in March of 1882. In Springfield again she sat at the fireside of the Edwards home with a few friends. Summer came, she weakened, lay abed many days racked with boils. She took off her wedding ring from a swollen finger. One Friday in July she walked across the room without help. But she wasn't getting better. For the next day she could neither walk nor talk nor eat. Paralysis crept up into her body.

In the room where she had sat so much with candle-light and shadow, the evening of all her years came a little after sunset on July 16, 1882. This was in the same house where nearly forty years earlier she was married. They carried a burial casket out over the threshold her feet touched as a bride—and that was all.

A newspaper had mentioned her wedding ring as taken off. "It is of Etruscan gold and is now quite thin from wear. It is inscribed with 'A. L. to Mary, Nov. 4, 1842. Love is Eternal.' The ring will be put on and probably be buried with her."

PART II

PART II

The Documents

WHEN the materials which go into the making of a biography are filtered through the mind of the author, something is invariably lost. A significant phrase from a letter, a paragraph perhaps, fits the biographer's immediate need; the balance of the document is rejected. Proper proportion—itself an approach to fidelity—and the necessity of keeping the finished sketch within readable limits make selection inescapable. Nevertheless, valuable lights on character are frequently sacrificed in the process. Letters are bits of self-portraiture, sometimes more effectively done, more convincing, than anything from the pen of another can possibly be. Often a few paragraphs which a newspaper writer struck off as a part of a day's routine have an authentic ring that defies duplication.

Particularly is this true in the case of Mary Todd. It is difficult, if not impossible, for another to convey quite the impression of buoyancy, of fine-drawn temperament, that her own early letters carry. Later correspondence furnishes a more convincing picture of her years of marriage than one is likely to derive from secondary accounts. The overwhelming grief occasioned by Lincoln's death, the virulence of the abuse which popular misunderstanding loaded upon her, her own mental deterioration—all these stand forth in high relief in the documents of the time.

In the autumn of 1839 Mary Todd arrived in Springfield to make her home with her sister, Mrs. Ninian W. Edwards. At about the same time Mercy Levering came on from Baltimore for an extended visit with her brother Lawrason and his family. The Leverings and the Edwardses lived adjacent to each other, and the two girls soon became firm friends. When they separated in the spring of 1840—Mercy Levering to return to Baltimore, Mary Todd to visit relatives in Missouri— they commenced a correspondence which continued until Mercy returned to Springfield in the autumn of 1841 as the bride of James C. Conkling.

Mary Todd's first contribution to this correspondence[1] was written from the home of her uncle, Judge David Todd, in Columbia, Missouri, where she found

---

[1] The three letters printed here are all that are now known to exist. They are in the collection of Oliver R. Barrett of Chicago, Illinois.

congenial company in her cousin Ann, Judge Todd's daughter, and other relatives.

Columbia July 23d 1840.

Many thanks Dearest Merce for your kind letter, yet in spite of the pleasure of hearing from you, it brought many feelings of sorrow and regret, to know that you were as near as St. Louis, & [I] was debarred the happiness of seeing one I love so well. A few days before receiving yours, Elizabeth wrote to me & spoke of the possibility of seeing you again as you did not quit these western wilds until August & then you would accompany your Brother home. In spite of the *agreeable visitation* I have already made, I had determined to forego all, once more to see you, and shorten my visit here. You will readily credit me Dearest, when I tell you my time has been most delightfully spent. This portion of the state is certainly most beautiful, and in my wanderings I never encountered more kindness & hospitality. As my visit was particularly to my relations & [I] did not expect to remain for any length of time, I was not anxious to mingle with the strange crowd, and form new associations so soon to be severed, yet every lady almost that called extended an invitation to us to spend an evening with them, so I have necessarily seen more society than I had anticipated. On yesterday we returned from a most agreeable excursion to Boonville, situated immediately on the river and a charming place. We remained a week, attended four parties, during the time. One was *particularly* distinguished for its brilliancy & *city like* doings. The house was very commodious four rooms & two halls, thrown open for the reception of the guests, in two, dancing was carried on with *untiring vigor,* kept up until 3 o'clock, however, Cousin & myself were more genteel [and] left rather earlier. *Your risibles* would have undergone a *considerable state* of *excitement,* were you to have seen the "poetry of motion" exercised in the dance. Had our grandfathers been present in the festive halls of mirth, they would undoubtedly have recognised the familiar airs of their youthful days, all the old Virginia reels that have been handed down to us by *tradition,* were played. Your cousin Sep methinks would have enjoyed the danse, no insinuations meant, save his extreme fondness for this fascinating amusement, and the rapid manner they hurried through the figures. At the end of each cotillion, I felt exhausted after such *desperate exertions* to keep pace with the music. Were Missouri my home, with the exception of St. Louis, Boonville would certainly in my estimation have the preference. A life on the river to me has always had a charm, so much excitement, and this *you* have deemed necessary to my well being; every day experience impresses me more fully with the belief. I would such were not my nature, for mine I fancy is to be a quiet lot, and happy indeed will I be, if it is, only cast near those, I *so dearly love.* My feelings & hopes are all so sanguine that in this dull world of reality tis best to dispell our delusive day dreams as soon as possible. Would it were in my power to follow your kind advice, my ever dear Merce and turn my thoughts from earthly vanities, to one higher than us all. Every day proves the fallacy of our enjoyments, & that we are living for pleasures that do not recompense us for the pursuit.—I wrote you a lengthy document, soon after reaching this place. As you did not mention having received it, I feared it had not reached you. The mail comes in to day, and I am on the wing of expectation, hoping to hear from my dear sister Fanny.[2] Dr Wallace I hear has been sick, & Fanny I fear is unable to play the part of devoted nurse at *this time,* to both child & husband.—Every week, since I left Springfield, have had the felicity of receiving various numbers of their interesting papers. Old Soldiers, Journals & even the *Hickory club,* has crossed my vision. This latter, rather astonished your friend, *there* I had deemed myself forgotten.—When I mention *some letters* I have received since leaving S- you will be somewhat surprised, as I *must confess* they were entirely *unlooked for.* This is *between ourselves,* my dearest, but of this more anon. Every day I am convinced this is a stranger world we live in, the *past* as the future is to me a mystery. How much I wish you were near, ever have I found yours a congenial heart. In your presence I have almost *thought aloud,* and the thought that paineth most is, that such may never be again, yet, I trust that a happier day will dawn, near you, I would be most happy to sojourn in our earthly pilgrimmage. To me it has ever appeared that those whose presence was the sunlight of my heart have departed— separated—far and wide, to meet when? In Boonville I met with two or three former schoolmates, endeared to me by

[2] Frances Todd, who married Dr. William S. Wallace of Springfield, Illinois, on May 21, 1839.

the ties of early memories, also several young gentlemen, I [illegible] well in Kentucky. I need not speak to you, of the pleasures of such agreeable meeting. Cousin Anne & myself did not *know* [illegible] whilst there. This, at all times I have deemed a hard lesson, yet in this instance, the task was still severer, to have so many beaux "dancing attendance" on us at one time, and the little throng were hosts within themselves. Our Sucker friends would have opened their orbs, at such strange doings. I there met with a young Cousin, by my mother's side, who has but a few weeks since, wended his way westward, a young lawyer, and gives hopes of bright promise. Already the old lawyers, have extended a *patronising* smile & I trust & feel that he may one day, ere long weave a bright chaplet of fame for his youthful brow.—Were you to see him, I almost fancy & hope that *others* in your eye would be forgotten. No other cousin save *him* would I deem worthy of your acceptance —and he has that Dear Merce which I have heard you say would be *indispensable,* good Morals & Religion and the most affectionate heart in the world, yet I much fear yours is a *gone case.* Though far separated, do not deem your confidence misplaced, tell me all—every thing, you know the deep interest I feel for you, time can never banish your remembrance, how desolate I shall feel on returning to Springfield without you, your kind and cheering presence has beguiled many a lonely hour of its length. Mrs. L-³ must feel lost, and little Anne too, has lost a play mate. Martha Jane I am told seldom wanders on the hill, still

³ Mrs. Lawrason Levering.

168

blest with her *little friend's* society. Be it so "I care not though she be dearer." Merce she can now have an opportunity of making *dead sets* at the youngsters. I can answer for the security of your claims, tell me, were my suspicions unfounded? To change our subject to one of a *still warmer* nature, did you ever feel such oppressive weather as we have had of late, though you perhaps did not experience the intensity of the heat. At this time, no doubt, you are sailing o'er the waters blue, what an agreeable trip will be yours dearest, & I trust every happiness may attend you. I shall expect a lengthy account of your journeyings, crossed and recrossed. I feel exacting, yet bear with me, my great desire to hear from you is a sufficient palliation for my fault, so at least I deem it. Cousin & myself take the world easy, as usual with me you know, allow but few of its cares, to mar *our serenity.* We regularly take our afternoon *siestas,* and soon find our spirits wafted to the land of dreams. Then will I think of thee. Still [it] does not require so mighty an effort, to bring you to mind, for the brightest associations of the [illegible] are connected with thee. Will Todd [4] has been here some part of the time, is now here, and sends his best respects, if not *love.* You will pardon the familiarity of the youth as in times past. He is agreeably surprised to find himself "not too young to enter society" here. That slight ever haunts him. He is uncertain as to whether he will locate himself in Missouri. Tis difficult at this time, to get any where into business,

[4] Probably William L. Todd, a son of Mary Todd's uncle, Dr. John Todd of Springfield, Illinois.

and perhaps he will yet again return homeward. There is a very lovely & interesting young lady, residing here whom rumor says will one day be a cousin of ours & *John Todd* is the happy man, surprised at her taste. He is certainly very clever, yet he did not shew off to the same advantage whilst with us, as here he was a general beau. Cousin Anne is betraying her womanly curiosity, wonders what I am scribbling so much about—I soon close without having said half enough. Though I can fancy you pale and exhausted—so in Mercy will spare you.—Ann says you cannot fail being pleased with Missouri, she is so much attached to her native State, that I fear nothing will ever draw her hence, not even *the leader in Israel,* though that will never be methinks.—She hopes one day not far distant with some faithful swain, you may pitch your tent here, and then she will have the happiness of seeing you, & with this wish she sends much love.—Uncle has just returned from Court, and insists upon our taking another jaunt as travelling is absolutely necessary to Cousin's health. I know not how this will be. Ere long I must quit this land. Your letter if you please direct to Springfield, as I am confident I shall be there ere you have time to receive & answer this, and do my dearest girl, write very soon. You know not the happiness one of your letters affords.—If you conclude to settle in Missouri, *I will do so too.* There is *one* being here, who cannot brook the mention of my return, an agreeable lawyer & grandson of *Patrick Henry—what an honor!* I shall never survive it—I wish you could see him, the most perfect original I ever met. My beaux have *always* been *hard bargains* at any rate. Uncle and others think, he surpasses his *noble ancestor* in *talents,* yet Merce I love him not, & my hand will never be given, where my heart is not.—Cousin A. has a most devoted here who watches her every look with a *lover's eye,* and I have long told her she was a coquette in a quiet way—and they are said to be the most dangerous ever.—Be as *unreserved* as you find me. I forget myself writing to you. Pass my imperfections lightly by, and excuse so miserable a production from your most attached friend

MARY

From Springfield James C. Conkling was writing to Mercy Levering every few days. Occasional passages throw illuminating light on Mary Todd and her friends. The extract which follows is taken from a letter dated September 21, 1840.[5]

I was reminded by what I had written of the first time I saw Miss Todd after her return.[6] It was on a Saturday evening at the Journal Office where some fifteen or twenty ladies were collected together to listen to the Tippecanoe Singing Club. It has lately become quite a place of resort, particularly when it is expected there will be any speeches. I had the honor of being called on that evening and made a few brief remarks. . . . But while on this topic, just let me state that there is a rumor that our friend Martha Jane

[5] The Conkling letters are owned by Mrs. Annie Bryan of Peoria, Illinois, a daughter.
[6] From Missouri.

is to change *her* name tomorrow (Tues) evening. I know nothing officially. I have no reason however to doubt it. . . . Since penning the last lines I have received official information from headquarters and tomorrow evening at 7½ P. M. Martha Jane will marry Mr. Abel. . . .

Well, I had no idea I should be instrumental more than once again in changing the name of a lady.[7] But last evening Miss Todd and myself, (standing partners you perceive) with the assistance of Parson Bergen in his usual dignified manner passed through the usual ceremonies of such an occasion. And about 10 o'clock we packed them in the stage and sent them off to Chicago. Peace and Happiness be with them. . . . But my official capacity on that occasion [the wedding] reminds me of my blooming partner who has just returned from Missouri. Verily, I believe the further West a young lady goes the better her health becomes. If she comes here she is sure to grow—if she visits Missouri she will soon grow out of your recollection and if she should visit the Rocky Mountains I know not what would become of her. Miss Todd certainly does improve astonishingly and soon bids fair to rival Mrs. Glenn if she does not exceed old Father Lambert. She regrets your absence very much and feels quite lonesome. And now Martha Jane has gone as well as yourself I do not doubt but she is quite solitary and were it not that Dr. Todd's daughter has returned from Kentucky she must feel the change very sensibly. She is the very creature of excite-

---

[7] This paragraph was written on September 23, the day after the marriage of Martha Jane Lowry and Sidney Abell.

ment you know and never enjoys herself more than when in society and surrounded by a company of merry friends.

The following passage, in which the marriage of James Campbell and Harriet Huntingdon is described, is taken from a letter dated October 24, 1840. "Miss T.," of course, is Mary Todd.

Another revolutionary hero gone! A week ago last Thursday evening our friend Mr. C. departed from the state of celibacy in which he had long been lingering. I assisted in performing the last offices and consigned him with all due ceremony to the happiness of a matrimonial life. I should feel truly bereaved and disconsolate did I imagine that I should be entirely deprived of his society. And if I do not make Mrs. C. feel jealous of me it will be because she has no more influence over him than myself. I have no notion of taking all my rambles alone or of spending all of my evenings in solitude and he was the only friend that I found at leisure at any moment, except bank hours, of pursuing the one, or indulging in the other. The party was very small. Miss T. was the only lady present unconnected with the family. Her presence reminded me of other days and even she did not appear as merry and joyous as usual. It appeared as if she looked around for former friends and asked "Where are they?" But Echo only answered "Where are they?" . . . and so you thought that a word of caution might be necessary for me if Miss T. and myself were partners much oftener, we might stand up once too often.

MARY LINCOLN

If that was your opinion before what must you think when you learn that *Miss Martha H* was my partner on this occasion?

The next letter is Mary Todd's. Internal evidence indicates that it was written during the week of December 13-20, 1840.

Springfield Decr. 1840-

Many, very many weary days have passed my ever dear Merce, since mine has been the pleasure of hearing from you. Some weeks since I received your kind, soul cheering epistle & had I been *then* told such a length of time would have intervened ere I had availed myself of an opportunity of replying to it, I would not have given credence to the tale, yet such has been the case & I feel I owe you many apologies & sincerely trust our further correspondence may be more punctual. My time has been much occupied of late, you will be surprised to learn, I have scarce a leisure moment to call my own. For several weeks this fall, a formidable supply of *sewing,* necessary to winter comfort, engaged our constant attention. Now the scene is changed. Mr. Edwards has a cousin from Alton spending the winter with us, a most interesting young lady, her fascinations, have drawn a concourse of beaux & company round us. Occasionally, I *feel as Miss Whitney,* we have too much of such useless commodities. You know it takes some time for habit to render us familiar with what we are not greatly accustomed to.—Could you step in upon us some evening in these "western wilds," you would be astonished at the

174

change, *time* has wrought on the hill.[8] I would my Dearest, you now were with us, be assured your name is most
frequently mentioned in our circle, *words of mine* are not
necessary to assure you of the loss I have sustained in your
society. On my return from Missouri, my time passed most
heavily. I feel quite made up in my present companion,
a congenial spirit I assure you. I know you would be pleased
with Matilda Edwards,[9] a lovelier girl I never saw. *Mr
Speed's* ever changing heart I suspect is about offering *its
young* affections at her shrine, with some others. There is
considerable acquisition in our society of *marriageable gentlemen,* unfortunately only "birds of passage." *Mr Webb,*[10]
a widower of modest merit, last winter, is our *principal
lion,* dances attendance very frequently. We expect a very
gay winter, evening before last my sister gave a most agreeable party, upwards of a hundred graced the festive scene.
I trust the period is not very distant when your presence
will be among us to cheer us & moreover I trust *our homes*
may be near, that as in times past, so may it *ever be,* that
our hearts will acknowledge the same kindred ties. Memory
oftimes reverts to by gone days, & with the past your
memory is intimately blended. Well did you say "time
has borne changes on its wing." Speed's "grey suit" has
gone the way of *all flesh,* an interesting suit of *Harrison
blues* have replaced his *sober livery, Lincoln's lincoln green*

[8] The eminence where both the Edwards and Levering homes were
situated. The Illinois Centennial Building now stands on the site.

[9] Daughter of Cyrus Edwards of Alton, Ninian W. Edwards' uncle.

[10] Edwin B. Webb of Carmi, Illinois—a man of some prominence as a
lawyer and politician.

have gone to dust, Mr Webb sports a *mourning* p[——?]
by way of reminding us *damsels,* that we *"cannot come it."*
Of the new recruits I need not mention, some few are
gifted & all in our humble estimation interesting. *Mr C-*[11]
seems to have *given up all,* when deprived of his "own particular star." I have not met him, to have a chat since
Martha Jane's marriage. I have often wished for the sake
of his society & of your *dear self* he would be more social.
Harriet Campbell appears to be enjoying all the sweets of
married life. *Mrs Abell* came down two or three weeks
since, have seen but very little of her. Her *silver tones,* the
other evening were not quite so captain like as was their
wont in former times. Why is it that married folks always
become so serious? Miss Lamb, report says is to be married
next week. *Mr Beauman* I caught a glimpse of a few days
since, looked *becomingly* happy at the prospect of the
change, that is about to await him. I am pleased she is
about perpetrating the *crime* of *matrimony,* like some of
our friends in *this place, M & L* for instance, I think she
will be much happier. I suppose like the rest of us *Whigs,*
though you seem rather to doubt my *faith,* you have been
rejoicing in the recent election of Gen Harrison, a cause
that has excited such deep interest in the nation and one of
such vital importance to our prosperity.—This fall I became
quite a *politician,* rather an unlady like profession, yet at
such a *crisis,* whose heart could remain untouched while the
energies of all were called in question?—You bid me pause,
in your last, on the banks of *"Lionel"* & there glean a use-

[11] James C. Conkling.

ful lesson, by marking the changes, the destroying hand of time has written on all. A moment's thought, would suffice to assure me, that all *is not,* as it then was. The icy hand of winter has set its seal upon the waters, the winds of Heaven visit the spot but roughly, the same stars shine down, yet not with the same liquid, mellow light as in the olden time. Some forms & memories that enhanced the place, have passed by, many weary miles are you dear Merce removed from us. The star of hope, must be a guiding *star,* and we must revel in the happy anticipations of a reunion, may the day be not far distant.—Once more, allow me my dear friend to wish you were with us. We have a pleasant jaunt in contemplation, to Jacksonville, next week there to spend a day or two. Mr Hardin & Browning are our leaders the van brought up by Miss E. my humble self, Webb, Lincoln & two or three others whom you know not. We are watching the clouds most anxiously trusting it may snow, so we may have a sleigh ride.—Will it not be pleasant?

Your Brother's family, are well, and all speak of you most frequently, & wonder when you expect to wander *westward.* We cannot do much longer without you, *your mate* misses you too much from her nest, not to marvel at your delay. Do trust a friend and be more communicative in your next, feeling as you must do the great interest I take in you, would you deny me the consolation of being a sharer in your joys & sorrows, may the latter be never known to you.—The State House is not quite completed, yet sufficiently so to allow the Legislature to meet within its walls. Springfield has improved astonishingly, have the addition of another *bell* to the Second Church. It rings so long & loud, that as in days past we cannot mistake the trysting hour.—I trust you do not allow your sister to sing you any more such melancholy dirges. I know by *sad experience* that such dolorous ditties only excite one's anxiety to see a beloved object, therefore tell her for the sympathetic feeling I entertain towards you dearest, bid her cease the strain.—The weather is miserably cold, & my stump of a pen keeps pace with the times. Pass my imperfections lightly as usual, I throw myself on your amiable nature, knowing that my shortcomings will be forgiven.—Fanny Wallace sends much love to you. Her little urchin, is almost a young lady in size. Elizabeth has not been well of late, suffering with a cold. I still am the same ruddy *pineknot,* only not quite so great an exuberance of flesh, as it once was my lot to contend with, although quite a sufficiency.—I must close. Write very, very soon if you love me.—Ever your attached friend   MARY.

In the interval between Mary Todd's letter and that from which the following extract is taken, her engagement with Lincoln was broken and his physical collapse took place. The passage is from a letter from Conkling to Mercy Levering, January 24, 1841.

Last evening I spent upon the Hill. Mrs. L. informed me she had lately written you and had given you some par-

ticulars about Abraham, Joshua and Jacob.[12] Poor L! how
are the mighty fallen! He was confined about a week, but
though he now appears again he is reduced and emaciated
in appearance and seems scarcely to possess strength enough
to speak above a whisper. His case at present is truly deplorable but what prospect there may be for ultimate relief
I cannot pretend to say. I doubt not but he can declare
"That loving is a painful thrill, And not to love more
painful still" but would not like to intimate that he has
experienced "That surely 'tis the worst of pain To love and
not be loved again."

And Joshua too is about to leave. I know not what dread-
ful blow may be inflicted upon the interests of our State
by his departure. But having taken a very prominent part
in the last political canvass I really fear that great convulsions and tumults will follow for the want of his superin-
tending care and protection.

On February 7 Mercy Levering replied from Baltimore in a letter which contains one allusion to Lincoln. It follows.

Yesterday I wrote a long letter to Bri- in answer to her
particulars about Abraham, Joshua, and Jacob to which you
refer. Poor A—I fear his is a blighted heart! perhaps if he
was as persevering as Mr. W-[13] he might finally be successful. And Joshua too, he has left the prairie state, really

[12] "Jacob Faithful" was Conkling himself.
[13] Edwin B. Webb. "Bri" was Mrs. Lawrason Levering.

I think the citizens of S- seem to be deserting it. But what more can one expect when the *Patriarchs* are beginning to move!

A month later Lincoln's condition was still the occasion for comment. Conkling referred to it in the following words when he wrote to Mercy Levering on March 7.

The Legislature have dispersed. Whether any persons regret it I cannot pretend to say. Miss Todd and her cousin Miss Edwards seemed to form the grand centre of attraction. Swarms of strangers who had little else to engage their attention hovered around them, to catch a *passing smile.* By the way, I do not think they were received, with even ordinary attention, if they did not obtain a *broad grin* or an *obstreporous laugh.* And L, poor hapless simple swain who loved most true but was not loved again—I suppose he will now endeavor to drown his cares among the intricacies and perplexities of the law. No more will the merry peal of laughter ascend *high in the air,* to greet his listening and delighted ears. He used to remind me sometimes of the pictures I formerly saw of old Father Jupiter, bending down from the clouds, to see what was going on below. And as an agreeable smile of satisfaction graced the countenance of the old heathen god, as he perceived the incense rising up—so the face of L. was occasionally distorted into a grin as he succeeded in eliciting applause from some of the fair votaries by whom he was surrounded. But alas! I fear his shrine will now be deserted and that he will withdraw himself from the society of us inferior mortals.

The final letter in this group was written by Mary Todd. It was mailed from Springfield on June 18, 1841.

Springfield June 1841.

When I reflect my own dear Merce, that months of change have passed by since I last wrote you, and that your letters during that time have been far, very far more unfrequent than I could have desired, these circumstances would lead an *unknowing one* to imagine that time had wrought its changes upon us, and lessened the love which I feel has ever been ours towards each other. Time and absence only serve to deepen the interest with which I have always regarded you & my greatest regret is that so many long & weary miles divide us.—My late silence would doubtless lead you to imagine that you were only occasionally remembered. I have been much alone of late and my thoughts have oft been with thee. Why I have not written oftener appears strange even to *me*, who should best know *myself*, that most difficult of all problems to solve. My evil genius Procrastination has whispered me to tarry til a more convenient season & spare you the infliction of a letter which daily experience convinces me would be "flat, stale & unprofitable," yet henceforth I trust it may not be thus with us. Were you aware of the delight given by hearing

181

from you, dearest Merce, surely you would more frequently cheer my sad spirit.—The last two or three months
have been of *interminable* length. After my gay companions of last winter departed, I was left much to the
solitude of my own thoughts, and some *lingering regrets*
over the past, which time can alone overshadow with its
healing balm. Thus has my *spring time* been passed. Summer in all its beauty has again come, the prairie land looks
as beautiful as it did in the olden time, when we strolled
together & derived so much of happiness from each other's
society—this is past & more than this. I can scarcely realize
that a year of change has gone by since we parted, may it
not be that another has rolled on, and we still remain
separated, the thought of meeting solaces many a lonely
hour.—I have much much to tell you, of all that is daily oc-
curring around us, that I scarcely know where the narrative
shall commence. At present a cousin of Mr Edward's from
Alton, is on a visit to us. The June Court is in session and
many distinguished strangers grace the gay capital. We have
an unusual number of agreeable visitors, some pleasant acquaintances of last winter, but in their midst the *winning
widower is not*.[14] *Rumor* says he with some others will
attend the Supreme Court next month. In your last, you
appeared impressed with the prevalent idea that we were
dearer to each other than friends. The idea was neither new
nor strange, dear Merce, the knowing world, have coupled
our names together for months past, merely through the
folly & belief of another, who strangely imagined we were

[14] Edwin B. Webb.

182

attached to each other. In your friendly & confiding ear allow me to whisper that my *heart can never be his*. I have deeply regretted that his constant visits, attentions &c should have given room for remarks, which were to me unpleasant. There being a slight difference of some eighteen or twenty summers in our years, would preclude all possibility of congeneality of feeling, without which I should never feel justifiable in resigning my happiness into the safe keeping of another, even should that other be, far too worthy for me, with his two *sweet little objections.*—We had such a continual round of company, gayety &c last winter, that after their departure the monotony of the place was almost unbearable. Now that I have become habituated to quiet, I have resumed my frequent & social visits to Mrs Levering, and if your ears do not oftimes burn, there can be no truth in the old adage, all, all reminds me so much of your dear, kind self. A few evenings since I was most forcibly reminded of you, by seeing *Jacob Faithful*. We spent the evening at Mrs Lamb's, and in one quiet sequestered nook in the room he was seated, sad & lonely. No doubt his thoughts were busy with you & the past. To me he has proved most *untrue* as I never see him, e'en for your own loved sake he *comes not.*—Mr Speed, our former most constant guest has been in Kentucky for some weeks past, will be here next month, on a visit *perhaps,* as he has some idea of deserting Illinois. His mother is anxious he should superintend her affairs. He takes a friend's privilege, of occasionally favouring me with a letter, in his last he spoke of his great desire of once more

inhabiting this region & of his possibility of soon returning.—*His* worthy friend,[15] deems me unworthy of notice,
as I have not met *him* in the gay world for months. With
the usual comfort of misery, imagine that others were as
seldom gladdened by his presence as my humble self, yet
I would that the case were different, that he would once
more resume his station in Society, that "Richard should
be himself again," much, much happiness would it afford
me.—My sister Fanny, returned some weeks since from
her visit east, her health & spirits much improved, regretted
much that the hurry of business prevented the Dr- visiting
Baltimore, as she was very desirous of seeing you. *Mrs
Beauman,* Miss Lamb, that was is now on a visit to Mrs
Mather, looks very well, says she is very happy, and much
pleased with her new home.—Mrs Abell, has been here,
for a great while, owing to the warm weather, or something, sports [?] wrappers, & looks quite dignified.—Our
agreeable friend Mrs Anderson was in town a few days
since spoke of having received a letter from you, and was
about doing herself the pleasure of replying to it. I have
never paid her a visit, since the time we went out together
with William Anderson, who is soon to be married to a
lady of Louisville—strange perversity of taste—Think you
not so? The interesting gentleman, whom Mrs Roberts
gave you for a beau is now a resident of this place, Mr
Trumbull, is Secretary of State, in lieu of *Judge Douglass,*
who has been rapidly promoted to office.—Now that your
fortune is made, I feel much disposed in your absence, to

15 Lincoln.

lay in my *claims,* as he is talented & agreeable & sometimes *countenances* me.—I regret to see that my paper is so rapidly disappearing, miserable scrawl as this has been, I feel much disposed to continue it, as with you, I always have so much to communicate. E. sends you much love & desires you would hasten your movements westward as your friends continue to remember you with the same unchanging affection.—Miss Whitney whom I have not visited since you left & for some time before, called up to day & requested me to accompany her as far as Peoria, on her bridal tour as she is to be married in a few days to a widower of some *ten months* standing, residing in the northern part of the state—Miss Rodney is also to be an attendant. As you may imagine I declined the honour and being strangers I was somewhat surprised at the request.— Your brother's family are all well. Write very, very soon to your ever attached friend

MARY—

Nearly seven years elapsed before Mary Todd wrote another letter which has been preserved. In the interval she had married Lincoln and had become the mother of two children, Robert Todd, born August 1, 1843, and Edward Baker, born March 10, 1846. Her husband had attained political prominence, and was serving his first and only term in Congress when the four letters which follow were written. Mrs. Lincoln and the two boys had accompanied him to Washington, but re-

MARY LINCOLN

turned to Lexington, Kentucky, for a visit at the Todd home before the end of the session.

Washington, April 16, 1848.

DEAR MARY:

In this troublesome world, we are never quite satisfied.[16] When you were here, I thought you hindered me some in attending to business; but now, having nothing but business—no vanity—it has grown exceedingly tasteless to me. I hate to sit down and direct documents, and I hate to stay in this old room by myself. You know I told you in last Sunday's letter I was going to make a little speech during the week, but the week has passed away without my getting a chance to do so, and now my interest in the subject has passed away too. Your second and third letters have been received since I wrote before. Dear Eddy thinks father is 'gone tapila.' Has any further discovery been made as to the breaking into your grandmother's house? If I were she I would not remain there alone. You mention that your Uncle John Parker is likely to be at Lexington. Don't forget to present him my very kindest regards.

I went yesterday to hunt the little plaid stockings as you wished, but found that McKnight has quit business and Allen had not a single pair of the description you give and only one plaid pair of any sort that I thought would fit 'Eddy's dear little feet.' I have a notion to make another trial tomorrow morning. If I could get them, I have an excellent chance of sending them. Mr. Warrich Tunstall of

16 Original in collection of Oliver R. Barrett. From *New Letters and Papers of Lincoln*, 41-43.

St. Louis is here. He is to leave early this week and to go by Lexington. He says he knows you, and will call to see you, and he voluntarily asked if I had not some package to send to you.

I wish you to enjoy yourself in every possible way, but is there no danger of wounding the feelings of your good father by being too openly intimate with the Wickliffe family?

Mrs. Broome has not removed yet, but she thinks of doing so tomorrow. All the house or rather all with whom you were on decided good terms send their love to you. The others say nothing. Very soon after you went away I got what I think a very pretty set of shirt-bosom studs— modest little ones, jet set in gold, only costing 50 cents a piece or $1.50 for the whole.

Suppose you do not prefix the 'hon.' to the address on your letters to me any more. I like the letters very much but I would rather they should not have that upon them. It is not necessary, as I suppose you have thought, to have them come free.

Are you entirely free from headache? That is good— good considering it is the first spring you have been free from it since we were acquainted. I am afraid you will get so well and fat and young as to be wanting to marry again. Tell Louisa I want her to watch you a little for me. Get weighed and write me how much you weigh.

I did not get rid of the impression of that foolish dream about dear Bobby till I got your letter written the same day. What did he and Eddy think of the little letters father sent them? Don't let the blessed fellows forget father.

A day or two ago Mr. Strong,[17] here in Congress, said to me that Matilda would visit here within two or three weeks. Suppose you write her a letter, and enclose it in one of mine, and if she comes I will deliver it to her, and if she does not, I will send it to her.

Most affectionately,

A. LINCOLN.

The following from Mrs. Lincoln is probably typical of the letters which she was writing to her husband at this time.

Lexington May- 48-

MY DEAR HUSBAND-

You will think indeed, that *old age* has set *its seal*,[18] upon my humble self, that in few or none of my letters, I can remember the day of the month, I must confess it as one of my peculiarities; I feel wearied & tired enough to know, that this is *Saturday night,* our babies are asleep, and as Aunt Maria B. is coming in for me tomorrow night, morning, I think the chances will be rather dull that I should answer your last letter tomorrow. I have just received a letter from Frances W. It related in an *especial* manner to *the box,* I had desired her to send, she thinks with you (as good persons generally agree) that it would cost more than it would come to, and it might be lost on the road. I rather expect she has examined the specified articles, and thinks

17 William Strong, of Reading, Pennsylvania, whom Matilda Edwards married.
18 Original owned by Oliver R. Barrett, Chicago, Illinois.

as *Levi* says, they are *hard bargains*. But it takes so many changes to do children, particularly in summer, that I thought it might save me a few stitches. I think I will write her a few lines this evening, directing her not to send them. She says Willie is just recovering from another spell of sickness, Mary or none of them were well. Springfield she reports as dull as usual. Uncle S- was to leave there on yesterday for Ky. Our little Eddy, has recovered from his little spell of sickness. Dear boy, I must tell you a little story about him. Boby in his wanderings to day, came across in a yard, a little kitten, *your hobby*. He says he asked a man for it, he brought it triumphantly to the house, so soon as Eddy spied it his *tenderness* broke forth, he made them bring it *water* fed it with bread himself, with his *own dear hands*. He was a delighted little creature over it. In the midst of his happiness Ma came in, she you must know dislikes the whole cat race. I thought in a very unfeeling manner, she ordered the servant near, to throw it out, which of *course,* was done. Ed- screaming & protesting loudly against the proceeding, *she* never appeared to mind his screams, which were long & loud, I assure you. Tis unusual for her *now a days,* to do any thing quite so striking. She is very obliging & accomodating, but if she thought any of us, were on her hands again, I believe she would be *worse* than ever. In the next moment she appeared in a good humor, I know she did not intend to offend me. By the way, she has just sent me up a glass of ice cream, for which this warm evening, I am duly grateful. The country is so delightful I am going to spend two or three weeks out here, it will doubtless benefit the children. Grandma has received a letter from Uncle James Parker of Miss saying he & his family would be up by the twenty fifth of June, would remain here some little time & go on to Philadelphia to take their oldest daughter there to school. I believe it would be a good chance for me to pack up & accompany them. You know I am so fond of *sight-seeing,* & I did not get to New York or Boston, or travel the lake route. But perhaps, dear husband, like the *irresistible Col Mc,* cannot do without his wife next winter, and must needs take her with him again. I expect you would cry aloud against it. How much, I wish instead of writing, we were together this evening, I feel very sad away from you. Ma & myself rode out to Mr Bell's splendid place this afternoon, to return a call, the house and grounds are magnificent, Frances W. would *have died* over their rare exotics. It is growing late, these summer eves are short. I expect my long *scrawls,* for truly such they are, weary you greatly. If you come on, in July or August *I* will take you to the springs. *Patty Webb's,* school in S- closes the first of July. I expect *Mr. Webb* [19] will come on for her. I must go down about that time & carry on quite a flirtation, you know *we,* always had a *penchant* that way. I must bid you good night. Do not fear the children, have forgotten you, I was only jesting. Even E- eyes brighten at the mention of your name. My love to all. Truly yours

M L-

[19] Edwin B. Webb. Patty, a daughter, was attending school in Shelbyville, Kentucky, at this time.

Lincoln's answer [20] reveals certain aspects of Mrs. Lincoln's personality more reliably than any reminiscence extant. It is not strange that William H. Herndon wrote "Not to be published" across the original letter.

My DEAR WIFE: Washington, June 12, 1848

On my return from Philadelphia yesterday, where in my anxiety I have been led to attend the Whig Convention I found your last letter. I was so tired and sleepy, having ridden all night, that I could not answer it till to-day; and now I have to do so in the H. R. The leading matter in your letter is your wish to return to this side of the Mountains. Will you be a *good girl* in all things, if I consent? Then come along, and that as *soon* as possible. Having got the idea in my head, I shall be impatient till I see you. You will not have money enough to bring you, but I presume your uncle will supply you and I will refund him here. By the way you do not mention whether you have received the fifty dollars I sent you. I do not much fear but that you got it; because the want of it would have induced you to say something in relation to it. If your uncle is already at Lexington, you might induce him to start in earlier than the first of July; he could stay in Kentucky longer on his return, and so make up for lost time. Since I began this letter, the H. R. has passed a resolution for adjourning on the 17th July, which probably will pass the Senate. I hope this letter will not be disagreeable to you; which, together

[20] Printed in Hertz, *Abraham Lincoln: A New Portrait*, II., 573.

with the circumstances under which I write, I hope will excuse me for not writing a longer one. Come on just as soon as you can—I want to see you and our dear *dear* boys very much. Every body here wants to see our dear Bobby.

Affectionately,

A. LINCOLN.

For some reason now hidden Mrs. Lincoln postponed her eastern trip, at first temporarily and then finally. Although Lincoln and his wife were to remain apart until October, the following letter[21] is the last of those which passed between them in that period, now known to exist.

My DEAR WIFE: Washington, July 2, 1848.

Your letter of last sunday came last night. On that day (sunday) I wrote the principal part of a letter to you, but did not finish it, or send it till tuesday, when I had provided a draft for $100 which I sent in it. It is now probable that on that day (tuesday) you started to Shelbyville; so that when the money reaches Lexington, you will not be there. Before leaving, did you make any provision about letters that might come to Lexington for you? Write me whether you got the draft, if you shall not have already done so, when this reaches you. Give my kindest regards to your uncle John, and all the family. Thinking of them reminds me that I saw your acquaintance, Newton, of

21 Original owned by the Library of the University of Chicago. Printed in Angle, *New Letters and Papers of Lincoln*, 45-46.

Arkansas, at the Philadelphia Convention. We had but a single interview, and that was so brief, and in so great a multitude of strange faces, that I am quite sure I should not recognize him, if I were to meet him again. He was a sort of Trinity, three in one, having the right, in his own person, to cast the three votes of Arkansas. Two or three days ago I sent your uncle John, and a few of our other friends each a copy of the speech I mentioned in my last letter; but I did not send any to you, thinking you would be on the road here, before it would reach you. I send you one now. Last Wednesday, P. H. Hood & Co. dunned me for a little bill of $5.38 cents, and Walter Harper & Co. another for $8.50 cents, for goods which they say you bought. I hesitated to pay them, because my recollection is that you told me when you went away, there was nothing left unpaid. Mention in your next letter whether they are right.

Mrs. Richardson is still here; and what is more, has a baby—so Richardson says, and he ought to know. I believe Mary Hewett has left here and gone to Boston. I met her on the street about fifteen or twenty days ago, and she told me she was going soon. I have seen nothing of her since.

The music in the Capitol grounds on saturdays, or, rather, the interest in it, is dwindling down to nothing. Yesterday evening the attendance was rather thin. Our two girls, whom you remember seeing first at Canisis, at the exhibition of the Ethiopian Serenaders, and whose peculiarities were the wearing of black fur bonnets, and never being seen in close company with other ladies, were at the music yesterday. One of them was attended by their brother, and the other had a member of Congress in tow. He went home with her; and if I were to guess, I would say, he went away a somewhat altered man—most likely in his pockets, and in some other particular. The fellow looked conscious of guilt, although I believe he was unconscious that everybody around knew who it was that had caught him.

I have had no letter from home, since I wrote you before, except short business letters, which have no interest for you.

By the way, you do not intend to do without a girl, because the one you had has left you? Get another as soon as you can to take charge of the dear codgers. Father expected to see you all sooner; but let it pass; stay as long as you please, and come when you please. Kiss and love the dear rascals.

Affectionately

A. Lincoln.

Something of the normal course of life in the Lincoln family is conveyed by three letters [22] from Mrs. Lincoln to Mrs. Emilie Todd Helm, a younger half-sister. Many things had happened between 1848 and 1856, when the first of these was written. A failure as a congressman, Lincoln had turned to the law, and had attained respectable rank at the bar of Illinois. Then, in 1854, came the repeal of the Kansas-Nebraska act, accompanied by widespread, bitter agitation of the

[22] From Helm, *Mary, Wife of Lincoln*, 120-26.

slavery question. Lincoln plunged into politics again, although it was two years before he allied himself with the newly-formed Republican party. By the summer of 1856, however, he had definitely committed himself, and in the presidential campaign of that year he canvassed Illinois as a Frémont elector. Meeting defeat so far as the head of the ticket was concerned, the Republicans swept the state offices.

An incidental result of professional success and political prominence—social position—is evident in the following letters, in which governors, bankers, men of affairs and their wives and daughters figure prominently.

Springfield, November 23, [1856]

With much pleasure, my dear Emilie, I acknowledge the receipt of one of your ever acceptable letters, and notwithstanding many weeks have passed since writing you, I have frequently intended doing so and you have been often in my thoughts. Mr. Edwards expressed great pleasure at meeting you last summer. You know you have a very warm place in his heart. You have been such a wanderer around with your good husband and a letter might have failed to reach you. I must try to devise some excuses for my past silence, forgetfulness you know it could not be. Besides there is a great deal in getting out of the habit of letter writing; once I was very fond of it. Nothing pleases me better than to receive a letter from an absent friend, so remember dear Emilie, when you desire to be particularly acceptable, write me one of your agreeable missives and do not wait for a return of each from a staid matron and moreover the mother of three noisy boys. Your husband like some of the rest of ours has a great taste for politics and has taken much interest in the late contest which has resulted very much as I expected, not hoped, although Mr. Lincoln is or was a Fremont man, you must not include him with so many of those who belong to that party, an Abolitionist. In principle he is far from it, all he desires is that slavery shall not be extended, let it remain where it is. My weak woman's heart was too Southern in feeling to sympathize with any but Filmore. I have always been his great admirer; he made so good a President and is so just a man and feels the necessity of keeping the foreigners within bounds. If some of you Kentuckians had to deal with the "Wild Irish" as we housekeepers are some times called upon to do, the South would certainly elect Mr. Filmore next time. The Democrats in our State have been defeated in their Governor so there is a crumb of comfort for each and all. What day is so dark that there is no ray of sunshine to penetrate the gloom? Speaking of politics, Governors, etc., reminds me of your questions relative to Lydia M. The hour of her patient lover's deliverance is at hand, they are to be married privately I expect. Some of us who had a handsome dress for the season thought it would be in good taste for Mrs. Matteson [23] in consideration of their being about to leave their present habitation to give

[23] Wife of the Democratic governor, whose term had just ended.

a general reception. Lydia has always been so retiring that she would be very averse to a public display. This fall in visiting Mrs. M. I met a sister of Mrs. McGinnis, a very pretty well bred woman from Joliet, she spoke of having met Margaret Kellogg [24] in Kentucky. Frances Wallace returned two or three days ago from her visit to Pennsylvania where she has been spending the fall. Mr. Edwards' family are well. Mr. Baker and Julia [25] are still with them. Miss Iles was married some three weeks since (I expect you do not remember her) which gave rise to some two or three parties. Mr. Scott is frequently here rather playing the devoted to Julia. I suspect, whether anything serious I do not know, the family would not be averse to him. Charley R. was on a visit to him in Lexington. He, it is said, is to be married this winter to Jennie Barrett, a lovely girl, you remember her.

I am sorry to hear that dear mother is frequently indisposed. I hope she has recovered from her lameness. Tell her when you see her that our old acquaintance Mr. —— took tea with us an evening or two since and made particular enquiries about her. Still as rough and uncultivated as ever although some years since married an accomplished Georgia belle with the advantages of some winters in Washington. Mother and I when last together spoke of our Minister, Mr. Smith, who finding his salary of some

[24] Margaret Todd, half-sister of Mrs. Lincoln, who married Charles Kellogg.

[25] Julia Edwards, daughter of Ninian W. Edwards. She married Edwin L. Baker.

197

$1600 inadequate has resigned the Church. Uncle and some few others are desirous of getting Dr. Brown your former pastor in Lexington. Within the last year both he and his wife have been a great deal here. He has purchased land and appears rather identified with the Country.

But I am speaking of things that will not interest you in the least. If you do not bring yourself and your husband to see us very soon we will think you are not as proud of him as rumor says you should be. Do write soon in return for this long and I fear dull letter from yours truly,

MARY LINCOLN.

Springfield, February 16, [1857]

Think not, dear Emilie, altho' weeks have passed since your welcome letter was received that you had been forgotten or that I have not daily proposed writing you, yet something has always occurred to oppose my good resolutions. This winter has certainly passed most rapidly. Spring, if we can call the month of March such, is nearly here. The first part of the winter was unusually quiet owing to so much sickness among children. With scarlet fever in several families some two or three children were swept away.

Within the last three weeks there has been a party almost every night and some two or three grand fetes are coming off this week. I may perhaps surprise you when I mention that I am recovering from the slight fatigue of a very large and I really believe a very handsome entertainment, at least our friends flatter us by saying so. About five hundred were invited, yet owing to an unlucky rain three hundred

only favored us by their presence and the same evening in
Jacksonville, Colonel Warren gave a bridal party to his son
who married Miss Birchall of this place which occasion
robbed us of some of our friends. You will think we have
enlarged our borders since you were here. Three evenings
since, Governor Bissell gave a very large party, I thought
of you frequently that evening when I saw so many of
your acquaintances beautifully dressed and dancing away
very happily and as enquiries were made about you during
the evening by both beaux and belles you could not fail to
be remembered. I wish you would write me more frequently and tell me all about yourself. You have so much
leisure and such a literary husband that you will become
a regular blue. Your old laugh will soften the solemnity
of such a character and the old Emilie of former times
will show herself. Miss Dunlap is spending the winter with
her sister Mrs. Mc looking very pretty but the beaux do
not appear so numerous as the winter you passed here.
Within the last two or three weeks I have often wished
that Dedee [26] was here, yet the first part of the winter was
so quiet that I feared she would not have enjoyed herself.
I hope another winter both Kitty [27] and Dedee will come
out and we will endeavor to make it as pleasant as possible for them.

Dr. and Mrs. Brown also Mr. Dwight Brown and his
wife, are residing here. The former has charge of the First
Church, whether the arrangement will suit all around re-

[26] Elodie Todd, another half-sister.
[27] Katherine Todd, youngest of Mrs. Lincoln's half-sisters.

mains to be proven. I must hasten to conclude as I am interrupted by company. Hoping to be remembered to your husband, I remain, Yours truly, MARY LINCOLN.

Springfield, September 20, [1857]

MY DEAR EMILIE:

So long a time has passed since your last letter that I scarcely know how to ask you to excuse my silence. . . . I only pray you to return good for evil and let me hear from you more frequently. Do write me all the news, I feel anxious to hear from you. The summer has so strangely and rapidly passed away. Some portion of it was spent most pleasantly in traveling East.[28] We visited Niagara, Canada, New York and other points of interest. When I saw the large steamers at the New York landings I felt in my heart inclined to sigh that poverty was my portion. How I long to go to Europe. I often laugh and tell Mr. Lincoln that I am determined my next husband shall be rich.

You can scarcely imagine a place improving more rapidly than ours. Almost palaces of homes have been reared since you were here, hundreds of houses have been going up this season and some of them very elegant. Governor Matteson's house is just being completed, the whole place has cost him, he says, $100,000, but he is now worth a million. I saw Elizabeth this afternoon. Julia and Mr. Baker are in Peoria, at the fair, from thence go to St. Louis. At the

[28] Mrs. Lincoln accompanied Lincoln on a trip he made to New York in July, where he made arrangement with the executives of the Illinois Central Railroad for the payment of a large fee for legal services.

county fair here last week, Julia's last quilt (which makes her third one) a very handsome silk one, took the premium. She trusts for the like fate at Peoria and St. Louis. She has nothing but her dear Husband and silk quilts to occupy her time. How different the daily routine of some of our lives are. It is getting very late, dear Emilie, and I must close my little billet. Shall I apologize for this scrawl? I know I ought to be ashamed of it. When you read this, like a good sister, sit down and write me a good long letter, all about yourself. Mr. L. is not at home, this makes the fourth week, he has been in Chicago. Remember me to your Husband.

Yours affectionately,

MARY L.

Two brief notes to O. M. Hatch, Secretary of State of Illinois, add detail to the picture of Mary Lincoln as wife and mother. Both were written in 1859.[29]

MR HATCH.   Monday Morning

If you are going up to Chicago to day, & should meet Mr L- there, will you say to him, that our *dear little Taddie,* is quite sick. The Dr. thinks it may prove a *slight* attack of *lung* fever. I am feeling troubled & it would be a comfort to have him, *at home.* He passed a bad night. I do not like his symptoms, and will be glad, if he hurries home.

Truly your friend

M. L.

[29] Originals in possession of Pascal E. Hatch, Springfield, Illinois.

Mr. Hatch.   Monday afternoon Oct 3d

By way of impressing upon your mind, that friends must
not be *entirely* forgotten, I would be pleased to have you
wander up our way, to see us this evening, altho' I have
not the inducements of meeting company to offer you, or
Mr Lincoln to welcome you, yet if you are disengaged, I
should like to see you.

Respectfully

Mary Lincoln.

Before eight months had passed the Republican
party, in convention at Chicago, nominated Abraham
Lincoln for the Presidency. Mark W. Delahay, returning to his home in Kansas, brought two of the convention flags to Springfield, and thus gave rise to com-
plications which Mrs. Lincoln sought to straighten out
in the following note.[30]

Mr Delahay   Springfield May 25th 60

  Dear Sir.

One of my boys, appears to claim prior possession of the
smallest flag, is inconsolable for its absence. As I believe it
is too small to do you any service, and as he is so urgent
to have it again—and as I am sure, the largest one, will be
quite sufficient, I will ask you to send it to us, the first
opportunity you may have, especially as he claims it, and
I feel it is as necessary to keep one's word with a child, as

---

[30] Original owned by Oliver R. Barrett, Chicago, Illinois.

with a grown person. Hoping you reached home safely, I remain yours respectfully,

MARY LINCOLN.

The year 1861 came, and brought with it, for Mary Lincoln, all the responsibilities that go with life in the White House. From the beginning there were indications of trouble. Five days after the inauguration, for instance, *Frank Leslie's Illustrated Newspaper* made public the attitude of the wife of the American representative of the Rothschilds. "We are requested to state," it announced, "that Mrs. August Belmont did not call on Mrs. Lincoln during her recent stay at the Astor House." Perhaps incidents like this were responsible for the nostalgia evident in the following note [31] to Mrs. S. H. Melvin of Springfield, who had named an infant daughter after her former neighbor.

Washington April 2, 1861-

MY DEAR MRS. MELVIN:

Cap Todd leaves to day for S- & I take the liberty of enclosing some photographs of the boys, also, a little bonnet cap for my sweet little name-sake. Thousands of soldiers are guarding us, and if there is safety in numbers we have every reason, to feel secure. We can only hope for peace! Our boys, remember your dear little sons, with much

[31] Printed in facsimile in *Illinois Central Magazine*, February, 1929.

affection. I trust the day *may come,* when they will be re-united. I had intended requesting Mr Melvin to have given me a promise, that on our return to S- we could be able to secure *our particular pew,* to which I was very much at-tached, and which we occupied some ten years. May I hope that he will be able to do so.

With kind regards to your family & all friends, I remain ever sincerely

MARY LINCOLN.

With the war Mary Lincoln was placed in a position more difficult than any other woman of the White House has ever had to endure, for with half-brothers in the Confederate service, she was under constant sus-picion, if not of disloyalty, at least of divided sympathy. Yet the following letter [32] shows clearly enough the unjustness of the rumors that she was but half-hearted in her allegiance.

Executive Mansion,
June 20, 1861.

MY DEAR SIR:

It gives me great pleasure to be the medium of transmis-sion of these weapons, to be used in the defense of national sovereignty upon the soil of Kentucky.

Though some years have passed since I left my native State, I have never ceased to contemplate her progress in happiness and prosperity with sentiments of fond and filial pride. In every effort of industrial energy, in every

[32] From Clark, *Abraham Lincoln in the National Capital,* 74-75.

enterprise of honor and valor my heart has been with her. And I rejoice in the consciousness that, at this time, when the institutions to whose fostering care we owe all we have of happiness and glory are rudely assailed by ungrateful and paricidal hands, the State of Kentucky, ever true and loyal, furnishes to the insulted flag of the Union a guard of her best and bravest sons. On every field the prowess of the Kentuckians has been manifested. In the holy cause of national defense they must be invincible.

Please accept, sir, these weapons as a token of the love I shall never cease to cherish for my mother State, of the pride with which I have always regarded the exploits of her sons, and the confidence which I feel in the ultimate loyalty of her people, who, while never forgetting the homage which their beloved State may justly claim, still remember the higher and grander allegiance due to our common country.

Yours, very sincerely,

COL. JOHN FRY.   MARY LINCOLN.

A place-seekers' quarrel was not above the attention of Mrs. Lincoln, as the following letter [33] to Caleb B. Smith, Secretary of the Interior, reveals. The principals were Watts, the White House gardener, and W. S. Wood, a protégé of Seward who had been in charge of the special train which took Lincoln from Springfield to Washington.

[33] Original owned by Wilfred C. Leland, Detroit, Michigan.

Sept 8th [1861]

Executive Mansion

Hon C. B. Smith:

Dear Sir,

You will kindly excuse me for troubling you, but I much regret that Mr. Wood still pursues the attack, and tries to bring the charge of dishonesty upon Mr. Watts, who in all his accounts with us, has been rigidly exact. Circumstances have proved that Mr. Wood is the last man who should bring a charge against any one, very especially against one who has been tried & always proved exact in his dealings. From remarks made by eye witnesses, in reference to Wood, he is either deranged or drinking. Many testify that he is acting very strangely, & as he is *now known* not to be the right man, he is trying to place a just man on a level with himself. Major French, who has long known Mr. Watts, will bear testimony to his good name. I heard much of Wood in N. York—and all agree that he is not a good man. He is bitterly disappointed that we read him aright & that he is displaced—and is capable of saying anything against those who tried to befriend him when he was so undeserving.

I remain very sincerely your friend

Mary Lincoln.

To Elizabeth Todd Grimsley, a cousin who visited the Lincolns in Washington for several weeks after the inauguration, Mary Lincoln wrote intimately—and unwisely.[34]

[34] This letter was privately printed by H. E. Barker, Springfield, Illinois, 1917.

THE DOCUMENTS

MY DEAR LIZZIE:

I have been intending writing you for some days. I have been quite sick with chills for some days, this is my day of rest so I am sitting up. I am beginning to feel very weak. If they cannot be broken in a few days, Mr. Lincoln wants me to go North and remain until cold weather. When so much is demanded of me I cannot afford to be delicate, if a different climate will restore my health. If at the close of this week I am still sick, I expect I will go up to Boston, take quarters at the Revere House for two or three weeks and return here in November. I trust, however, I may not be under the necessity, yet I am feeling very far from well. September & early in October are always considered unhealthy months here, my racked frame certainly bears evidence to the fact. Have just received a note from Willis, with all his weaknesses he is kind hearted. Gov. Newell & Halstead are frequently here as *who is not?* I presume you are aware your brother is elected to Congress. I received a letter from Elizabeth E.[35] the other day. Very kind & aff. yet very *characteristic*. Said if rents and means permitted, she would like to make us a visit, I believe for a season. I am weary of *intrigue,* when she is by herself she can be very agreeable, especially when her mind is not dwelling on the merits of fair daughters and a talented son-in-law. Such personages always *speak for themselves.* I often regret E. P. E. little weaknesses, after all, since the election she is the only one of my sisters who has appeared

[35] Elizabeth Todd Edwards.

to be pleased with our advancement. You know this to be so. Notwithstanding Dr. Wallace has received his portion in life from the Administration,[36] yet Frances always remains quiet. E. in her letter said Frances often spoke of Mr. L's kindness in giving him his place. She little knows what a hard battle I had for it, and how near he came getting nothing. Poor unfortunate Ann, inasmuch as she possesses such a miserable disposition and so false a tongue. How far dear Lizzie are we removed from such a person. Even if Smith [37] succeeds in being a rich man, what advantage will it be to him, who has gained it in some cases most unjustly, and with such a woman, whom no one respects, whose tongue for so many years, has been considered "no slander" and as a child and young girl could not be outdone in falsehood, "Truly the Leopard cannot change his spots." She is so seldom in my thoughts. I have so much more, that is attractive, both in bodily presence, and my minds eye, to interest me. I grieve for those who have to come in contact with her malice, yet even that is so well understood, the object of her *wrath,* generally rises, with good people, in proportion to her *vindictiveness.* What will you name the hill on which I must be placed. Her, putting it on that ground with Mrs. Brown, was only to hide her envious feeling toward you. Tell Ann for me, to quote her own expression, she is becoming still further removed from "Queen Victoria's Court."

How foolish between us to be discussing, such a person.

[36] An appointment as paymaster of volunteers.
[37] C. M. Smith, whom Ann Todd had married.

Yet really it is amusing, in how many forms, human nature can appear before us. Nicolay told me, that Caleb Smith, said to him, a few days since that he had just received a letter from Kellogg, of Cin. that he did not know why he had not received his appointment as Consul. Is not the idea preposterous? Did I tell you that "Hollis" has been here, came to see me frequently, and always inquired with much interest, after you. The "Cap" also dined here a few days since, still as refined and elegant as ever. I have so much to tell you, I do not know, what first to write about. Wykoff, the "Chevalier," enlightened me about Baker's and Julia's proceedings in New York in Feb. Looked a little quizzical, about her not remaining in W. as she expected a long stay and much gayety. Did you say, she only numbered 5 *months*. I thought she had gently insinuated, when she was here. Hill Lamon, is now in Ill. mustering recruits. I know you will be sorry to hear, that our colored Mantua-maker, Elizabeth, lost her only son and child in the battle of Lex., Mo. She is heart broken. She is a very remarkable woman herself. The weather is so beautiful, why is it, that we cannot feel well. The air feels very much like the early days when I used to have chills in Ill., those days have passed, and I know I have no cause to grieve over my lot. If the country was only peaceful, all would be well. If I thought, sending your Father, a pass, would bring him here, I would do so with much pleasure. Give my best love to them both. Mrs. Don Piatt, calls here in an hour's time. I must mount my white Cachmere and receive her. We now occupy the stately guest room. She spoke last winter

of the miserably furnished rooms. I think she will be astonished at the change. I am not well enough to go down.
Write very soon and very often to,

your attached cousin,

MARY LINCOLN.

P. S. William has given me $3.00 to hand you. I will have
it in bill shape, to send you in a few days, when I write
next. Strange he called upon you.

Mrs. Lincoln's propensity to take a hand in matters
outside her proper sphere was the cause of no little embarrassment to Lincoln. The letter [38] which follows is
an example.

Oct 3d 61.

Executive Mansion.

COL. SCOTT:

A friend of mine, has written me from Kentucky, that
he himself has, from 500 to 1,000 of the finest young Ky
horses. He is a good Union man & wishes to dispose of
them to the Government, at Gov. prices. If you could favor
me with the authority to Major Belger, Quarter Master at
Baltimore, to buy the horses at government prices, subject
to Government inspection, I would be much obliged to
you.

Being a native of Kentucky, it would be a great pride to
me, to know that this selection had been made. I ask this as
an especial favor. Lieut Watts, is going to Baltimore this
evening, and it would give me great pleasure, if he could

[38] Original owned by Oliver R. Barrett.

hand the order to Major Belger. In the battle for the Union, it would gratify, to see the horses used, from my native state. Hoping I will receive a favorable answer, I remain

Yours very sincerely MARY LINCOLN.

Second only to Greeley's *Tribune* in influence was James Gordon Bennett's New York *Herald*. After bitterly opposing Lincoln's election, Bennett carried his opposition to the administration to such lengths that his life and newspaper plant were both threatened by ardent partisans. After Sumter, however, he reversed his position and supported the Lincoln administration with a fair degree of consistency throughout the war.

About the time the following letter [39] was written sarcastic articles about the intimacy between Mrs. Lincoln and Mrs. James Gordon Bennett, and their habit of exchanging flowers, were going the rounds of the papers.

Oct 25th 61.
Executive Mansion.

MR BENNETT

DEAR SIR:

It is with feelings of more than ordinary gratitude, that I venture to address you, a note, expressive of my thanks for the kind support and consideration, extended towards the Administration, by you, at a time when your powerful

[39] Original in Barton Library at the University of Chicago Library.

influence would be sensibly felt. In the hour of peace, the kind words of a friend are always acceptable, how much more so, when a "man's foes, are those of their own household," when treason and rebellion, threaten our beloved land, our freedom & rights are invaded and every sacred right, is trampled upon! Clouds and darkness surround us, yet Heaven is just, and the day of triumph will *surely* come, when justice & truth will be vindicated. Our wrongs will be made right, and we will once more, taste the blessings of freedom, of which the degraded rebels, would deprive us.

My own nature is very sensitive; have always tried to secure the best wishes of all, with whom through life, I have been associated; need I repeat to you, my thanks, in my own individual case, when I meet, in the columns of your paper, a kind reply, to some uncalled for attack, upon one so *little desirous* of newspaper notoriety, as my inoffensive self. I trust it may be my good fortune, at some not very distant day, to welcome both Mrs. Bennett & yourself to Washington; the President would be equally as much pleased to meet you. With an apology, for so long, trespassing upon your time, I remain, dear Mr Bennett, yours very respectfully

MARY LINCOLN.

The recipient of the following note [40] was the successor and agent in New York of Mathew B. Brady, famous photographer.

[40] Original in the Chicago Historical Society.

THE DOCUMENTS

Washington, [1861?]

Mr. Anthony

Dear Sir—

At Mr. Brady's gallery here, in the city, they tell me, they sent on some of my photographs. On yesterday the principal persons at the establishment told me they would send you a dispatch to have them destroyed. You will certainly oblige me, by doing so. The only one at all possible is the one, standing, with the large figured dress—back almost turned —showing only side face. You will readily remark which is the one. This you might retain. On Monday I will sit for another, which we will send you, if you will destroy the others. Please answer.

Very respcty

Mrs. Lincoln

The following letter [41] was written one day after the death of Willie Lincoln. It is safe to assume that Mrs. Lincoln never saw it, yet it has value, showing as it does what one segment of the population thought of the woman in the White House.

Washington City   Feb 21st 62

Silence and sadness uninterrupted reigns in and around the Executive Mansion. The halls where all was merryment & gaiety but a few brief days ago, and inmates looking forward to a still brighter 22nd in commemorating a victory which had been the cause of frantick agony to mothers

[41] Original owned by Oliver R. Barrett, Chicago, Ill.

& wives, all changed, *now* the darkness of night holds un-
disputed possession, instead of the bugle and fife harbingers
of glee and exaltation over a downtroden people, comes the
muffled drum and the wail of the heartstricken mother
calling after her lost one ever and anon you hear the low
voice asking where is my child. "Echo answers where"

I who have been a mother and wept out my hearts blood
by the death bed of an idolised son can answer, gone to
the portals of bliss, there to be carried into the presence of
a *merciful* Father attended by angels and archangels. An
inquiry arrises in our rebellious hearts. *Why has this
sacri*fice been required? *I* already feel why to wean a dev-
otee from the vain frivolities of life; but child of *fortune*
why has it been required of you! the still small voice of
conscience *answers*. The angel of *death* hovered around
your threshold day after day in mercy *threatening* yet
dreading to strike the blow, it is but a just retaliation you
would not listen to the prayers of the poor broken hearted
southern mothers which day after day ascended up to
God, *they* beged for mercy some to spare an *only* boy,
others wep't for son after son slain in battle. Oh! northern
mother *you* were permitted to minister to the wants and
alleviate the pains of that dying child but there is the child
of that poor southern mother who had been nurtured in
the lap of warmth and comfort lying on the chill bare
ground weltering in his lifes blood, no mother, no kind
friend to wet his parched lips, no smooth hand to wipe
away the dampness of death which is gathering o'er his
polished brow, *no* wreath, *no* flowers scattered over his

lonely bier, *no* silk flanel winding sheet, but *instead,* a soiled, blood deluged shirt and a shallow sepulchre is all that covers that mothers boy.

Now afflicted mother look on that bowed and fallen flower and think of the poor southern mother returning to the widowed, childless, desolate home (made desolate by the fires of an invading foe)—and let a prayer go up to an infinite and holy God to stop this *unholy* war, let your days and nights be devoted to offerings of balm & sympathy to the bleeding hearts of your persecuted sisters of the south, if so the avenging hand of a God of justice may be stayed, the faint flame of life that still flickers in the pulse of that little casket which now remains an object of solicitude and care, *may* grow brighter & he may be spared to comfort you in your sorrow; but let this miserable war go on and "your house will be unto you desolate" the blood of the butchered and mangled on their own soil cryes for revenge the mother in her frantick grief calls down the vengeance of an angry God on your house.

Oh! wife, mother, stop this sheding brothers blood. After your angel child shall have been laid in a carefully prepared grave think of the miserable scanty covering of clay awarded to the sons of a southern mother, and when his little toys are carefully placed away in a well selected resting place let them remain as emblems of peace, purity, and innocence, but pause & contrast them with the implements of death the sword, the bayonet, and the knife all of which have become playthings to deal death and destruction to our southern homes. Oh! God I say again the blood that still stains the ground of our sister states still calls for vengeance. Oh! entreat your husband to still this awful tumult and the manes of departed spirits will be appeased and mothers and orphans will rise up and call you blessed.

A Friend.

Time after time Mrs. Lincoln asked for appointments or objected to those which were contemplated.[42]

March 10 [1862?]
Executive Mansion.
Hon Mr Watson.

Having been acquainted, with the family of Mrs Redwood, in earlier years, and as she is very solicitous, to procure writing from your Department, for one of her Daughters—Will you not confer a favor upon me, by granting her request? By so doing, you will greatly oblige   yours Res-

Mrs Lincoln.

To Mrs. John C. Sprigg, a Springfield neighbor, Mrs. Lincoln gave way to the grief which nearly prostrated her for weeks after the death of her son Willie.

May 29th [1862] [43]
Executive Mansion.
My Dear Mrs. Sprigg:

Your very welcome letter was received two weeks since, and my sadness & ill health have alone prevented my reply-

[42] Original letter owned by Oliver R. Barrett.
[43] Printed in facsimile in Goltz, *Incidents in the Life of Mary Todd Lincoln.*

216

ing to it. We have met with so overwhelming an affliction in the death of our beloved Willie a being too precious for earth, that I am so completely unnerved, that I can scarcely command myself to write. What would I give to see you & talk to you, in our crushing bereavement, if any one's presence could afford comfort—it would be yours. You were always a good friend & dearly have I loved you. All that human skill could do, was done for our sainted boy. I fully believe the severe illness, he passed through, now, almost two years since, was but a warning to us, that one so pure, was not to remain long here and at the same time, he was *lent* us a little longer—to try us & wean us from a world, whose chains were fastening around us & when the blow came, it found us so unprepared to meet it. Our home is very beautiful, the grounds around us are enchanting, the world still smiles & pays homage, yet the charm is dispelled—everything appears a mockery, the idolised one, is not with us, he has fulfilled his mission and we are left desolate. When I think over his short but happy childhood, how much comfort, he always was to me, and how fearfully, I always found my hopes concentrating on so good a boy as he was—when I can bring myself to realise that he has indeed passed away, my question to myself is, "can life be endured?" Dear little Taddie who was so devoted to his darling Brother, although as deeply afflicted as ourselves, bears up and teaches us a lesson, in enduring the stroke, to which we *must submit*. Robert will be home from Cambridge in about 6 weeks and will spend his vacation with us. He has grown & improved more than any one you ever saw. Will we ever meet, & talk together as *we have* done. *Time* time how many sad changes it brings. The 1st of July, we go out to the "Soldiers' Home," a very charming place 2½ miles from the city, several hundred feet, above, our present situation, to pass the summer. I dread that it will be a greater resort than here, *if possible,* when we are in sorrow, quiet is very necessary to us. Mr Dubois, I suppose has reached home, ere this. I see by the papers that Mr *Burch* is married. We have some pieces of furniture, still remaining at his house, may I ask a favor of you— It is this—If Mr Black can have room for them, can they be moved, to any place above his store, where he may have room for them. The sofa, at Mr Burch's was new, a few months before we left. May I also ask you, to speak to Mr Black, and see if the 8 boxes we left with him, are all there. I fear we have been troublesome friends. I send you a list of the articles sent me by Mr B. If you feel the least delicacy about this—I will not wish you to do it. Whenever you have leisure, I hope you will write me. With love to all, I remain ever your attached friend

MARY LINCOLN.

A year later the memory of Willie Lincoln's death was still fresh. Mrs. Gideon Welles, wife of the Secretary of the Navy, was one of the few women of official Washington with whom Mrs. Lincoln was on entirely friendly terms.

THE DOCUMENTS

Feb 21st 63-

Executive Mansion

My Dear Mrs Welles:[44]

Allow me to thank you for your sympathising & kindly remembrance of *yesterday,* when I felt so broken hearted. Only those who have passed through such bereavements, can realise, how the heart bleeds at the return, of these anniversaries.—I have never been able, to express to you, how I grieved over your trouble, our precious lambs, if we could only realise, how far happier they *now* are than when on earth! Heaven helps the sorrowing, and how full the land is, of such! Any morning, you may have leisure, I should like to see you. I would enjoy, a little conversation with you.

Ever sincerely,

Mary Lincoln.

The following letter,[45] undated and to an unknown correspondent, reveals the principal cause of the financial difficulties in which Mrs. Lincoln was later to find herself.

Executive Mansion

My Dear Madame

Your bonnets were received on yesterday. The black with colors, I liked very much. Also the black crape. I wished a much finer blk straw bonnet for mourning— without the gloss. Could you not get such a one? I want you to send me a bow of blk crape, for the top of the blk straw bonnet, *exactly* like the one, on top the blk crape

---

[44] From Clark, *Abraham Lincoln in the National Capital.*
[45] Original in the Historical Society of Pennsylvania, Philadelphia, Pa.

219

bonnet—of the *same crape* two bows on each side of the loup, bound, like the other. I wrote you about the veils—did you receive the letter. I want you to select me the *very finest,* & blackest & lightest long crape veil & bordered as they bring them. Please get me the finest that can be obtained. Want a *very very* fine blk crape veil, round corners & folds around. Want one of very fine blk silknet—with folds around for summer—round at corners & short. The *long veil* I should like to have by Friday—want it very fine—blk & light—please send *this,* immediately.

I liked the undersleeves & collars. Please have me *two more,* white & blk collars mixed, with cuffs to match—no undersleeves. I want the genteelest & tastiest you can find or have made. I liked the style of the blk & white reversed. Do not forget the bow, for the bonnet. And the long veil, I want immediately. I have your money ready for you.

Very truly yours
Mrs Lincoln.

During the latter part of Lincoln's Presidency Mrs. Lincoln conceived a deep admiration for Charles Sumner. The courtly bearing and polished manners of the handsome senator from Massachusetts had a strong attraction for her, and she welcomed him to the White House. On several occasions she sent him notes like the following.[46]

[46] From Morrow, *Mary Todd Lincoln,* 46-47.

THE DOCUMENTS

HON. CHARLES SUMNER,

MY DEAR SIR:

Words are scarcely an atonement for the inadvertent manner in which I addressed you yesterday. Therefore, I pray you, accept this little peace offering for your table: a few fresh flowers brought up by the gardener. I am aware that you do not usually frequent large crowds or attend receptions. They are certainly *somewhat* of an annoyance but a necessity which of course in this house cannot be dispensed with. Yet in reference to your special attendance my words were mere badinage. We have no good news from that brave youth, Col. Dahlgren. Fears are now entertained that he is certainly killed. Trusting that your kind nature will excuse me, I remain,

Respectfully,

MARY LINCOLN.

Mary Lincoln never succeeded in learning the difference between the President and the President's wife. She greatly feared that Gen. Nathaniel P. Banks, in Washington for some months in the fall of 1864, would be appointed to a cabinet position. She used what influence she possessed to defeat his appointment, and announced the final decision to Murat Halstead of the Cincinnati *Commercial* with obvious gratitude.[47]

[47] Original owned by Oliver R. Barrett.

MR HALSTEAD— Nov 24th [1864]

I write you in great haste, to say, that after all the excitement, Gen Banks, is to be returned to his command, at New Orleans, and the *Great Nation,* will be comforted with the idea, that he is not to be in the Cabinet. With kind regards to Mrs H- I remain your friend

MRS LINCOLN-

Even Sumner was called on upon occasion, as the following letter [48] testifies.

Executive Mansion,
Sunday, March 19, 1865.

SENATOR SUMNER,

MY DEAR SIR:

Whilst appointments are being made and vacancies filled, I trust you will not deem me intrusive by suggesting your *quiet* perseverance and that of your influential friends in the claim of Mr J. Jay. Our good friend, Baron Gerolt, called to see me yesterday and proposed bringing the new Austrian Minister to pay his respects this evening. Hoping the charming music in "Faust" compensated you for the two or three hours passed away from your studies, which in Mr. Lincoln's case I never regret,

I remain, very truly,

MARY LINCOLN.

From the time a few days before the first inauguration that Mrs. Lincoln first made use of the "colored

48 From Morrow, *Mary Todd Lincoln,* 47.

mantuamaker," Elizabeth Keckley, her regard for her grew steadily. The following letter [49] of recommendation was written to George Harrington, Assistant Secretary of the Treasury.

Hon Sec Harrington   Executive Mansion
Dear Sir

I am under many obligations to you, for your frequent kindnesses to me, and will only request you to add another name, in the place of *Ellen Shehan,* & will promise, not to trouble you again. The woman, who is most estimable, is named Elizabeth Keckley, although colored, is very industrious, & has just had an interview with Gov Chase, who says he will see you & I am sure, it rests with you. She is very unobtrusive, and will perform her duties, faithfully. I do not believe, I am making a vain request of you— and I will not again trouble you.

Please insert her name in place of the other. I presume you will not object, to her not entering upon her duties, until the middle of April. You see Mr Harrington, I am calculating on your kindly agreeing to my proposal.

Very Respectfully
Mrs. Lincoln.

The following letter [50] suggests the pleasures which Mary Lincoln might have found in life had its normal course not been interrupted.

[49] Original in the Illinois State Historical Library.
[50] From Morrow, *Mary Todd Lincoln,* 48.

MARY LINCOLN

SENATOR SUMNER,
MY DEAR SIR:

The President and myself are about leaving for "City Point" and I cannot but devoutly hope that change of air and rest may have a beneficial effect on my good Husband's health. On our return, about Wednesday, we hope you will be inclined to accompany us to the Italian Opera. "Ernani" is set aside for that evening. Perhaps we will have a large private box and some one or two other agreeable friends will join us.

From the "State Department" yesterday, Mr. Lincoln received Louis Napoleon's recent work, the *Life of Julius Caesar*. It has been sent in pamphlet form and is to be bound. When it has been returned to us, if you will allow us the liberty of sending it to you to read, you will doubtless be interested in it. In the coming summer, when we shall be left to our solitude I shall peruse it myself for I have so sadly neglected the little French I fancied so familiar to me.

Judge Haines called last evening to say farewell. He has been so kind a friend that I am quite as attached to him as if he were a relative.

Very Truly,

MARY LINCOLN.

Please excuse this very hasty note,

M. L.

Within three weeks came the catastrophe which shattered Mary Lincoln's life. How it came about that Lincoln was at the theatre on the night of April 14, what his last words were, and how overwhelming was the grief of Mrs. Lincoln are told in a letter from Dr. Anson G. Henry to his wife.[51] In Springfield, before he went West in the early fifties, Henry had been Lincoln's physician and intimate friend. Lincoln appointed him Surveyor-General of Washington Territory in 1861. In 1863 Henry visited Washington, and the old friendship was resumed. In 1865 he was again at the capital, seeking advancement. Upon Lincoln's death Mrs. Lincoln turned to him eagerly, and he was her constant attendant for several weeks.

Washington D. C.
April 19th 1865

MY DEAR WIFE

Today has been the saddest day of my life, if indeed one day can be sadder than another of the sad days that has shrouded the nation in gloom. I have no words to express what I feel, and how much I now long to fold you to my bosom and mingle my burning tears with yours for the loss of our greatest, best & most kind & loving friend Abraham Lincoln. Now that he has gone to the spirit land we realize how much we loved him and how worthy he was of our love & confidence.

[51] Original owned by Oliver R. Barrett.

225

I was in Richmond on the night of his assassination. The next day in the afternoon I went down to City Point & met the sad news. I was so stunned by the blow that I could not realize that he was dead untill I saw him lying in the Guests Chamber cold & still in the embrace of Death. Then the terrible truth flashed upon me, & the fountain of tears was broken up and I wept like a child refusing to be comforted, remaining riveted to the spot untill led away by those who came in for the purpose of placing the body in the coffin. I felt that a mountain load had been suddenly lifted from my heart. I had never before realized the luxury of tears, & I never before wept in the bitterness of heart & soul, & God grant that I may never have cause to so weep again.

After recovering my composure, I sought the presence of poor heart broken Mrs. Lincoln. I found her in bed more composed than I had anticipated, but the moment I came within her reach she threw her arms around my neck & wept most hysterically for several minutes, and this completely unmanned me again, but my sympathy was to her most consoling, and for a half hour she talked very composedly about what had transpired between her and [her] Husband the day & evening of his death, which I will tell you when we meet. She says he was more cheerful and joyous that day and evening than he had been for years. When at dinner he complained of being worn out with the incessant toils of the day, and proposed to go to the Theatre and have a laugh over the Country Cousin. She says she discouraged going, on account of a bad headache, but he insisted that he must go, for if he stayd at home he would have no rest, for he would be obliged to see company all the evening as usual. Finding that he had decided to go, she could not think of having him go without her, never having felt so unwilling to be away from him. She sat close to him and was leaning on his lap when the fatal shot was fired, his last words being in answer to her question, "What will Miss Harris think of my hanging on to you so" —"She wont think anything about it," and said accompanied with one of his kind and affectionate smiles. Yes, that look & expression is stamped upon her soul too indelibly to ever be effaced by time, and its recollection will never fail to sooth and comfort her in her hours of darkest affliction. God in his mercy will sanctify this personal & national affliction for great good, and this is my greatest and almost only consolation under the terrible bereavement.

I feel that there is no selfishness mixed up with my sorrow. The loss of Mr. Lincoln will not affect my personal interests unfavorably. I have good reason to believe that President Johnson will do all for me that President Lincoln could or would have done, but the great attraction for remaining here has been taken away, yet it would not be right to refuse to stay here as the representative of our Pacific interests in the Departments, should the Delegation insist upon it, as they undoubtedly will. At least so says Judge Williams. The matter wont be settled until Mr. Harlan takes charge of the Department of the Interior on the 15th of May. This was the understanding between

Harlan & Mr. Lincoln when I left for Richmond. It may *possibly* turn out that Johnson wont ratify the arrangement, but I dont think he will refuse. The general impression is, that he will, as near as possible, carry out Mr. Lincoln's policy & plans. In other words, finish up the work the immortal Lincoln had begun and so nearly completed. The great body of the Nation will demand this of him.

You must my Dear Dear Wife bear our separation with all the patience possible. Let us thank God that we are permitted to commune together in this way, and that should it be the will of providence that we do not meet again on earth, that by his all prevailing grace and mercy we will meet in Heaven.

ANSON

P. S. I forgot to tell you that I followed the hearse in the funeral procession in the third carriage as one of the family. This place was assigned me by the Marshall, as I suppose on the suggestion of Mrs. Lincoln. I was seated with the mourners in the East Room when the Funeral Ceremonies were performed. I send you a copy of them enclosed— The sermon of Doctor Gurley.

In the following letter [52] to Andrew Johnson Mrs. Lincoln interceded for a man upon whom she was soon to bestow her entire confidence. Since the death of Willie Lincoln, Alexander Williamson had held a minor position in the Treasury Department.

[52] Original in the Library of Congress.

THE DOCUMENTS

Executive Mansion
April 29, 1865.

MY DEAR SIR

The bearer Mr. Alexr. Williamson was for more than four years connected with our family in the capacity of tutor to my late son Willie and latterly to Tad. He enjoyed the complete confidence and had the best wishes of my late husband, so much so that about the middle of March when he had made up his mind to make certain prominent appointments in connection with the "Bureau of Refugees, Freedmen and Abandoned Lands," he in a conversation with Mr. W. in the library, told him that he would "not forget him." I am most desirous that the promise should be fulfilled.

Mr. W. has all along been a devoted friend of our family and an unconditional friend of the Union, and as such I leave him and his case with perfect confidence in your hands.

I am
My dear Sir
Yours very Truly
MARY LINCOLN

His Excellency
A. JOHNSON.

As soon as she left Washington and took up her residence in Chicago, Mrs. Lincoln commenced a correspondence with Williamson. The newspaper article which aroused the anger so evident in the following letter [53] purported to be an interview with Captain

[53] Original owned by Oliver R. Barrett.

Stackpole, who had charge of the White House and grounds during the war, in which the Captain described how Lincoln had once exercised "Executive clemency" to save Tad from a whipping.

Hyde Park Hotel.
June 15th 1865.

MR. WILLIAMSON,
MY DEAR SIR:

Taddie has just received the name of the "Bucktail," & bids me write & thank you truly, for *all* your kindness to him. He says two or three lessons a day & is at length seized with the desire to *read* & *write*—which with his *natural* brightness, will be *half* the battle with him. I hope he will be able to write by fall so that he may be able to write you a letter inviting you *out here* to see him. For all your great kindness to my darling boys, may Heaven forever bless you! I am sure my angel boy, in Heaven, loves you as dearly as ever. *He* was too pure for Earth & God recalled his own. How deeply we have been made to drink of the bitter cup of affliction is known to all, if it were not for my two remaining sons, I would pray the Father, to take me too hence. Taddie has a lovely nature & I have not the least trouble in managing him, he is all love & gentleness. Robert, in our day of sorrow and adversity, manifests himself as he really is, a youth of great nobleness. I was very much surprised in yesterday's evening Chicago Journal, to see this article I enclose, purporting to come from Stackpole. My Beloved Husband's great tenderness & gentleness of character, is well established & in his great love for his children, it is well known, that I bore an equal part. His love for me, was in the same proportion, yet, when I read a story which gives S- as the author, saying I threatened to *whip* Taddie, for cutting up *copper-toed* shoes, such articles as my boys never wore—I am surprised. It is a new story— that in my life I have ever whipped a child. In the first place *they* never required it. A gentle, loving word, was all sufficient with them—and if I have erred, it has been, in being too indulgent. I trust if S- has ever got up such a story, even in jest, he will discontinue it. I have relied on him as a friend. Do not, I pray you, let him have the piece, but return it to me. It would please *Hanson* the R- man, to have such a piece, it may have been copied from his paper. As to Copperheadism, I really believe it would have been a happier day for us now, & my idolized husband would *now* have been living, if those, en masse holding office, would have abhorred & sternly treated these Copper-heads as I would have done.

M. L.

After spending several weeks with Mrs. Lincoln as her personal physician and adviser, Doctor Henry gave up hope of a better appointment at the hands of the new administration and started on the long trip to his home at Olympia, Washington Territory. While he was *en route*—he chose the Isthmus route—Mrs. Lincoln wrote him two letters.[54] Both are marked by such

[54] Originals owned by Oliver R. Barrett.

bitterness, and such unnecessary financial concern, that they can hardly be accepted as the products of a normal mind.

Hyde Park Place
July 17th 1865

MY DEAR DR:

I had hoped to have sent this letter by today's Steamer, but have been so seriously indisposed this week, that this is the first day of it, I have been sitting up. *General* Todd, called to see us, ten days since, said he had a conversation with Sec Harlan, the day before leaving, that was the Monday after you sailed. He expressed *great regret,* that you had *so suddenly* left, said *he had* intended doing something for you. Robert immediately wrote to him and insisted, that it was not too late & that *he* considered it due, his Father's memory, that *you* should be provided for, in *W*. Altho' it has been over a week since this was written, not a word, have we heard from *him*. I see, by the papers, this week, that *some* man from Iowa, has been put in Dole's place, and that *Holloway,* has resigned.—*Much,* doubtless, to old Newton's delight—*another, this last* is, of the selfish ones.

Mr Harlan, has acted in the most contemptible way! It has become so much so with every one, that when I write to Wash- on any subject or business, I receive no reply. It is so, with Robert also. No *such sorrow,* was ever visited upon a people or family, as when we were bereaved of my darling husband, every day causes me to feel still more crushed & broken hearted. If it was not for dear little

Taddie, I would pray to die, I am so miserable. I still remain closeted in my rooms, take an occasional walk, in the park & as usual see no one. What have I, in my misery, to do with the outside world? I must not fail to thank you, for your most interesting letter from New York, it is well for us, that you passed a day or two there, & saw those you did. Mr Bentley wrote me from Detroit, one day this week, said he would probably, be in Chicago, next week. He appears to be a very kind hearted man. *Judge* Davis, has been holding court in Chicago, called out, & said *very complacently,* I am glad, to see you are so well situated out *here* & remarked, that there was not the *least indication,* that C- or *any other place,* would *bestow* a house & we would have to *content* ourselves, with boarding. I replied, "I board *no longer,* than next spring in *Ill, after that,* if we have still to be *vagrants,* I prefer being so, in any state, rather than where *every man* in the State, owes my Husband a deep debt of gratitude." He said, will you take Robt with you too? I replied, "most certainly, he goes, where I do."—There is no doubt he, Judge D, enters *entirely* into the feelings of the *S* clique. I mentioned, that I had understood, that *Smith* had been making himself as silly & malicious as ever, by endeavouring to turn my best friends in N. Y. against me. He said "not at all, he could not believe it"—I told him very emphatically, *"it was so."* I did not mention any names to him. With all our overwhelming sorrows, what enemies, we *do* have to contend with!—I can assure them here, that it is from no feeling of gratitude or love, for *them,* that I have returned *here.*—

Judge D is entirely selfish, and would rather, I really believe, prefer to see us, as we are, without a home, or the prospect of one, rather than have us comfortable—it is endurance vile—I assure you—and no prospect of a remedy.

I believe in my heart, that you are really the only disinterested, sincere friend, left us. I trust for all your kindness, I will be enabled to repay some of it. It was very painful to us, I assure you, to find that you had to return home. I had fondly hoped, that you would have been settled in W. and we would have received frequent visits from you & Mrs. Henry, whom I remember with much affection. Alas, alas, our families are both situated alike, nothing but disappointments before us—and if myself & sons, are specimens, of American justice, God help other people. I have written to Sen Williams, and have as yet, had no reply. I have requested him to inform me, of the first safe means, of sending some articles to you—our *poor boxes,* I fear, are long destined, to remain in the warehouse. I thought it best, not to send, for the present, those claims to Mr Brooks. Some months later, perhaps, it would be better. Anything *we do* is seized on—an especial way, of "being cared for, by the American people." Robert is so worried, that I am sick so much, that he has purchased a neat covered buggy, in which he can drive his horse, otherwise, he says he would sell the horse. As it was his Father's *last* gift, I could not consent to this, although I expect we will hear remarks, about our purchasing a buggy. I do hope, dear Doctor, you will write to us very frequently, what would I not give, to have one of our old chats together again. R- often remarks the same. I cannot express, how lonely & desolate we are. And you have been almost our only friend in our deep, deep affliction. Please present much love to Mrs Henry, who must indeed be rejoiced to see you. I will write you again in a few days, after seeing Bentley, *if he calls*. Do write at least once a week. Robt & Tad send much love.

Your truly attached friend

MARY LINCOLN.

Hyde Park Place
July 26th 65.

MY DEAR DR:

Although I wrote you, a few days since, by the Overland Route, yet remembering that a steamer sails next Saturday, I have concluded to send you a few lines. I did not receive your letter from Panama and I have written to Senator Williams & he has not replied. I have nothing new, just now to tell you. *This place* has become a complete Babal & I grieve, that *necessity* requires us, to live in this way. Bentley, from the Detroit Convention, came over to C—as usual, he was "hoping on, hoping ever." There is a very dim prospect of success I think. I see that one of the Editors of the Springfield *Mass,* R paper, accompanies Mr Colfax, and is now, with him in California. This Mr Bowles, will throw cold water, I fear on any of your or the Tribune's efforts in Cal. Taddie is not at home, the scarlet fever, is in the house & a lady who boards here, the daughter of Dr Boone, & niece of Mrs Judge Thomas, who formerly lived in S. now in C. proposed for fear of the disease, taking Taddie, up to her Mother's, in the country. I am so miserable, it is painful to part with him, even for a day, yet it is best, he should be away. Taddie, has made many warm friends, in the house. I live as secluded as ever—as a matter of course. I long for a home, where I can bury myself & my sorrows. Sec Harlan wrote R. a letter, full of all manner of excuses about *not* appointing you—*he* is intensely selfish & I trust, I shall never see any of them again. I am sure, as *we* are not now in power, *they* do not desire it. Gov Oglesby is in Chicago, and it appeared in two of the leading journals of the city, yesterday, purporting to be copied, from "Boston Transcript," that Mrs Lincoln had already from the estate $100,000, and the paper was authorized to state, no more contributions would be received. It, of course, emanated from Springfield, and those people know, we have no home! If you hear of any person, going to California or W. T. please advise me. I wish to send you what I have promised. I again reiterate, that when *you* left, our only true friend departed. Do write very often & give my best love to Mrs Henry. The world looks darker to me than ever & my heart aches, for my bereaved sons.

Poor Robert, has borne his sorrows, manfully, yet with a broken heart. I wish to goodness, yourself & family, could have remained on this side.—But, as it was *our* earnest wish, they, *at W.* saw fit to disappoint us.

Your attached friend
MARY LINCOLN.

Mrs Trumbull has not *yet* honored me with a call, should she ever deign, she would not be received. She is indeed "a whited sepulchre."

Again in the following letter [55] Mrs. Lincoln recurred to the matter of finances, a subject which was to be an obsession with her for years to come, and to find a place in nearly every letter she wrote.

Chicago, Aug. 17th/65

MR. WILLIAMSON,
MY DEAR SIR:

Your letter, was received on yesterday. We were quite surprised to learn of your speedy return to the U. S. I trust, you found your Mother, in good health. Taddie is well & sends you a photograph of himself, just taken. He is growing very fast & I am sorry to say, he does not apply himself to his studies, with as much interest as he should. We intend that he shall attend school, regularly after the 1st of Sep. Your idea about the carriage, is very correct. I did not wish a notice of it, to appear, in the W. C. but in Forney's Phil paper. There are too many Secessionists in W. to care, for any thing, belonging to us. As you may suppose, no family ever felt their bereavement, more than we do. My heart is indeed broken, and without my beloved husband, I do not wish to live. Life, is indeed a heavy burden, & I do not care how soon, I am called hence.

I wish you to see Cuthbert & tell her, I thought according to her promise, she would have settled my business ere

[55] Original owned by Oliver R. Barrett.

237

this. We have to board, as our means will not enable us to purchase a home—each of us, have only $500 a year—hence, where everything is so expensive, we can only board, in the plainest manner, on it. I explain to you, exactly & truly, how we are circumstanced, a greater portion of our means, is unavailable, consisting, in a house in S. & some wild lands in Iowa. Notwithstanding my great & good husband's life, was sacrificed for his country, we are left to struggle, in a manner entirely new to us—and a noble people would pronounce our manner of life, *undeserved*. Roving Generals have elegant mansions showered upon them, and the American people—leave the family of the Martyred President, to struggle as best they may! Strange justice this. I hope the day may yet come, when I can repay *your* kindness to us. At present, seeking lodging, from one place to another, is insupportable, and added to my afflicting sorrow, rendered life very desolate. My poor sad boys, are the only remaining ties, to a world rendered so miserable by my great loss. You need not show Cuthbert the *letter* or papers—please return them to me—talk to her. R & Taddie wish to be remembered.

Your friend—

M. L.

Need of money soon led Mrs. Lincoln into a series of major indiscretions. The first of these—the sale of the Presidential carriage—is recorded in the following letter.[56]

[56] Original in the collection of Wilfred C. Leland, Detroit, Mich.

THE DOCUMENTS

Mess. H. Leeds & Miner

Gentlemen—

Your letter, relative to the carriage, has been received. Considering it was so much out of repair, I think it sold very well. Can you inform me, who was the purchaser? As to Mr. Williamson—for the last four years, he was tutor to my little boys. My husband & myself always regarded him as an upright, intelligent man. When leaving Washington, last May, I directed the servant woman to present him in my name (and in consideration, for the high reverence, he Mr. W. always entertained for the President) a shawl & dressing gown. In doing so I felt he would cherish & always retain these relics of so great and good a man. My astonishment was very great I assure you, when you mentioned that these articles were for sale. Mr. W. certainly did not reflect when he proposed such a thing. I wish you would write to him and remonstrate upon so strange a proceeding. Hoping again to hear from you, on the subject, I remain very respectfully.

Mrs. A. Lincoln

I am feeling very anxious, after again looking over your letter, about Mr. Williamson's *proposed sale,* of these little relics—it sounds very badly *to me,* who in my deep affliction, am naturally very sensitive. If possible it *must be prevented.*

M. L.

MARY LINCOLN

In this letter to Francis B. Carpenter [57] Mrs. Lincoln again described the transformation which peace had wrought in Lincoln, and the buoyancy which characterized him on the day he was shot. Carpenter had spent six months in the White House painting a picture of the signing of the Emancipation Proclamation, and was now engaged on a group picture of the Lincoln family.

Chicago Nov 15th [1865]

MR. CARPENTER
MY DEAR SIR:

Your last letter, has been received. It would be utterly impossible for me, in my present nervous state, to sit for a photograph—although, I should like to oblige you, very much. There is an excellent painted likeness of me, at Brady's in N. Y. taken in *1861*—have you ever seen it? I am sure you will like it & I believe, it was taken, in a black velvet. I enclose you one of my precious, sainted Willie. You have doubtless heard, how *very* handsome a boy, he was considered—with a pure, gentle nature, always unearthly & an intellect *far, far* beyond his years. When I reflect, as I am always doing, upon the overwhelming loss, of that *most* idolized boy, and the crushing blow, that deprived me, of my *all in all,* in this life, I wonder that I retain my reason & live. There are hours of each day, that my mind, cannot be brought to realize, that *He,* who is

[57] From Honoré Willsie Morrow, "Lincoln's Last Day," in *Hearst's International-Cosmopolitan,* February, 1930.

considered so great and good a God, has *thus* seen fit to afflict us! How difficult it is to be reconciled to such a bereavement, how much sooner, each one of our stricken family, if the choice had been left to us, would have preferred "passing away," ourselves.

It strikes me strangely, how such a rumor, should be circulated—that Robert is in Europe. The thought of leaving home, I am sure, has never *once,* entered his mind. He is diligently applying himself, to his law studies—a most devoted Son & brother. Every thing, is *so fabulously* high *here,* that his third of the estate, an income of $1800 apiece —with taxes deducted. It requires the most rigid economy, with Robert & the rest of us to clothe ourselves, plainly & weekly settle our board-bills. Is not this, a sad change for us! As a matter of course living, every where now, in the U. S. is high—Yet I cannot express to you, how painful to me it is, to have *no* quiet home, where I can freely indulge my sorrows—*this* is, yet another, of the crosses appointed unto me. With my beloved husband, I should have had a heart for any fate, if "need be." Dear little Taddie was named, for my husband's father, Thomas Lincoln—no *T* for a middle name—was nicknamed Taddie by his loving Father. Taddie is learning to be as diligent in his studies, as he used to be *at play,* in the W. H. He appears to be rapidly making up, for the great amount of time, he lost in W. As you are aware, *he* was always a *marked character.* Two or three weeks since, a lady in an adjoining room, gave him a copy of Mr. Raymond's, life of the President, for me to read & return to her. After reading it, I remarked to

Robert, in Taddie's presence, that it was *the most* correct history, of his Father, that had been written. Taddie immediately spoke up & said "Mother, I am going to save all the little money, you give me and get one of them." R. told him he need not, as he would buy a copy. I press the poor little fellow closer, *if possible,* to my heart, in memory of the sainted Father, who loved *him so very dearly,* as well as the rest of us. How I wish you could have seen my dear husband, the last three weeks of his life! Having a realizing sense, that the unnatural rebellion, was near its close, & being most of the time, *away* from W. where he had endured such conflicts of mind, within the last four years, feeling *so encouraged,* he freely gave vent to his cheerfulness. Down the Potomac, he was almost boyish in his mirth & reminded me, of his original nature, what I had always remembered of him, in our own home—free from care, surrounded by those he loved so well & by *whom,* he was so idolized. *The Friday* I never saw him so supremely cheerful—his manner was even playful. At three o'clock, in the afternoon, he drove out with me in the open carriage. In starting, I asked him, if any one, should accompany us. He immediately replied—"No, I prefer to ride by ourselves to day." During the drive he was so gay, that I said to him, laughingly, "Dear Husband, you almost startle me, by your great cheerfulness;" he replied "and well I may feel so, Mary, I consider *this day,* the war has come to a close"—and then added, "We must *both,* be more cheerful in the future—between the war & the loss of our darling Willie—we have both, been very miserable." Every word, then uttered, is deeply engraven, on my poor broken heart. In the evening, his mind, was fixed upon having some relaxation & bent on the theatre. Yet I firmly believe, that if he had remained, at the W. H. on that night of darkness, when the fiends prevailed he would have been horribly *cut to pieces.* Those fiends, had too long contemplated, this inhuman murder, to have allowed, *him,* to escape. Robert informs me, that the best likeness of himself, is at Goldin's, in Washington, taken last spring. We have none, unframed. The attitude in the one, you sent me, of myself, is very good, my hands are always *made* in *them,* very large and I look too stern. The drapery of the dress, was *not,* sufficiently flowing—and my hair, should not be so low down, on the forehead & so much dressed. I am sending you a long & most hastily written letter, which I pray you excuse. My sons desire to be remembered to you. Whilst I remain

Very Sincerely

MARY LINCOLN.

The first writer of real competence to publish a biography of Lincoln was J. G. Holland, editor of the *Century Magazine.* Shortly after Lincoln's death Holland spent several weeks in Springfield interviewing Lincoln's old neighbors, and particularly his former law partner, William H. Herndon. When his book appeared he sent Mrs. Lincoln a copy, which she acknowledged in a letter [58] as valuable for its evasions as for its direct statements.

Private- Chicago Dec 4th 1865

Dr. J. G. Holland

My dear Sir:

The Biography of my deeply lamented husband, which you have so kindly sent me, has been received and read with very great interest. After a careful perusal of the work, I find the statements, in *most* instances, so very correct, that I feel quite surprised, as to the extent of your *minute* information. From the description of my husband's early struggles, which he has so frequently described to me, to the foolish and uncalled for rencontre, with Gen Shields, all are truthfully portrayed. This *last* event, occurred about six months, before our marriage, when, Mr Lincoln thought, he had some right, to assume to be *my* champion, even on frivolous occasions. The poor Genl., in our little gay circle, was oftentimes, the subject of mirth & even song —and we were *then* surrounded, by several of those, who have since been appreciated, by the *world*. The Genl. was very impulsive & on the occasion referred to, had placed himself before us, in so ridiculous a light, that the love of the ludicrous had been excited within me & I presume, I gave vent to it, in some *very* silly lines. After the reconciliation, between the *contending* parties, Mr L & myself mutually agreed, never to refer to it & except in an occa-

[58] Original in the Barton Library at the University of Chicago Library.

sional light manner, between us it was never mentioned. I am surprised, at *so* distant a day, you should have ever heard of the circumstance.

It is exceedingly painful to me, *now,* suffering under such an overwhelming bereavement, to recall *that* happy time. My beloved husband, had so entirely devoted himself to me, for two years before my marriage, that I doubtless trespassed, many times & oft, upon his great tenderness & amiability of character. There never existed a more loving & devoted husband & such a Father, has seldom been bestowed on children. Crushed and bowed to the earth, with our *great great* sorrow, for the sake of my poor afflicted boys, I have to strive, to live on, and comfort them, as well as I can. You are aware, that with all the President's deep feeling, he was *not* a demonstrative man, when he felt most deeply, he expressed the least. There are some very good persons, who are inclined to magnify conversations & incidents, connected with their slight acquaintance, with this great & good man. For instance, the purported conversations, between the President & the Hospital nurse, it was not *his* nature, to commit his griefs and religious feelings so fully to words & that with an entire stranger. Even between ourselves, when our deep & touching sorrows, were *one* & the same, his expressions were few. Also the lengthy account, of the lady, who *very* wisely persisted, in claiming a hospital, for her State. My husband never had the time, to discuss these matters, so lengthily with any person or persons—too many of them came daily, in review before him. And again, I cannot understand, how strangely his temper, could be at so complete a variance, from what it always was, in the home circle. There, he was always so gentle & kind. Before closing this long letter, which I fear will weary you ere you get through it—allow me again to assure you, of the great satisfaction the perusal of your Memoirs have given me. I remain very truly & gratefully,

MARY LINCOLN.

Further comment on Lincoln's duel with Shields marks a second letter [59] to Francis B. Carpenter.

MR CARPENTER   Chicago. Dec. 8th 1865.
MY DEAR SIR:

The saddest of *all my very sad* days, has passed, Thanksgiving day, and by way of diverting my mind & memory, from the recollection of *yesterday,* I have concluded, to reply, to your very kind note, so recently received. Only those, who have suffered & lost, what made life so well worth living for, can fully understand the return of Anniversaries, that recall the past so vividly to the mind & make the day of general praise & rejoicing, so painful, to the sufferer. But I will not complain, or return to my sorrows. I must endeavour to make the best, of the life that is left me, for the sake of my sons, who have had so much, to try them. I thought you would be satisfied, with the likenesses of my darling little boys, Willie & Taddie, taken in 1861 —they will answer very well, for the picture you propose

[59] From Honoré Willsie Morrow, "Lincoln's Last Day," in *Hearst's International-Cosmopolitan,* February, 1930.

246

painting. Even in *that* likeness of Willie, justice is not done him, he was a very beautiful boy, with a most *spiritual* expression of face. He was a most peculiarly religious child, with great amiability & cheerfulness of character. It is impossible, for *time,* to alleviate the anguish, of *such ir- reparable losses*—only the grace of God, can calm our grief & still the tempest. I wish you could have known that dear boy, for *child,* he scarcely seemed to me. So unlike little Taddie, yet so devoted to him. Their love for each other, was charming to behold. Taddie was quite worried about the expression, he was said to have made use of, on *that* Sabbath morning, he says "His Father was always so happy, when he was alone, with his Mother and himself, that he scarcely believes, he said it." In his great grief, it is impossible for him to remember, all his utterances. I have been reading Dr. Holland's Memoirs, of my husband—and was quite surprised, at the mention of a circumstance in the "Long ago," the publication of which, would have an- noyed the President, very much. You may have heard, of the little coterie, we had in Springfield years since, who have all since, in a greater or less degree, distinguished themselves, in the political world. Genl Hardin, Baker, Douglas, Trumbull—Shields and my great & glorious hus- band, always a "World above them all," these men con- stituted our society. Shields was always a subject of mirth, his impulsiveness & drolleries were irresistible. On one occasion, he made himself so conspicuous, that I committed his follies, to rhyme & some person, looking over the silly verses carried them off & had them published in the daily paper of the place. The sarcastic allusions irritated Shields & he demanded the author, of the Editor. The latter, requesting a few days for reflection, repaired to Mr. Lincoln, who having heard of it, through me, immediately told the Editor, that "he would be responsible." A few days after this, Mr. L. almost forgetting the circumstance, went off some two hundred miles to court, and to make a foolish story, very short, was followed by Shields, demanding satisfaction. Mr. L- accepted, scarcely knowing what he was doing, they repaired to St. Louis, to "Bloody Island," with their "long swords," the choice of weapons, being left to Mr. L-, the challenged party. Genl Hardin, my cousin, stepped in their midst & effected a reconciliation. No doubt, much to *their* satisfaction. This affair, always annoyed my husband's peaceful nerves, and as it occured six months, before we were married, he said he felt, he could do no less, than be my champion. However, if the same cause, had transpired a year & half before, it would doubtless have been the same result, as our mutual relations were *then,* the same. Last February, an officer of our army, presented himself in the drawing room of the W. H. on one of those fortunate & especial occasions, when the President, was able to respond to my urgent invitation, to accompany me to the drawing room, if "only for an hour." This Genl in the course of conversation, said, playfully, to my husband "Mr. President, is it true, as I have heard that you, once went out, to fight a duel & all for the sake of the lady by your side." Mr. Lincoln, with a flushed face, replied, "I do not deny it, but if you desire my friendship, you will never mention it again." Immediately after the occurence, months before we were married, *we* mutually agreed, on no occasion to allude to it & gradually it ceased to be mentioned. In the long lapse of years, I marvel that Dr. H. should have heard, of this very unnecessary episode, in my lamented husband's life. All this is between ourselves. I must say, I was greatly surprised, to see a simple letter of mine, written when my heart was bursting, with its great sorrow, in print. I will forgive you—in the hope, it may never occur again. If we are ever sufficiently well situated, to invite our friends to see us, I hope you will visit us, accompanied by Mrs. C. and I can tell you many things, of my dearly beloved husband, that I have not sufficient time or calmness, to commit to paper. Taddie is greatly mortified, that you have exposed his little waywardness, but he is a dear amiable loving boy, after all, and I presume, will forgive.

Your friend,

MARY LINCOLN.

During the summer and fall of 1865 prominent men in the East interested themselves in raising money for Mrs. Lincoln by means of a fund to which those who wanted to aid in alleviating her reputed distress were asked to contribute one dollar each. Benjamin B. Sherman, a New York merchant and banker, was treasurer. In the end, $10,747.77 was transmitted to her.

MARY LINCOLN

Chicago, Ill.
December 26, 1865.

BENJAMIN B. SHERMAN [60]

MY DEAR SIR:

Although my son wrote you a letter on yesterday, I have concluded to write and thank you, most gratefully, for your kind interest in our deeply afflicted family. We have, indeed, lost our all; the idolized husband and father is no more with us, and, if possible, our adverse fate and the great injustice of a people who owed so much to my beloved husband does not contribute toward lessening our heavy trials. Sir Morton Pelo gave a farewell dinner to his friends in New York in return for their polite attentions to him. We are homeless, and in return for the sacrifices my great and noble husband made, both in his life and in his death, the paltry first year's salary is offered us; under the circumstances, such injustice has been done us as calls the blush to any true, loyal heart. The sum is in reality only $20,000, as the first month's salary was paid my husband, and I presume the tax on it will be deducted from it. The interest of it will be about $1,500. I am humiliated when I think that we are destined to be forever homeless. I can write no more. I remain, very respectfully,

MARY LINCOLN.

P. S.—I omitted to say, my dear Mr. Sherman, mentioning to you what has been told me several times lately; persons apparently reliable saying that to their knowledge $10,000 in money toward the dollar fund had been raised in Boston. I mention this so that you might write to Boston to ascer-

[60] From the New York *Times*, December 17, 1922.

tain the truth of this report. Knowing my anxiety to have a home where we could at least have some privacy and your good feeling for us in our distress will, I am sure, induce you to write about this to B. Excuse my troubling you in this matter &c. I agree with R. it is best not to advertise; if there is anything at such an hour as this, it will be forthcoming.

M. L.

Perhaps Mrs. Lincoln's most familiar correspondent, for several years after Lincoln's death, was Mrs. J. H. Orne, of Philadelphia.

The following letter,[61] one of the first of a large number, reveals Mrs. Lincoln's first steps in an enterprise which was to make her the object of bitter reproach—the sale of her own wearing apparel.

MY DEAR MRS. ORNE: Chicago Jan 4th 66

I wrote you a hurried line, this morning, enclosing a very few hairs, from my beloved husband's head. I regret, I have so few to spare you, as I have only a bunch, as large as one of our fingers. I was told before I left Washington, that quite a quantity was cut off, to be reserved for me, was placed in the wardrobe, in the guest room, at the W. H. As some officers were present at the time, it was presumed, it was taken, from where it was placed. Your appreciative heart will prize, even the few hairs, I send you. May Heaven bless you, for *thus* having reverenced my

[61] Original owned by Oliver R. Barrett.

great and good husband. I enclose you a scrap from this morning's paper. The country, is certainly "growing smaller by degrees, & beautifully less." I almost wish, that the *necessities* of the case, did not require me, to retain the small portion, so *ungraciously* bestowed upon me. I have passed the last two mornings, my dear friend, at a warehouse a mile distant among the few goods we have, trying to assort them & see what disposition, I can make of them. *For,* boarding in such narrow quarters & so curtailed for means, I must dispose of every thing, not necessary, to be retained. As I was leaving off black, last March, I find myself, with several dress patterns on hand. If I am not asking too great a favor, should I send them on to you, to be placed in a store for disposal—would I be imposing, too much, on your great goodness. The price of living here is fabulous, board is quite as high, as in Wash. and our last resort, a plain yet genteel boarding, does not exempt us, from charges, that I shall have to exert myself, in the future, to meet. I will write no more to day, for I became so thoroughly chilled on yesterday that my limbs ache with pain and I am sure, the terrible trials we are passing through, will only pain your gentle heart, by the recapitulation.

With much love, I remain
always truly
Mary Lincoln.

Something of Mrs. Lincoln's state of mind can be gained from her treatment of the following elaborately embellished state document. In May, 1867, it was found in an ash barrel in front of her house in Chicago.[62]

> Executive Mansion
> Washington, January 12, 1866

To Mrs. MARY LINCOLN,
   CHICAGO, ILLINOIS
MADAM,

Pursuant to the request of Congress therein contained, I have the honor to transmit a copy of the Resolutions of that Body, of the 18th of last month, passed upon the occasion of the violent and tragic death of ABRAHAM LINCOLN, late President of the United States.

In accordance with the further request contained in the Resolutions, I also have the honor to assure you of the profound sympathy of the two Houses of Congress, for your deep personal affliction, and of their sincere condolence for the late national bereavement.

> I have the honor to be,
>   Madam,
>   Your very obedient servant
>   ANDREW JOHNSON.

The lack of restraint which characterized Mrs. Lincoln in the years after 1865 is painfully evident in the following letter [63] to Alexander Williamson. Most of it is devoted to Col. Benjamin B. French, who, as

---

[62] Original in the Library of the University of Chicago.
[63] Original owned by Oliver R. Barrett.

Commissioner of Public Buildings, was charged with
the general supervision of the White House.

Mr. Williamson,   Chicago, Jany 26th 1866.

My Dear Sir:

Your last note was received on yesterday. I had seen the
"Herald" article before, when I was in the W. H. I felt it
was a degredation to have to submit to such abominable
furniture as if it had been my own, even occupying the
humblest cabin would not have given it room. That villian-
ous & criminal falsehood was gotten up by the *party* who
wished to have *all* the spoils to themselves—and in consequence was rewarded in *truly American* style, by *quite* a
$100,000—to fit up the W. H. We will see, how much of
it will be used for *that purpose. His Yankee* pockets, are
capacious, perhaps his love for gain will be discovered ere
long. I am receiving letters *now,* constantly, on *this* subject, and it is being traced to the smooth-faced Com—all
those barbarous stories, of W. H. depredations. The New
York World did not lose, I imagine, by its correspondence.
He was kicked out of the *place* in Pierce's time—and if
Johnson knows what he is about, he will not have him
remain long where he is. Everyone, understanding the
miserable state of W. H. furniture & knowing from whence
those villanous falsehoods emanated, & better still, appreci-
ating me & knowing, that I desire *only,* what is my own—
this week, I have received letters from most of my distinguished friends, of course *not* alluding to such low stuff

254

as French & his surroundings are. *He* is every obsequious, to the *new* powers—and a *blunderer, I* always found him at receptions. *He* has secured $75,000—which should have been mine—and deprives me of a home, yet *such* a *villain* does not always prosper. In consequence of his *recent* success he can afford to place himself, pompously, in newspapers. Eh bien! "let him laugh who wins." *This* communication is confidential—but keep your *eyes* open to the *house* & proceedings generally. All you write me is as safe as if never written. *Old Newton* is another old scamp, and both have worked, against me. Be quiet about all *this,* & you can soon judge for yourself. How heartless & hollow I have found all those who were so much indebted to us! If I had not this great overwhelming sorrow upon me, and knowing what I now do, I should have no desire to return to a world so entirely selfish, and who would prefer to attack an innocent & helpless woman, in her deep affliction, than a strong man, who could soon *quiet* the assailant.

Dear little Taddie goes to school, and does not miss an hour. He is already very much beloved in C-, his teacher speaks of him in the highest & most affectionate terms. One of the Bucktails resides here, and T takes great comfort in visiting him. He is married and keeps house.

Watch for Mr. Andrews at the hotels, and write him 47 Wall St. N. Y. I wish all my business settled early in Feb- no matter how poor I am left. Quiet the *Wash.* creditors until then. *After that* never a cent will I owe. Andrews is influential, & guess can see me through all. I see that *Han-*

scom, another of the low, sycophantic *timeservers,* is writing the Johnsons.

What a world this is! Write me longer, and more especially, show my letters to no one & be quiet about contents I pray you.

Yr friend,

M. L.

Occasional contacts with Charles Sumner continued. The following letter [64] was found among the papers of John Greenleaf Whittier.

Chicago, April 2nd 1866

HON. CHARLES SUMNER
MY DEAR SIR:

I am reminded whilst reading this simple & natural poem, "Snow-Bound" that its author, Whittier, is a resident of your State & doubtless a personal friend of yours; and presuming that amidst the cares and anxieties of the past winter this little volume may have escaped yr notice, therefore I take the liberty of sending it to you. I thank you kindly for your speech you sent me. I have already read it with much interest. How much misfortune would we be spared as a Nation if our faithless & unscrupulous President entertained the same views as yourself & all other true patriots. Unfortunately he is endeavoring to ignore all the good that has been accomplished, and return the slave to his bondage. The contemptible act of refusing the freedmen of Richmond the privilege of celebrating the anniversary of their freedom is but too sure an indication of *his*

[64] Printed in *The Independent,* Vol. 54, 2803.

feeling towards the oppressed race. His wicked efforts will fail & justice & liberty triumph.

How sad & melancholy at this particular time the death of our noble friend Senator Foot! Such good men at any time can be ill spared but when each & every voice is needed to silence the traitors that still infest our land, his loss is very painful. His "passing-away" was peaceful & triumphant; so much in unison with his well-spent life that it appears most sinful to wish him back. How many of the cherished friends of my beloved husband have within the past year entered into their rest and been reunited to *one* they loved so well whilst here.

I am forgetting myself in writing you so lengthy a note, when I had merely intended a few lines.

With apologies & assurance of friendship, I remain always truly

MARY LINCOLN

The two letters which Mrs. Lincoln wrote to Dr. A. G. Henry in the summer of 1865 were never received, for Henry was lost at sea when the steamer on which he was returning sank off the coast of California. Mrs. Lincoln felt his loss deeply, and, as the following letter [65] to Noah Brooks shows, entertained a real sympathy for his widow. The claims to which she referred were "wildcat" stocks which she had bought in the days of prosperity.

[65] From Brooks, *Washington in Lincoln's Time*, 124.

Chicago, May 11, 1866

NOAH BROOKS, ESQ.,
SAN FRANCISCO.

MY DEAR SIR:

A few days since I received a very sad letter from Mrs. Henry, in which she vividly portrays her great desolation and dependence upon others for every earthly comfort. I am induced to enclose you the Nevada claims and also a petroleum claim, hoping you may be able to secure a purchaser for them, in which case I will most cheerfully give Mrs. Henry some of the proceeds. I am aware that I am taxing your kindness very greatly, yet the remembrance of your great esteem for my beloved husband and Dr. Henry would excuse the intrusion upon you. I wish you were not so far removed from us—true friends, in these overwhelming days of affliction, I find to be very rare. I find myself clinging more tenderly to the memory of those who, if not so remote, would be more friendly.

I hope you will be able to visit Mrs. Henry the coming summer. I, sometimes, in my wildness and grief, am tempted to believe that it is some *terrible, terrible* dream, and that my idolized husband will return to me. Poor Dr. Henry! he who wept so truly and freely with us in our great misfortune, how soon he was called to join the beloved one who had so recently "gone before"! In my own great sorrow, how often have I prayed for death to end my misery.

My sons are well and a great comfort to me. Robert and Taddie remember you very kindly. I hope you will write to us more frequently. I am well aware of the deep sympathy you feel for us and the great affection and confidence my husband cherished for you draws you very near to us. With apologies for troubling you as I am now doing, I remain, always, sincerely your friend,

MARY LINCOLN.

The tone of the following note to David Davis, administrator of the Lincoln estate, indicates that such strictures as Mrs. Lincoln had passed upon him in previous letters were the consequence of her unsettled mental state rather than an expression of her true feeling.[66]

HON DAVID DAVIS   Chicago   Aug 20th 66.

MY DEAR SIR:

Quite a severe indisposition, has prevented an earlier acknowledgment, of your kindness, in so soon acceding to my request & procuring through the favor of Mr Jones, a pass for my sons & myself to Springfield. Also your letter of Aug 17th enclosing a check, for $1,000, was duly received, for which I will send you, a more formal receipt. We propose going down to S- about the time, the *"royal progress,"* is expected here. It will be quite as well to be absent from the city on *that* occasion. I will endeavor whilst in S. to see Mr Conkling, on the subject of the guardianship. I remain, with great respect, very truly

MARY LINCOLN.

[66] Original in estate files, Sangamon County Probate Court.

Three weeks before David Davis filed his first inventory of the Lincoln estate—showing personal property alone of more than $85,000—Mrs. Lincoln wrote the following despairing letter [67] to Alexander Williamson.

Chicago, Nov 5-1866.

MR. WILLIAMSON,

MY DEAR SIR:

Your note with enclosure is just received. It appears to me, to be an impossibility, *under the* circumstances, if my necessities *were* made known to the rich and generous men of N. Y. and Boston, that the demands would not be met. A poor return for my beloved husband's services to his country. If you knew how debts were staring me in the face, which I cannot meet & depending, as I have been doing, on Col Howe's assistance to settle them, you would understand how, being unable to meet them as a matter of course, with my great need upon me, I cannot do what under other circumstances, with a well filled purse, I should like to do—help you about your house. I borrowed money, at a high rate of interest, to purchase this house at a moderate cost & am unable to keep it, so I shall relinquish it very soon—which I deeply regret being compelled to do. My income is about equal to your salary—and there is no place more expensive than Chicago, anywhere. So the "shoe pinches" with us all. For the last three months, to meet the most ordinary expenses, I have had to part with my

[67] Original owned by Oliver R. Barrett.

clothing and I assure you I am at the end of *that line*—all that is left are simple things enough, but as gifts of my precious husband, only absolute starvation would induce me to part with them. If I am not assisted ere long, I shall give up every thing to meet every indebtedness formed here, take my little Taddie in the Spring and go, where I can live cheaper. I sometimes think of Germany, where Tad can be educated at a moderate rate & certainly I can keep him & myself at a more moderate cost than here. How little did my good husband ever imagine *his family* would be reduced to *this,* last extremity. I am now suffering so much mortification and with my great sorrow upon me, that in this country, situated as I am, unable to meet what I am owing & the simplest daily necessities, I cannot endure it much longer, and my pride will compel me to leave the land—a necessity most painful to me, and which I shrink from. You will understand, in a measure, my situation, but it would be impossible, for you fully to do so. If my purse, was equal to my good will, you would have what little assistance I could give. As it is alas! with unpaid bills pressing upon me.—I wish I could forget myself.

I write in great haste & remain Truly

Yr friend

M. L.

Mrs. Lincoln's letters to Francis B. Carpenter were singularly free from the obsessions which had taken possession of her. The last one known to exist follows:[68]

Private

Chicago, *25th Dec* 1866

F. B. CARPENTER, ESQ

MY DEAR SIR:

Your very kind letter was received a day or two since & I address you, whilst all the world is rejoicing over the return of an anniversary so welcome to the glad world generally, my desolate broken heart, feels more than ever its great, great sorrow. I write you to day, to thank you, for the most perfect likeness of my beloved husband, that I have ever seen, the resemblance is so accurate, that it will require far more calmness, than I can now command, to have it continually placed before me. Time, only increases my great anguish of mind, over the fearful loss sustained, in the death of my idolized husband.

As regards the volume you so kindly sent my "little Taddie," I feel that many apologies, are due you. When it was received, I was suffering from chills and just as my health was being partially restored, your last kind favor, was received. I had the pleasure of a call from Mr Arnold recently, whom you doubtless remember, he spoke of you, very pleasantly.

Knowing how precious the memory of my sainted husband is to you, may I request the acceptance of a simple

[68] From a photostatic copy in the possession of Mrs. Honoré Willsie Morrow, New York City.

memento, which was *his,* and has been handled by *him.* It is a very plain cane, yet it has his name upon it, and will be treasured by you & yours. *This day,* is so sad to me, separated from my husband—that I can scarcely compose myself to write—even to you—so connected as you were for months, with the White House, and so many painful associations, that distract my brain.

With many happy returns of this day, to yourself and Mrs. Carpenter, I remain

Very truly your friend

"P. S."   MARY LINCOLN

The cane will be sent by Express to you, tomorrow, to your address.

M. L.

In the autumn of 1867 the news of Mrs. Lincoln's ill-fated "old clothes speculation" broke upon a shocked but avid public. Driven by the delusion of financial want, she asked Elizabeth Keckley, who had now become a confidante, to meet her in New York in early September and help arrange for the disposal of part of her wardrobe. After various adventures under the assumed name of Mrs. Clarke, arrangements were made with Brady and Keyes, 609 Broadway, for the sale of a number of shawls and dresses and a quantity of jewelry, but not until Mrs. Lincoln had made known her identity.

263

Before public announcement of the proposed sale was made, Mrs. Lincoln yielded to the advice of Brady and Keyes and wrote several letters to be shown by them to prominent politicians who, they argued, would pay good prices rather than have the story of her poverty widely advertised. Two of these letters follow.[69] Although the first is dated Chicago, both were written in New York, where Mrs. Lincoln and Mrs. Keckley were moving from one hotel to another in an effort to avoid reporters.

W. H. BRADY, ESQ.   Chicago, September 22, 1867.

You write me that reporters are after you concerning my goods deposited with you—which, in consideration of my urgent wants, I assure you I am compelled to relinquish—and also that there is a fear that these newsmen will seize upon the painful circumstances of your having these articles placed in your hands to injure the Republican party politically. In the cause of this party, and for universal freedom, my beloved husband's precious life was sacrificed, nor for the world would I do anything to injure the cause. My heart is very anxious for its success, notwithstanding the very men for whom my noble husband did so much unhesitatingly deprived me of all means of support and left me in a pitiless condition. The necessities of life are upon me, urgent and imperative, and I am scarcely removed from want—so different from the lot

[69] From the New York *World*, October 3, 1867.

my loving and devoted husband would have assigned me —and I find myself left to struggle for myself. I am compelled to pursue the only course left me—immediately within the next week to sell these goods, and if not wholly disposed of by Wednesday, October 30th, on that day please sell them at auction, after advertising *very largely* that they are my goods.

Very respectfully,

Mrs. A. Lincoln.

Private

September 25.

W. H. Brady, Esq.:

I have reflected upon your remarks, and have concluded to leave everything to your good judgment and excellent sense. My great, great sorrow and loss have made me painfully sensitive; but as my feelings and pecuniary comfort were never regarded or even recognized in the midst of my overwhelming bereavement, now that I am pressed in a most startling manner for means of common subsistence, I do not know why I should shrink from an opportunity of improving my trying position. Being assured that all you do will be appropriately executed, and in a manner that will not startle me very greatly and excite as little comment as possible, again I shall leave all in your hands. I am passing through a very painful ordeal, which the country, in remembrance of my noble and elevated husband, should have spared me. I remain, with great respect, very truly,

Mrs. Lincoln.

265

P. S.—As you mention that my goods have been valued at $24,000, I will be willing to make a reduction of $8,000, and relinquish them for $16,000 in five-twenties—*nothing less*. If *this* is not accomplished, I will continue to advertise largely until every article is sold. I must have means to live, at least in a *medium* comfortable state.

Mrs. L.

Though freely shown, the foregoing letters failed to bring forth a single dollar. Accordingly, Mrs. Lincoln gave Brady permission to publish them in the New York *World*. A more inept choice could not have been made, for the *World,* militantly Democratic, could hardly have been expected not to make the most of a matter so perfectly calculated to result in Republican embarrassment. And as if her letters alone were not severe enough, Mrs. Lincoln made a further statement which appeared in the issue of October 3, when the letters were made public. Asked what her feelings towards the Republican party were, she permitted herself to be quoted as follows: "I could not relinquish my attachment for the party to which my husband belonged, and in whose cause his precious life was sacrificed, notwithstanding it is composed of such men as Weed, Raymond and Seward, who nominally belong to it, and who to accomplish their purposes would drag it down to the lowest depths of degradation. The late President thoroughly detested these men, and had become fully aware before his death of their treachery and falseness."

Thus the project became entangled in partisan politics. All over the country the Republican press rose to the defense of the party's course. Most severe in its strictures, and, because of the position of its author, most important, was the counter-attack of Thurlow Weed. Weed's statement was printed in the New York *Commercial Advertiser* on October 4, and widely reprinted throughout the nation.

We have never approached a question with half the sorrow that this awakens. To vindicate, shield and protect "Heaven's best gift to man" is a grateful duty, while to even reprove, and much more to assail a woman, is painful, and if without a perfect justification, unmanly.

If the American Congress or the American people have failed to meet the pecuniary expectations of Mr. Lincoln's widow, it is because that personage failed, during his life and since his death, to inspire either respect or confidence. They should not, therefore, be subjected to reproach, and rest under the imputation of ingratitude. Had Mrs. Lincoln, while in power, borne herself becomingly, the suggestion of a Lincoln fund, by voluntary contributions, would have been promptly responded to. The national heart was warm. It gushed out in liberal endowments for

Grant and Farragut. It would as cheerfully have met the appeal in favor of Mrs. Lincoln if it had not intuitively closed and chilled.

In her conversations Mrs. Lincoln is represented as bitterly denouncing Secretary Seward, for which, of course, there is no warrant or excuse, for he wrongs no man, and much less is he capable of injustice, wrong, or even unkindness, to woman.

But we happen to know—the late Caleb B. Smith, then Secretary of the Interior, being our informant—a fact which incensed Mrs. Lincoln against Mr. Seward. The President gave the Prince Napoleon a dinner, for which Mrs. Lincoln sent to the Secretary of the Interior for payment of a bill of some $900. This demand, though wholly illegal, coming from the President's wife, embarrassed the Secretary, who called upon the Secretary of State for advice, where he learned that Mr. Seward had also dined the Prince, having the same number of guests and giving them a duplicate of the dinner at the White House. In fact, Mr. Seward ordered both dinners from the same restaurant, and by his own bill knew the cost of each. For what Mr. Seward paid $300, Mrs. Lincoln demanded $900. But whether three or nine hundred, the claim was alike illegal, and could not be paid. For this, however, Mrs. Lincoln quarreled with Secretaries Smith and Seward. This amount, however, was subsequently covered up in a gardener's account, but occasioned scandal, which respect for Mr. Lincoln measurably suppressed.

Though Mr. Lincoln left an estate which enabled his

family to live quite as comfortably as they had ever lived, Congress and the people would have promptly and cheerfully provided munificently for them if Mrs. Lincoln herself, with every advantage that high position gave her, had made friends or inspired respect. And this last exhibition proves how instinctively right the popular estimate of her character was.

The fact for which Mrs. Lincoln seeks large publicity, namely, that she received presents valued at $24,000, is a pregnant and suggestive one—suggestive, at least, of offices and contracts, unless the more charitable construction is reached through the assumption that they were expressions of regard and friendship. But it is not known that the wife of the President, however estimable, was so loaded with shawls, laces, furs, diamonds, rings, &c.

Individually, we are obliged to Mrs. Lincoln for an expression of her ill-will. It is pleasant to remember that we were always out of favor in that quarter. And it is equally pleasant to remember that we possessed the friendship of Mr. Lincoln to the last hour of his life, without paying court, as others did, to Mrs. Lincoln, and in spite of her constant efforts to disturb our relations.

This mortifying revelation will go abroad, and, as is natural, the press of Europe will make the most of it, in depreciating the ingratitude of our government and the want of liberality in the American people. This consideration alone constrains us to discharge the unpleasant duty of showing that neither the government nor the people are justly obnoxious to these accusations.

269

In this connection the comment of the Illinois *State Journal* is significant, not only because it was edited by the husband of Mrs. Lincoln's own niece, but also because it spoke authoritatively on the state of her finances.

We were not at first disposed ourselves to make any comments upon this strange and mortifying publication [the *World* story], though we felt sure, from what we knew of the pecuniary circumstances of Mr. Lincoln at the time of his death, that the statements put forth in the *World* were not true, and that they should be received by the public with very considerable allowance. A Republican contemporary, however, insists, now that the subject has been brought thus prominently before the public, that 'it should not be permitted to sleep without a statement of facts from some authenticated source, or a thorough investigation,' urging that 'this is demanded not only by the honor of the Republican party, which is assailed in the article of the *World,* but of the whole Nation.' In this view, we have deemed that the publication of the inventory of the estate of Mr. Lincoln, as filed by Judge Davis, the administrator, in the office of the Clerk of the County Court of Sangamon County, would not only not be out of place but would be the easiest and the surest way of placing the facts before the public. We therefore give it below. It was filed on the 29th of November, 1866, by 'N. W. Matheny, clerk,' and recorded in Book 4 of Inventories, page 70:—

THE DOCUMENTS

Inventory of the estate of Abraham Lincoln, late President of the United States, so far as the same has come to my knowledge.   DAVID DAVIS, Administrator.

In registered bonds bearing 6 per cent. payable
   in coin $57,000.00
In temporary loan bearing six per cent. in currency 2,781.04
In Treasury warrants, issued to him for salary
   and not paid, as follows:
No. 554 .... 1,981.67
  " 826 .... 1,981.67
  " 900 .... 1,976.22
  " 1217 .... 1,981.67
Draft of National Bank of Springfield 133.00
Balance of salary received from the Treasurer of
   the United States 847.83
Claims *vs* Robert Irwin of Springfield, which Mr.
   Condell paid 9,044.41
Balance in hands of Riggs, banker, at Washington 1,373.53
Balance in hands of First National Bank, Washington 881.66

                                        $79,482.70

This sum is all invested in United States securities bearing interest.
Also the following:

N. B. Judd's note, dated Sept. 1, 1859, bearing 10
   per cent. interest, for $3,000.00
Thomas J. Turner, (Freeport), July 1, 1858, due
   November 1, 1858; interest 10 per ct. 400.00

A. & J. Haines, (Pekin), two notes for $200 each, one due October 15th, 1858, the other January 1st, 1859 .... $400.00

With the following credits:
February 16, '59, $50; May 2, '59, $50; July 14, '59, $100; September 12, '59, $50; August 13, '60, $50.

M. B. Church, (Springfield), November 5th, 1864, at five months, given at Washington 260.00

Jas. H. & J. S. McDaniel, (Sangamon co.), April 23, 1863, 1 day, 10 per cent. int. 250.00

Golden Patterson, (Vermilion co.), April 25, '59, due one year after date 60.00

Milton Davis, (Vermilion co.), November 7, '57, due December 25, '57, 10 per cent., with credit of $30, March 28th, '59 .... 80.00

John P. Mercer, (Shelbyville), May 25, 1852 ...... 7.69

REAL ESTATE IN ILLINOIS

Mr. Lincoln's homestead in Springfield, Ill., on lot 5 and part of lot 7, in block 10, E. Iles' addition to Springfield. Lot 3, in block 19, town of Lincoln, Logan county, Ill.

REAL ESTATE IN IOWA

Crawford county, Iowa.—120 acres east half, north-east and north-west, north-east, section 18, town 84, range 39.

Tama county.—40 acres, description not recollected. Certificate of entry in hands of C. H. Moore, of Clinton, DeWitt county, Ill.

DAVID DAVIS, Adm'r, etc.

THE DOCUMENTS

The following is a transcript of the oath filed by Judge Davis, upon taking out letters of administration:

State of Illinois,   }
Sangamon County. }

David Davis being duly sworn deposes and says that Abraham Lincoln, late of the county of Sangamon and State of Illinois, is dead, and that he died on or about the 14th day of April, A. D., 1865, intestate, as it is said, and that his estate will probably amount to the sum of $85,000; that said Abraham Lincoln left at the time of his decease, Mary Lincoln, his widow, and Robert T. Lincoln and Thomas Lincoln, his children.

(Signed,)   DAVID DAVIS,
Subscribed and sworn to before me this 14th day of June, A. D., 1865.

(Signed,)   N. W. MATHENY, Clerk.

The above figures speak for themselves. To be added to them however is the $25,000, which was appropriated by the last Congress on account of Mr. Lincoln's salary, making altogether the total value of the personal estate to be about *one hundred and ten thousand dollars,* to say nothing of the real estate described in the schedule above. So that the statement made in the *World* that Mr. Lincoln saved nothing and left nothing from his salary and that Mrs. Lincoln has no resources but what remains from the appropriation of Congress, $22,000, and the rents of the homestead, returning altogether but $1,700 per year, can not possibly be true. That Mr. Lincoln did not leave his family wealthy is very evident, but no one in view of the above

inventory will say that they are in the deplorable condition
of "want" and "destitution," in regard to which the public
has with so much astonishment, just been informed.

We say this much, not for the purpose of preventing
"personal contributions" from being made to Mrs. Lincoln,
if she desires them, much less to deter Congress from making a further appropriation for her support, which we
should be glad to have it do; but simply in order that the
people of the nation may not suppose that Mrs. Lincoln is
in anything like destitute circumstances. Her income may
not be sufficient to meet all her wants and necessities,
but it is certainly large enough to maintain her at least
as comfortably as she lived before going to Washington.

Meanwhile Mrs. Lincoln had fled from New York
to Chicago. On the train she had the ill-fortune to meet
Charles Sumner. Her mortification, and her feelings
generally, she made known in a letter which she wrote
to Mrs. Keckley soon after her arrival.[70]

Chicago, October 6th.
My Dear Lizzie:
My ink is like myself and my spirits failing, so I write
you to-day with a pencil. I had a solitary ride to this place,
as you may imagine, varied by one or two amusing incidents. I found, after you left me, I could not continue in
the car in which you left me, owing to every seat's berth

[70] From Keckley, *Behind the Scenes*, 296-301.

being engaged; so, being simple *Mrs.* Clarke, I had to eat 'humble pie' in a car less commodious. My thoughts were too much with my 'dry goods and interests' at 609 Broadway, to care much for my surroundings, as uncomfortable as they were. In front of me sat a middle-aged, gray-haired, respectable-looking gentleman, who, for the whole morning, had the page of the *World* before him which contained my letters and business concerns. About four hours before arriving at Chicago, a consequential-looking man, of formidable size, seated himself by him, and it appears they were entirely unknown to each other. The well-fed looking individual opened the conversation with the man who had read the *World* so attentively, and the conversation soon grew warm and earnest. The war and its devastation engaged them. The bluffy individual, doubtless a Republican who had pocketed his many thousands, spoke of the widows of the land, made so by the war. My reading man remarked to him:

'Are you aware that Mrs. Lincoln is in indigent circumstances, and has to sell her clothing and jewelry to gain means to make life more endurable?'

The well-conditioned man replied: 'I do not blame her for selling her clothing, if she wishes it. I suppose *when sold* she will convert the proceeds into five-twenties to enable her to have means to be buried.'

The *World* man turned towards him with a searching glance, and replied, with the haughtiest manner: 'That woman is not dead yet.'

The discomfited individual looked down, never spoke

another word, and in half an hour left his seat, and did not return.

I give you word for word as the conversation occured. May it be found through the execution of my friends, Messrs. Brady and Keyes, that 'that woman is not yet dead,' and being alive, she speaketh and gaineth valuable hearers. Such is life! Those who have been injured, how gladly the injurer would consign them to mother earth and forgetfulness! Hoping I should not be recognized at Fort Wayne, I thought I would get out at dinner for a cup of tea. . . . I went into the dining-room alone, and was ushered up to the table, where, at its head, sat a very elegant-looking gentleman—at his side a middle-aged lady. My black veil was doubled over my face. I had taken my seat next to him—he at the head of the table, I at his left hand. I immediately *felt* a pair of eyes was gazing at me. I looked him full in the face, and the glance was earnestly returned. I sipped my water, and said: "Mr. S., is this indeed you?" His face was as pale as the table-cloth. We entered into conversation, when I asked him how long since he had left Chicago. He replied, "Two weeks since." He said, "How strange you should be on the train and I not know it!"

As soon as I could escape from the table, I did so by saying, "I must secure a cup of tea for a lady friend with me who has a head-ache." I had scarcely returned to the car, when he entered it with a cup of tea borne by his own aristocratic hands. I was a good deal annoyed by seeing him, and he was so agitated that he spilled half of the cup over my *elegantly gloved* hands. *He* looked very sad, and I fancied 609 Broadway occupied his thoughts. I apologized for the absent lady who wished the cup, by saying that "in my absence she had slipped out for it." His heart was in his eyes, notwithstanding my veiled face. Pity for me, I fear, has something to do with all this. I never saw his manner *so* gentle and sad. This was nearly evening, and I did not see him again, as he returned to the lady, who was his sister-in-law from the East. . . . What evil spirit possessed me to go out and get that cup of tea? When he left me, *woman-like* I tossed the cup of tea out of the window, and tucked my head down and shed *bitter tears.* . . . At the depot my darling little Taddie was waiting for me, and his voice never sounded so sweet. . . . My dear Lizzie, do visit Mr. Brady each morning at nine o'clock, and urge them all you can. I see by the papers Stewart has returned. To-morrow I will send the invoice of goods, which please to not give up. How much I miss you, tongue cannot tell. Forget my fright and nervousness of the evening before. Of course you were as innocent as a child in all you did. I consider you my best living friend, and I am struggling to be enabled some day to repay you. Write me often, as you promised.

Always truly yours,

M. L.

As soon as she was aware of the extent of the criticism which her action had brought upon her, Mrs. Lincoln lost the buoyancy which her decision to resort to desperate measures had given her. In its place came anger—and despair.

MY DEAR LIZZIE: [71] Chicago, Sunday Oct. 13.

I am greatly disappointed, having only received one letter from you since we parted, which was dated the day after. Day after day 1 sent to Mrs. F. for letters. After your promise of writing to me every other day, I can scarcely understand it. I hope to-morrow will bring me a letter from you. How much I miss you cannot be expressed. I hope you have arrived safely in Washington, and will tell me everything. . . . Was there ever such cruel newspaper abuse lavished upon an unoffending woman as has been showered upon my devoted head? The people of this ungrateful country are like the "dogs in the manger;" will neither do anything themselves, nor allow me to improve my own condition. What a Government we have! All their abuse lavished upon me only lowers themselves in the estimation of all true-hearted people. The Springfield *Journal* had an editorial a few days since, with the important information that Mrs. Lincoln had been known to be *deranged* for years, and should be *pitied* for all her strange *acts*. I should have been *all right* if I had allowed *them* to take possession of the White House. In the comfortable stealings by contracts from the Government, these low creatures are allowed to hurl their malicious wrath at me, with no one to defend me or protect me, if I should starve. These people injure themselves far more than they could do me, by

[71] From Keckley, *Behind the Scenes*, 336-39.

their lies and villany. Their aim is to prevent my goods being sold, or anything being done for me. *In this,* I very much fear, they have succeeded.

Write me, my dear friend, your candid opinion about everything. I wished to be made better off, quite as much to improve your condition as well as for myself. . . . Two weeks ago, dear Lizzie, we were in that *den* of discomfort and dirt. *Now* we are far asunder. Every other day, for the past week, I have had a chill, brought on by excitement and suffering of mind. In the midst of it I have moved into my winter quarters, and am now very comfortably situated. My parlor and bedroom are very sweetly furnished. I am lodged in a handsome house, a very kind, good, *quiet* family, and their meals are excellent. I consider myself fortunate in all this. I feel assured that the Republicans, who, to cover up their own perfidy and neglect, have used every villanous falsehood in their power to injure me— I fear they have *more* than succeeded, but if their day of reckoning does not come in this world, it *will surely* in the next. . . .

Saturday.—I have determined to shed no more tears over all their cruel falsehoods, yet, just now, I feel almost forsaken by God and man—except by the *latter* to be vilified. Write me all that Keyes and Brady think of the result. For myself, after *such* abuse, I *expect* nothing. Oh! that I could see you. Write me, dear Lizzie, if only a line; I cannot understand your silence. Hereafter direct your letters to Mrs. A. Lincoln, 460 West Washington street, Chicago, Ill., care of D. Cole. Remember 460. I am always so anxious to hear from you, I am feeling so *friendless* in the world. I remain always your affectionate friend.

M. L.

The flood of unfavorable publicity which greeted Mrs. Lincoln's venture assured its failure. Only a few articles were sold, and those brought low prices. In the spring of 1868 her goods were returned, and Brady and Keyes collected $820.00 for their expenses and for advances which they had made. Thus, besides making her an object of national scorn and causing her weeks of anguish, Mrs. Lincoln's ill-advised project actually cost her money.

Illuminating in the light it throws on Mrs. Lincoln's attitude toward her husband's family is the following note,[72] addressed to Mrs. Sally Lincoln, Coles Co., Charleston, Illinois; Widow of Thomas Lincoln.

Dec 20th 1867.

Enclosed is the Express receipt—also ten dollars which please accept for the making of the dress &c &c. An answer is requested, whether the box, money &c &c has been received & oblige

Mrs. Lincoln

Mrs A Lincoln's address is 460 West Washington St., Chicago, Ill.

[72] Original owned by Oliver R. Barrett, Chicago, Illinois.

The failure of Mrs. Lincoln's clothing sale left her physically exhausted, yet, as the letter [73] which follows indicates, she was in better mental health than she had been for many months. Her correspondent was Mrs. Albert S. White, whom she had known in Washington during the war. In 1864 Lincoln had appointed White, at the time a congressman from Indiana, to a federal judgeship. He had died a few months later.

MY DEAR MRS. WHITE:　　　　　Chicago, May 2d. [1868]

It has been quite a time, since I have had the pleasure of hearing from you & in fact, I believe you are owing me a letter. This, however will not deter me from writing you to day, as serious considerations prompt me to do so. I *am permitted* to sit up, whilst I write you a few lines as for the past three weeks, I have been seriously sick. (My disease is of a womanly nature, which you will understand has been) [74] greatly accelerated by the last three years of mental suffering. Since the birth of my youngest son, for about twelve years I have been more or less a sufferer. My physician, Dr Clarke, a brother of Mrs Lippincut (Grace Greenwood) told me on yesterday, that he must prescribe an entire change of air, scene, &c for me. He thought going abroad—would alone benefit me—& advised me, as soon as I could bear the change, to go to Scotland for the summer. Our old Minister, a very good and intellectual man, resides

[73] Original in the Barton Library at the University of Chicago Library.
[74] These words are crossed out in the original.

there & has been always writing that I should visit Scotland —and has promised to accompany me to some places of interest in that country. I have also a first Cousin in Edinburgh Mrs Judge Dickinson, of Cincinnati—who is at present residing there. If I go, I shall be accompanied by my youngest son—a very promising, lovely boy of 15. In the autumn, I shall place him, in some desirable school. In the winter, if my health continues so delicate, I shall pass it in the South of Europe. I am thus minute—as I am anxious that we should understand each other. Your daughter, Mrs Mack, wrote me, that she proposed going to Europe, early in the Autumn; hoping that you had intended accompanying her—I write this almost unintelligible note. How dearly I would love to have you go over at the time I do, I fear from what my physician tells me, I cannot delay it longer than the 1st of July. Will you not consider the subject and join me at *that* time? We both, have many pleasant friends in E. and a summer tour in S. & early in the Autumn in Switzerland, would be delightful. I am only anticipating, a visit to Europe which my dear husband, intended we should take at the end of his term, with myself. *Ill health* and much sorrow, forces me *now* to go & I earnestly hope you will favorably consider what I have written & give me an immediate reply. This proposition from me, does not argue *a debt of $70,000!!* as *the colored* historian asserts. It was Judge Davis (the administrator's) particular pride that only $11 (eleven dollars) was owing on my husband's estate—and that for a country newspaper, which he knew nothing about. If such a debt or any debts existed, what good fairy, would have canceled them? It is my comfort to know, that I do not owe, a dollar in the world, but what little I have, I intend enjoying—and can make myself more comfortable in Europe, than I can for the same amount of means in Chicago, which if possible surpasses, N. Y.—in high prices. My health *now* demands the change & I do hope, my dear Mrs W- we may cross the Ocean together &c. This communication, I am sure you will regard as entirely confidential. Through what fearful trials I have been recently passing! My trust has been in our Heavenly Father & he has sustained me. Hoping to hear from you, I remain

Always truly yours

MARY LINCOLN

July found Mrs. Lincoln still in the United States, worse rather than better in health.[75]

Cresson, Penn.
July 18th, '68.

MY DEAR MRS. WHITE:

Your letter, as well as your recently written book, has been forwarded to me in this beautiful Alleghany Mountain retreat. The work has interested me very greatly and your great grief on the occasion of the death of so lovely and Christian a daughter is very natural. My beloved husband's devotion to me was so great that it always inclined him to view with consideration all those whom I liked.— Towards your family, in conversing with him, I never

[75] This letter is owned by Alfred Meyer, Highland Park, Ill.

failed to express a great regard, and he therefore felt an interest in yourselves, as well as your daughter, from whom you were called upon to be separated in her far distant home. I only wish, she had visited Washington more frequently and that Mr. Lincoln and myself could have become better acquainted with her—alas! alas! the ways of Providence are inscrutable.

We sail from Baltimore the 1st of August and in my very feeble health I am endeavoring to catch every mountain breeze, in hopes that strength may be given me, for the sea voyage before me. In my hours of great bodily suffering, which now occur quite frequently, I often fancy I shall not much longer be separated from my idolized husband, who has only "Gone before" and I am certain is fondly watching and waiting for our re-union, nevermore to be separated. Can it be, that one, with whom every association since I was fifteen years old, has been connected,[76] and who was only happy when I was in his presence, does not watch over my sorrows and yearn for the time, when they will be over? If we had sailed from New York, I should have hoped to have seen you. As it is, I shall indulge in the anticipation of hearing from you occasionally, whilst abroad. My address until the 1st of October will be Edinburgh, Scotland. My dear Mrs. White, I have brooded over my great, great loss so much, that with others, I now feel assured, the change that I am now about making, is the

---

[76] A curious statement. Mrs. Lincoln could not have met Lincoln before 1837, when she was nineteen, and it is unlikely that she knew him more than casually before 1839.

only thing left me to prolong my life. And I have two noble, devoted sons who would be very desolate without me. Hoping to hear from you very soon, I always remain your affectionate friend

MARY LINCOLN.

P. S. Will you be able to decipher this scrawl? I am suffering so much, I am scarcely able to sit up.

M. L.

A month later the European trip still remained a thing of the future.[77]

Altoona Penn.

Aug. 19, '68.

MY DEAR MRS. WHITE:

Your telegram has been received, & I greatly regret to hear of your indisposition. As you are aware I am peculiarly situated, being exceedingly anxious to witness the marriage of my son—with a young lady, who is so charming & whom I love so much. The terror of having to proceed to *Washington* to witness it, almost overpowers me. My little son is so anxious to remain, until that event takes place & perhaps the regret I may also feel in the future that I had not gratified them all by remaining, has quite determined me. Of course it will be the 1st of Oct. before I sail. I will then go immediately to Carlsbad & place myself under medical treatment & place my little son in school—somewhere in Germany. I write you hastily, for I am feeling this morning, much indisposed. The intervening time, I shall endeavour

[77] This letter is in the Barton Library at the University of Chicago Library.

to take care of my health & will remain in this mountanous region. If I do not continue so well, may return to Bedford. I have half promised Gov & Mrs Curtin, with whom we came up from Bedford a few days since to join them at a charming retreat on the Susquehanna. I hope to hear from you & if you will direct your letters *here,* they will be forwarded me. I can scarcely express to you, what a source of comfort they are to me. With much love, I remain always truly yours

MARY LINCOLN.

Abroad at last, Mrs. Lincoln decided to resort to the last possibility of increasing her income—a pension from the United States. The application was addressed to the Vice-President.

SIR:

I herewith most respectfully present to the honorable Senate of the United States an application for a pension. I am a widow of a President of the United States whose life was sacrificed to his country's service. That sad calamity has very much impaired my health and by the advice of my physician I have come over to Germany to try the mineral waters and during the winter to go to Italy. But my financial means do not permit me to take advantage of the advice given me nor can I live in a style becoming to the widow of a Chief Executive of a great nation, although I live as economically as I can. In consideration of the great services my deeply lamented husband has rendered to the United States, and of the fearful loss I have sustained by his untimely death, I respectfully submit to your honorable body this petition.

Mrs. A. Lincoln,
Frankfurt, Germany.

During her stay abroad Mrs. Lincoln resumed correspondence with Mrs. Orne, then on a protracted visit to Paris. The following [78] is one of the first of a long series of letters.

Frankfurt   Oct 23d 69.
My dear Mrs. Orne:

Notwithstanding the disadvantageous circumstances under which I am now labouring I hasten to reply to your last most acceptable letter, received so gladly on yesterday. The first finger of my right hand is painfully sore, enveloped in cloths—all arising from the smallest prick of a needle. *It* (*the finger*) has been to consult with a physician and the salve administered with him, I trust will prove efficaceous. It is very much inflamed & I scarcely closed my eyes during the night. Last week, sick most of the time & this week unable to use my hand and I am feeling so anxious *all* the time about that very precious little Mary in A—for her time of trouble has surely now come—and I do not know why, but I am fearing a suffering time for her. She is so innocent & lovely in character, my son is greatly blessed in so sweet a young wife—and she writes me that she never imagined *such* devotion, as she receives from him.

[78] Original owned by Oliver R. Barrett, Chicago, Ill.

When I had gone out on yesterday, about my painful finger, the New Consul & his wife called. I found their cards. *She* is a sister of *Mrs.* Ben Butler. Very soon—I expect to return it. From what Mrs Glazen tells me, I am prepared to like her. Pray, present ever so much love to your very sweet daughter—with kind regards to your brother & a world of love to your dear self—I remain always most affectionately.

M. L.

In February, 1869, Charles Sumner presented Mrs. Lincoln's petition for a pension to the Senate, and introduced a bill providing that $5,000 annually should be given her for the balance of her life. The bill was defeated. Mrs. Lincoln hoped that he would introduce another bill when the new Congress met in December, 1869. She hoped also that Mrs. Orne would be able to do something towards the passage of the bill through her brother Charles O'Neill, a member of the House, and other influential relatives and friends. Her anxiety is apparent in the letters which follow.

MY DEAR MRS ORNE: [79] Frankfurt Nov. 7th 1869.

Instead of writing you a dull uninteresting letter this *unusually* bright morning, how much more agreeable to me, it would be, if we were only together, with hours before us, to indulge in a long pleasant conversation. I am

[79] Original owned by Oliver R. Barrett, Chicago, Ill.

anxiously, most *anxiously,* waiting that you should redeem your promise of "soon returning to Germany." But knowing your loving, *motherly* heart as I do, I have my fears, that you will remain some little time longer in Paris. Although I am sure Dear Sallie, would study *far* better if you were away. It is the same, I know as regards my boy, but I am so differently situated from you and have to accomodate myself, to the sad & unpropitious circumstances of the case. If that brighter day *should* come *ere* long I hope *that day* of "thanksgiving & praise" will be passed together. I am well aware, I have not a friend *in the world,* who would as gladly rejoice as yourself over my changed fortunes. I hope you will oblige me, in the event of your receiving *any* intimation, either favorably or *if unfortunately adverse,* to my interests whatever the opinion may be—*inform me.* I know you to be good & true & that you would not for an instant, that I should be deceived by false expectations. You will, I am sure, unite your prayers with mine—that all may be well. If we succeed I shall be more indebted to *you & yours*—than to any one else. Sumner *has been considered,* to be a man, who entertains but *one idea,* at a time— (entirely between ourselves) *I* know him to be, all that is excellent, yet *by this time,* my claims *may* have passed out of his mind & his thoughts may be absorbed in *Cuba* & something else. Your husband, your brother Charles & your other Phil Members, will agitate & make it effectual —I know—*ere* Congress becomes *immersed* in other business. *On this subject,* my dear friend, I will not trouble you again—only—when you indite your "farewell address"

to your own family & *perhaps Col* Forney on *the* subject—
close your portfolio & come to Frankfurt. It appears a
weary, weary age, since I lost you.—A week ago, I received the welcome news from my son that on the 15th
of October our dear Mary became the mother of a sweet
little daughter—after great suffering of eight hours & she
was doing *well*—Heaven be praised, for *that* mercy. *She*
is a dear child to me, indeed. He wrote after a sleepless
night & *four hours* after the birth of the child therefore
no names were mentioned—but as *the other Grandmama
presided* with the Dr & nurse over the advent of the darling
child perhaps *she* may consider *herself* entitled to the name
—surely myself, as *one Grandmother* (how very queer that
sounds *to me*) being named Mary, the mother of the child
Mary, the child being called so too, would be rather too
much in the beginning. Mrs. Harlan, has written me a few
times & signed herself always, *A. E. H.* whether the *A.*
stands for *Angelica* or *Anastasia* I know not. I abominate
ugly names—if *they can* be avoided. I write you, my dear
Mrs Orne, always confidentially. With a great deal of love
to Susie, and hoping that she has now entirely recovered,
I pray that it may be so. I have called on the Webster's
& like them very much. My fingers are well. Write please
so soon as you receive this. Very affectionately your friend,

MARY LINCOLN.

THE DOCUMENTS

MY VERY DEAR FRIEND: [80]

Your kind letter was received last evening, with much pleasure, you may be sure. Yet it found me confined to my bed, with a neuralgic headache, which was not lessened, when my darling boy produced a *late London* paper published about *ten* days since, announcing that "Mrs Lincoln, was soon to be married to the Baden Count"—with so unpronounceable a name, that I could not *attempt* to remember it. The same evil spirit, that originated this rumor last spring, is evidently again at work, and in the most malignant form too—probably anticipating, that by *this* time, Congress might be turning their attention to my *sad & unfortunate* case. The notice was in a budget of items of an Anglo-American paper—and is without doubt *just now* being republished with *such* eagerness in *our* public journals. I tremble lest my name coupled with a person whom I have never seen or never expect to do so may not entirely ruin my prospects of any future comfort, for believe me, at present I am in the most trying & humiliating position—which you well know. In my indignation last evening, if means had allowed, I would have sent a telegram to our good friend Col Forney, that "Mrs Lincoln was unacquainted with such a person." As it was, I passed a sleepless, miserable night & must remain very quiet to day—as I have fever upon me—with great & burning pain in my spine—with no one near me to hand me a glass of water if I was dying.

[80] Original in Illinois State Historical Library, Springfield, Ill.

The *hour* you receive this *note* will you write to Col Forney & your brother—so that mention may be made, that Mrs. L. sees no gentlemen & knows no such person as *this Count*. It is evidently a most *malignant invention*. When I am able to sit up I will write you more fully regarding the contents of your last &c. I fancy, my dear friend, you yourself are a *little* wavering, regarding your *former hopes & anticipations. Withhold* nothing from me. My health has again become so poor that I do not expect to rally—if defeat comes. Perhaps when the end comes, we can hope that it will be, "well with me."

Please have your letter go off by *next* Saturday's—Dec 18th—steamer. I fear *this* new trouble may create mischief. I am in much pain—*do write* me, often. With much love, I remain always, most affectionately yours,

MARY LINCOLN.

In her anxiety to ensure the passage of the pension bill, Mrs. Lincoln turned also to Mrs. White.[81]

Frankfort-a-Main
Jany 30th, 1870

MY DEAR MRS. WHITE:

In this land of strangers, words are powerless to express the great pleasure I feel when I receive letters from the friends, so dearly loved, separated by the broad Atlantic. Notwithstanding *our* acquaintance first commenced, in prosperity, with our beloved husbands by our side, with not

---

[81] From a typewritten copy in the Barton Library at the University of Chicago Library.

a cloud to mar our happiness, yet we met as strangers, surrounded by the cold heartless throng, but even then we
were drawn to each other and sorrow and adversity finds
us true and undivided in our friendship for each other.
My thoughts so often wander to you & I sometimes feel as
if I would give worlds, to have daily communion with you,
who have alike with myself been so *deeply, deeply* bereaved. We can at least write to each other, that satisfaction
is at least not denied us. I can fully understand & appreciate your feelings, returning to Wash. in sorrow & gloom
after having visited it in former years, surrounded by all
the delights, that make life so precious. I am so broken
hearted myself that there is no suffering of mind, I cannot
fully sympathize with. In *God's Own Time* the veil will
be removed, and the chastenings that are now so grievous
to be bourne will be made clear to us. In that great Hereafter, our present sorrow, will be turned into joy. "Life &
Immortality" will be brought to light. "Over the river" our
loved ones are watching and waiting for us, but yet the
time of that reunion appears so far distant. With sorrow,
as a companion, the time passes, but slowly. We have ♥·d
a cold wintr⌐ here, and as in this country, the comforts of
our homelife, in America, are *most* imperfectly understood, suffering greatly with neuralgia myself, the winter
has passed most unpleasantly. It is a great pleasure to me
to receive the kind remembrances of Mrs. Admiral
D[ahlgren]. I have considered her one of our most amiable, accomplished & intellectual women. She requires to
be known, to be understood. And she has a grand husband,

293

do you not think so? If I had known you were going to
Washington, knowing how much you delight in bene-
fitting others, I would have requested you to see Genl.
Butler & urge him to favor my cause. Should any business
for me be brought up before the *House,* I believe you are
well acquainted with him & I am greatly disposed to ask
you to write to him. *He* is one of our noblest and most
patriotic men & would not desire to see the widow of the
great and good man who did so much to save his Country,
in the Rebellion, *so* very embarrassingly & painfully and I
may say Humiliatingly situated as I now am, surely *his*
kind and powerful voice will be raised in my behalf. Please
dear Mrs. White, write him so soon as you receive this, on
this subject. I would be so deeply grateful to you, & if it
was ever in my power, would *so* love to oblige you in any
way. I feel that by making this request I am taking a great
liberty with you. Your great heart will, I am sure, kindly
excuse. I fear you will be unable to decipher this scrawl.
With kind regards to your daughters, & *ever so much love*
to yourself, I remain always aff. yours,

M. L.

Please write soon and *burn this*

Another of the letters which went to Mrs. Orne
every few days follows.[82]

MY VERY DEAR FRIEND: Frankfurt Feb 18th 1870

Now that I am again *en rapport* with you, I fear you will
weary of my frequent letters. Confined to my room, as I

[82] Original owned by Alexander W. Hannah, Chicago, Ill.

now am, you can imagine that with so much solitude &
weary, anxious thoughts, I am having a *very sorry* time
of it.

Your description of your journey over the famous Cornice
road was most interesting to me. Thank Heaven no accidents befel your party, I am just in such a nervous state,
that I can see *every* precipice, you have passed over and
appreciate all your fears, by the way side. Now, I hope your
dear roving ladyship, will take a good rest, where you are
and that *in the spring,* if such a season of balmy sunshine
will *ever* come, after such an interminable winter, we may
again meet. What a pleasure, that will be, to me! Of course
you found a formidable budget of letters, from your loved
ones at home. I shall soon hope to hear from you & I am
sure you will *candidly* inform me, of what your friends
consider to be, *my prospects* in Wash. Your letter dear
friend, *was a week* in reaching me, dated *Genoa,* it has
even a *London* postmark, upon it—*I am not jesting.* You
omitted "Germany" on your letter—which as I am anxious
to receive *all letters* that you write me, I hope you will in
the future *avoid.* If I continue, in this strain, this hastily
written note, may turn out a sermon. Of course you have
read with interest of Prince Arthur's visit to Wash &c &c.
I do not see Mrs Sprague's name, among the gay notices
of the winter. Is she in Wash—or South? I hope her truelly
kind hearted husband, will favor our interests. Our best,
most reliable papers, contradict the reckless assertion of
Fisk, that Grant or his wife, had anything to do, with the
gold operation! What freedom & insolence there is, in our

American Press—I have always, had a curiosity to know what villanous & malignant falsehoods, that "World" article contained. Something base of course. Ignorance of their lying malice, is best for me. I see the name, of *a* "Mrs Smith," *said* to be a cousin of Mrs Grant, flourishing largely in the *Court* Circle this winter. *Is it our* Mrs Smith—who tried to thrust herself, so much in former times, upon public notice? I hope to receive some long letters now, from you. *Do not* disappoint me.

With a great deal of love for your daughters & any quantity for yourself, who both in prosperity & adversity have been so true to me in your friendship. The "cup of cold water," to the parched lips & the loving words to the suffering ones of earth are always recorded in the *Great Book of Remembrance.*

Affectionately yours

MARY LINCOLN

Mary Harlan Lincoln, Mrs. Lincoln's daughter-in-law, was the one person who could turn her thoughts from herself and call forth the best aspects of her normal nature. Letters, marked by affection and understanding, went to her frequently. A typical one follows.[83]

MY VERY DEAR MARY: Frankfurt March 22 [1870]

After a most tedious journey from Nice of constant travel for three days, I arrived here this morning. Of course,

[83] From Helm, *Mary, Wife of Lincoln,* 280-83.

THE DOCUMENTS

I sent immediately for my Taddie and as he has just left
me for an hour, I feel that I cannot refrain from writing
you, for your most welcome letter of March 1st has just
been read. It pains me beyond expression, to learn of your
recent illness and I deeply deplore that I was not with you
to wait upon you. My dear child, do take good care of
your precious health—*even the thought* of you at this great
distance is a great alleviation to the sorrow I am enduring.

I may quietly return to you, as it is, nothing can please
me in what is beyond doubt most necessary at the present
time both to my health and to my peace of mind—this
change of scene. My thoughts have been constantly with
you for months past, and, oh! how I have wished day by
day, that you could be with me and enjoy the air and the
sunshine of the lovely climate I have just left. It would
have been utterly impossible for me with my present health
and sad state of mind, to have taken the least interest in
Italian cities this winter. I return to find my dear boy much
grown in even so short a time and I am pained to see his
face thinner, although he retains his usual bright complexion. He is doubtless greatly improving in his studies,
yet I am very sure the food he gets at his school does not
agree with him. This you may be sure is a most painful
belief to me. When I am here, I can always give him his
dinner as he has their permission to be absent. His presence
has become so necessary even to my life. In two days' time
he will have his Easter vacation for ten days and he is
urging me to take him *somewhere* at that time and if I

were not so fatigued would gladly consent to do so, but I suppose it will end in my acquiescing with his wishes. . . .

Do oblige me by considering me as a mother for you are very dear to me as a daughter. *Anything* and *everything* is yours—if you will consider them worth an acceptance. My mind was so distracted with my grief in that house, 375, I cannot remember where anything was put. It will be such a relief to me to know that articles can be used and enjoyed by you. . . . Remember everything is yours and feeling so fully assured as you must be of my love, will you now, my dear girl, consider them as such? Oh! that I could be with you! for with the lonely life I impose upon myself, separation from those I love so much, at this trying, heart-rending time, is excruciating pain. If when we meet I find you restored to health I will feel in a measure compensated for the dreary absence. I am glad you enjoyed your visit to Springfield. They are all so pleasantly situated—so hospitable and so fully prepared to receive you with the greatest affection. Do make the promised visit to Mrs. Edwards —in the summer and then go to the seaside and rest quietly for a month, no less time. Let me beseech you, dear Mary, to take care of your health.

My head aches now for the tears I have shed this morning in thinking of you and our loving boy. Taddie with his great good heart loves you so devotedly. I shall try to think of you as with your dear mother while it is so cold in Chicago at present. I know they will be careful of you. I never see anything particularly pretty—that I do not wish it was yours. My spirit is very willing but my purse not very extensive.

I am pained to hear of Bettie Stuart's death. She was a most amiable woman, and her father is a very dearly loved cousin—a most affectionate relative. Did you see Mrs. Lizzie Brown in Springfield?—a very sweet woman. I shall, dear Mary, await most anxiously news from you. If I do not hear soon I shall imagine every trouble. If you will write to dear Taddie, you will gratify him very much.

Referring to that speech Mrs. —— made you last winter that housekeeping and babies were an uncomfortable state of existence for a young married lady I think her experience was different from most mothers who consider that in the outset in life—a nice home—loving husband and precious child are the happiest stages of life. I fear she has grown moody, but at the same time I hope you will have a good rest and enjoy yourself *free* for a year or more to come. The Doctor has just left me and says he wonders to find me sitting up.

You should go out *every day* and enjoy yourself—you are so *very young* and should be as gay as a lark. Trouble comes soon enough, my dear child, and you must enjoy life, whenever you can. We all love you so very much—and you are blessed with a devoted husband and darling child—*so do go out* and enjoy the sunshine. I do so hope your dear mother has recovered her health. When I can I will write to her. Do, I pray you, write frequently. I do wish you would take out the double India shawl, with a red center, which I never wore and make faithful use of it.

MARY LINCOLN.

In the face of much opposition Charles Sumner finally got his bill for a pension to Mrs. Lincoln passed, although he was forced to consent to the reduction of the amount to $3,000. It was approved July 14, 1870. The effect on Mrs. Lincoln's state of mind was apparent at once. Her letters became brighter, less introspective, and her interests broadened. The two which follow [84] —to a Louisville woman who had recently married Paul R. Shipman, the former associate editor of the Louisville *Journal*—reveal a different woman than the Mary Lincoln of a few months earlier.

Frankfurt am Main,
June 29, 1870.

MY DEAR MRS. SHIPMAN:

Although weary months have passed since your very kind and welcome letter was received, yet notwithstanding it has so long remained unanswered, you have been very frequently in my thoughts and I have been mentally wishing you such a world of happiness in your new marriage relations. Your letter in the early spring found me quite an invalid and I have just returned from a long visit to the Marienbad baths and waters in Bohemia and I find

[84] From Helm, *Mary, Wife of Lincoln*, 284 and 287.

my health greatly benefited. I can well imagine how greatly you have enjoyed your journeyings in Europe and I truly hope we may meet whilst we are both abroad. You with your life so filled with love and happiness, whilst I alas am but a weary exile. Without my beloved husband's presence, the world is filled with gloom and dreariness for me. I am going with my young son in a day or two into the country to remain for some weeks. If you will kindly write me and direct to care of Philip Nicoll Schmidt, Bankers, Frankfurt, Am Main, Germany, I will receive it. The name of the gentleman you have married is too prominent a one in America not to be familiar to me and associated with one so highly gifted as Mr. Prentice was. The gems of poetry he has written will always fill our minds and hearts with remembrance of him. Dickens too has passed away. How much delight it would give me to meet you this summer. Do you ever hear from our amiable and lovely friend, Mrs. Speed? With compliments to Mr. Shipman and many affectionate congratulations to yourself,

I remain always truly yours,

MARY LINCOLN.

Leamington, England.
October 27, '70.

MY DEAR MRS. SHIPMAN:

Your very kind and welcome letter of September 27 has just been received from Frankfurt. I cannot express to you how deeply I regret not being in Frankfurt when you were there. I have been absent most of the time from Germany since last June, have been occasionally in London but this I have considered my resting place. I am exceedingly anxious to meet you, and if you could not come here to the loveliest garden spot of Europe I would run up any time to London. In three hours and a half we arrive there passing through Oxford. Very possibly you may have been here,—surrounded by Kenilworth Castle, Warwick Castle, Stratford-on-Avon, nine miles distant, and only a very pleasant drive. My son of course is here with me. I have been fortunate enough to secure a very fine English tutor for him, who comes to us very highly recommended, a very fine scholar and a gentlemanly, conscientious man. He recites his lessons with his tutor seven hours of each day, so you can imagine that I see very little of my dear, good son. If he improves as he is doing I shall be satisfied. Many Americans are always here. One especial family with whom I have been very intimate for years, has been with me all the time. Again I repeat, I long to see you. My remembrance of you is of a very agreeable nature, and in this strange land those whom we have formerly loved become doubly dear. Hoping that I may soon hear from you, my dear friend, and with compliments for your husband and much love for yourself,

Your affectionate friend,

MARY LINCOLN.

In the spring of 1871 Mrs. Lincoln returned to America, bringing Tad with her. Shortly after her return she thanked Mrs. John A. Dahlgren for a copy of her book, "Thoughts on Female Suffrage," in a letter [85] in which she set forth her own opposition to the movement for votes for women.

Mrs. Dahlgren

Dear Madame,

I have read with great pleasure your *spirituelle brochure,* and can assure you of my entire sympathy in your eloquent opposition to what are falsely called woman's rights. As if we women in America, were not in the fullest possession of every right—even of that one which I think the French call, "le droit d'insolence." I would recommend our strong-minded sisters to take a trip to Savoy or Saxony, where I have seen women hitched to the plough or harnessed with dogs drawing little carts through the streets.

The movement seems to me however, one of those which should be treated with wholesome neglect, since should congress give them the privilege of voting—those, who would avail themselves of it, are sure to behave in so inconsequent a manner as to reduce the whole matter to an absurdity. I know not whether it is indolence or because I am so thoroughly anti-protestant but I never signed a protest against any thing in my life, however, out of respect for your talents and opinions, I shall avail myself of the first opportunity to lay this pamphlet & petition before my friend Mrs. Peter to get her signature at the head, and

[85] Original owned by Oliver R. Barrett, Chicago, Ill.

then try to obtain others—as also subscribers for the *True Women*.

Will you kindly mention to Mrs. Sherman, that her daughter left me hers and the other signatures; for which I thank her sincerely. They have been copied and are being bound to send to the Holy Father. We regret not to have seen more of Miss Sherman, who we were told, had left soon after she did us the honor of calling.

Accept dear lady the sincere sympathy and admiration of

Yours truly

MARY T. LINCOLN

Soon after arriving in the United States Tad Lincoln caught a severe cold, which quickly developed serious proportions. Mrs. Lincoln reported on his progress to Mrs. White.[86]

June 8th [1871]

MY DEAR MRS. WHITE: Clifton House, Chicago, Ill.

Feeling assured that you will hear of my beloved young son's illness and being well convinced of your anxiety regarding him, I take advantage of a quiet sleep, which he is enjoying, to write you regarding him. My dear boy, has been *very very* dangerously ill—attended by two excellent physicians, who have just left me, with the assurance, that he is better. May we *ever* be sufficiently grateful, should his precious life be spared. Dr Davis, a very eminent lung physician, says, that *thus far,* his lungs, are *not at all* dis-

[86] Original in the Barton Library at the University of Chicago Library.

eased although water has been formed on part of his left lung, which is gradually decreasing. His youth, and vigilant care, with the mercy of God, may ward off future trouble. With the *last* few years *so filled* with sorrow, *this* fresh anguish, bows me to the earth. I have been sitting up so constantly for the last ten nights, that I am unable to write you at length to day. I regret to hear of the illness of Mrs Walker's child. Ere this I trust it has entirely recovered. When you write please direct to room 21, the Clifton House. Please *burn* the letters, I have *recently* written you. In this *hard,* matter of fact world, such vain delusions must not be cherished. With ever so much love, believe me, your affectionate friend

MARY LINCOLN

Unable to throw off his cold, Tad Lincoln developed pneumonia. He died on July 15. For years Mrs. Lincoln had devoted her life to him, and his death was more than she could bear. Henceforward she was to be found on the dark side of the invisible line which separates normal minds from those which life has shattered.

The extent of the mental deterioration which took place between 1871 and 1875 was painfully evident at the insanity hearing which took place in May of the latter year. The following extracts[87] from the testimony show that Robert Lincoln took the only possible

[87] From the Chicago *Inter-Ocean,* May 20, 1875.

course. They show also, although faintly, something of the agony of the ordeal.

Dr. Willis Danforth testified that he was acquainted with Mrs. Lincoln; had called to see her Nov. 24, 1873, at her residence; she had strange imaginings; thought that some one was at work at her head; thought it was an Indian removing the bones of her face and pulling wires out; visited Mrs. Lincoln again Sept. 16, 1874; she was suffering from debility of the nervous system; complained that some one was taking steel springs from her head and would not let her rest; believed that she was going to die within a few days, and had been admonished to that effect by her husband; imagined that she heard raps on the table conveying the time of her death to her. She sat by the table and asked questions and repeated the supposed answer the table returned, although no one heard any sounds. When witness expressed a doubt as to the reliability of the information given, Mrs. Lincoln made what she termed a final test by putting the question to a glass goblet which was on the table. The goblet was found to be cracked, and that circumstance she regarded as a corroboration of the table raps. These were derangements not dependent on the condition of her body, not delirium arising from physical disease. A week ago called on Mrs. Lincoln at the Grand Pacific Hotel. She spoke rationally, and appeared to be in excellent health, and the hallucinations formerly noticeable seemed to have passed away. She said that her reason for returning from Florida was that her son was not well.

Suddenly she startled witness somewhat by saying that an attempt had been made to poison her on her journey from the South. She said that she had been very thirsty, and at a wayside station not far from Jacksonville, she obtained a cup of coffee; discovered there was poison in the coffee, and drank another cup, so that the overdose of poison might cause her to retch. Witness did not see any traces that she suffered from mineral poison. His professional opinion was that Mrs. Lincoln is insane. . . .

Dr. Isham testified that on March 12th he received a telegram from Mrs. Lincoln, at Jacksonville, Florida, as follows: "My belief is my son is ill: telegraph: I start for Chicago tomorrow." Mr. Lincoln was perfectly well, and the telegram rather startled witness then; wired her to that effect, and Mr. Lincoln sent a telegram telling her to remain in Florida until she was perfectly well; received another telegram one hour and a half after receipt of the first; it read: "My dearly beloved son, Robert T. Lincoln— Rouse yourself and live for your mother; you are all I have; from this hour all I have is yours. I pray every night that you may be spared to your mother."

Robert T. Lincoln, the petitioner, then took the witness stand. His face was pale; his eyes bore evidence that he had been weeping, and his whole manner was such as to affect all present. His mother looked upon him benignly, and never betrayed the emotion which must have filled her breast during the recital of the unfortunate and regretful scenes they were parties to. He testified that there was no reason his mother should think he was sick unless that she had seen some newspaper paragraph. He had not been sick in ten years. He did not want any money from his mother. He owed her money, that is, he had some in his hands in trust for her. Mother arrived from the South on March 15. When witness entered the car in which she was she appeared startled. She looked well and not fatigued after her journey of seventy-two hours. Asked her to come to witness' home. She declined and went to the Grand Pacific. Had supper together, and after it sat talking. She told him that at the first breakfast she had after leaving Jacksonville, an attempt was made to poison her. Occupied a room adjoining hers that night. She slept well that night, but subsequently was restless. Several nights she tapped at witness' bed-room door; she would be in her night gown. Told her to go back to her room. Twice in one night she roused him up. One night she aroused him, and asked that she might sleep in his room. He gave his mother his bed, and he slept on the lounge.

Here witness gave vent to his feelings in tears, and the scene was most touching.

He continued: Then I got Dr. Isham to attend her. On April 1 she ceased tapping at witness' room door, for witness told her she must not do it or he would leave the hotel. On that day he went to her room. She was not properly dressed. She left the room under some pretext, and the next thing he knew she was in the elevator going down to the office. Called back the elevator and endeavored to induce her to return to her room. She regarded witness' interference as impertinent; declined to leave the elevator.

Just then the bell rang several times. She was not in a condition of dress to be seen, and witness gently forced her out of the elevator by putting his arm around her waist. Maggie Gavin assisted him, and they got her into her room. She screamed, "You are going to murder me," and would not let Maggie Gavin leave the room to do her work. After awhile she said that the man who had taken her pocket-book promised to return it at 3 o'clock. Asked her who the man was. She replied he was the Wandering Jew; had seen him in Florida. Then she sat near the wall and for an hour professed to be repeating what this man was telling her through the wall. During the afternoon she slept. Since the fire she has kept her trunks and property in the Fidelity Safe Deposit Company's building. In the beginning of the last week in April he called on her. She said that all Chicago was going to be burned, and she intended to send her trunks to some country town—to Milwaukee. Told her that Milwaukee was too near Oshkosh, where there had been a terrible fire the night before. She said that witness' house, of all in Chicago, would be saved, and witness then suggested that was the best place to send the trunks. On the Saturday following she showed witness securities for $57,000 which she carried in her pocket. She has spent large sums of money lately; bought $600 worth of lace curtains; three watches costing $450; $700 worth of jewelry; $200 worth of Lubin's soaps and perfumeries, and a whole piece of silk. Witness had no doubt that she is insane.

Had had a conference with her cousin Major Stuart, of

Springfield, and Judge Davis, of the Supreme Court, as to the best thing to be done for her. They advised the present course.

Q. Do you regard it safe to allow your mother to remain as she is, unrestrained?

A. She has long been a source of much anxiety to me. [Again Mr. Lincoln was affected to tears.] I do not think it would be safe or proper. Have had a man watching her for the last three weeks, whose sole duty was to watch after her when she went on the street. She knew nothing about it. She has no home, and does not visit at witness' house because of a misunderstanding with his wife. Has always been exceedingly kind to witness. She has been of unsound mind since the death of father; has been irresponsible for past ten years. Regarded her as eccentric and unmanageable, never heeding witness' advice. Had no reason to make these purchases, for her trunks are filled with dresses and valuables of which she makes no use. She wears no jewelry and dresses in deep black.

After an absence of only a few minutes, the jury returned the following verdict.[88]

STATE OF ILLINOIS |
County of Cook |

We, the undersigned, jurors in the case of Mary Lincoln alleged to be insane, having heard the evidence in the case, are satisfied that the said Mary Lincoln is insane, and is a

[88] From the files of the Cook County Probate Court.

fit person to be sent to a State Hospital for the Insane; that she is a resident of the State of Illinois, and County of Cook; that her age is fifty six years; that the disease is of unknown duration; that the cause is unknown; that the disease is not with her hereditary; that she is not subject to epilepsy; that she does not manifest homicidal or suicidal tendencies, and that she is not a pauper.

L. J. Gage	S. C. Blake M. D.
J. McG. Adams	C. B. Farwell
S. B. Parkhurst	C. M. Henderson
	Jas. A. Mason
	D. R. Cameron Jurors
	Wm. Stewart
	S. M. Moore
	H. C. Durand
	Thomas Cogswell

Chicago, May 19th 1875

Whereupon the clerk opened the volume entitled "Lunatic Record" to page 96 and filled in the blanks. When he had finished the page read as follows.[89]

May 19th, 1875

IN THE MATTER OF THE ALLEGED }
   INSANITY OF Mary Lincoln

On reading and filing the petition, duly verified, of Robert T. Lincoln and the Certificate of Ralph N. Isham, a Physician, alleging among other matters that Mary Lin-

[89] From the records of the Cook County Probate Court.

coln, of the County of Cook, in the State of Illinois, is insane, and praying that a jury may be summoned to enquire into the truth of said allegations; and on motion, it is ordered that a Writ of Inquisition be issued to the Sheriff of Cook County, commanding him that he cause the said Mary Lincoln personally to appear before this Court, on the 19th day of May, 1875, at 2 o'clock P.M., to answer said allegations; and that a venire be issued, returnable at the same time, for 12 good and lawful men, one of whom shall be a physician, to serve as jurors in the matter of said enquiry, and also that a subpoena be issued to the wit. nesses named in said petition, commanding them to appear in Court at the same time, to testify in that behalf.

May 19th, 1875, 2 o'clock P. M.

And now comes the said Mary Lincoln, who is alleged to be insane, in custody of the Sheriff of Cook County; also comes B. F. Ayer Esq. on behalf of Robert T. Lincoln at whose instance she was arrested; and thereupon also come the jurors of a jury of good and lawful men, to wit:

S. C. Blake, a Doctor of Medicine, and Wm. Stewart
C. B. Farwell   C. M. Henderson   S. M. Moore
J. McG. Adams   Jas. A. Mason   H. C. Durand
S. B. Parkhurst D. R. Cameron   Thos. Cogswell
L. J. Gage, who after being duly empanelled and sworn according to law, and having heard the evidence adduced and the arguments of counsel, retire in charge of an officer of the Court to consider their verdict; and thereupon return

into Court, and in the presence of the said . . . . deliver
their verdict in the words and figures as follows, to wit:

STATE OF ILLINOIS, ⎱
County of Cook,   ⎰ *ss.*

We the undersigned, jurors in the case of Mary Lincoln
who is alleged to be insane, having heard the evidence
adduced, are satisfied that the said Mary Lincoln is insane,
and is a fit person to be sent to the State Hospital for the
Insane: that she is a resident of the County of Cook, in the
State of Illinois: that her age is 56 years; that her disease
is of unknown duration; that the cause is unknown; that
the disease is not with her hereditary; that she is not subject to epilepsy: that she does not manifest homicidal or
suicidal tendencies and that she is not a pauper.
Which Verdict is signed by each of the jurors above named.

Whereupon, upon the verdict aforesaid, it is considered
and adjudged by the Court that the said Mary Lincoln is
an insane person, and it is ordered that said Mary Lincoln
be committed to a State hospital for the Insane, and it is
further ordered that a summons be issued to the said Mary
Lincoln commanding her to appear before this Court and
show cause if any she has or can show why a conservator
should not be appointed to manage and control her estate.

The day after the hearing Mrs. Lincoln made an unsuccessful attempt to commit suicide. She was immediately taken to the private sanitarium of Dr. R. J. Patterson at Batavia, Illinois. After three months Doctor Pat-

terson felt that a public description of her condition was advisable. He wrote the following letter to the Chicago *Tribune.* The Illinois *State Journal,* of Springfield, reprinted it with favorable comment on "the most discreet, considerate and tender" care which the patient had been receiving.[90]

Batavia, Ill., Aug. 28, 1875.

To the Editor of the Chicago Tribune:

It is no fault of mine that the sad case of Mrs. Lincoln has been again in all the papers of the land, but now that so many incorrect statements have been made I deem it proper to correct some of them.

On the 19th of May last, Mrs. Lincoln, being in court, was declared "insane, and a fit subject for treatment in a State hospital for the insane." The warrant for commitment was at the request of her friends, directed to the undersigned, commanding him "forthwith to arrest and convey her to Bellevue Place, Batavia, Ills."

It has been publicly stated that I have "certified" to the recovery or mental soundness of Mrs. Lincoln. This is not true. She is certainly much improved, both mentally and physically; but I have not at any time regarded her as a person of sound mind. I heard all the testimony at the trial, May 19, and saw no reason then to doubt the correctness of the verdict of the jury. I believe her now to be insane.

The question of Mrs. Lincoln's removal from this place, notwithstanding her mental impairment, has received care-

[90] September 1 and 2, 1875.

ful consideration from her conservator, Mr. Robert T. Lincoln, and myself. The proposition having been made that she should go and live with her sister, Mrs. Edwards, in Springfield, I at once said, if she would do this in good faith, and thus secure a quiet home for herself, I should favor it, "unless her condition should change for the worse." This was written to Mr. Robert T. Lincoln in a letter addressed to him on the 9th inst. And this is all there is of the "certificate" of Mrs. Lincoln. In accordance with the above conditional sanction of the proposition for removal, I have occasion to know that Robert T. Lincoln made efforts to perfect arrangements for the transfer of Mrs. Lincoln to Springfield.

It is well known that there are certain insane persons who need what in medico-legal science is termed interdiction, which does not necessarily imply restraint. If time should show that Mrs. Lincoln needs only the former, without the latter, all will rejoice to see any possible enlargement of her privileges. And now, although the conditions upon which, on the 9th inst., I favored her removal have been modified by the presence of a greater degree of mental perturbation than at that time existed, I am still unwilling to throw any obstacle in the way of giving her an opportunity to have a home with her sister. But I am willing to record the opinion that such is the character of her malady she will not be content to do this, and that the experiment, if made, will result only in giving the coveted opportunity to make extended rambles, to renew the indulgence of her purchasing mania and other morbid mental manifestations.

In regard to the treatment of Mrs. Lincoln while under my care, it has been stated that she has been "kept in close confinement," "virtually imprisoned behind gates and bars," "locked by her jailer as a prisoner," "incarcerated," etc., etc. These and other like harsh terms are not used in the interest of truth. They are unjust, and do no credit to those who apply them to the case of Mrs. Lincoln. She need not remain indoors unless by her own choice more than two or three waking hours of any day. A carriage is always at her command. She may ride or walk when and where she pleases, on condition that she shall return at proper hours, and be accompanied by some suitable person or persons. She received calls from ladies of her acquaintance in Batavia, and may return them. She has been called upon by Gen. Farnsworth, of St. Charles, and by some of her relatives in Springfield. She has had, until the 16th inst., private unrestricted personal intercourse with Judge Bradwell, who, in a threatening and insulting letter to me, calls himself "her legal adviser and friend." The wife of Judge Bradwell, until the date above named, has been permitted to visit Mrs. Lincoln, write her numerous letters, bear messages and packages of letters from her, and lodge over night with her in her room.

As to "guarded windows" I have only to say they are made as unobjectionable as it is possible to make them. A light ornamental screen was at first placed before Mrs. Lincoln's windows. These were subsequently removed. But when it is remembered that the same evening on which Mrs. Lincoln was declared insane she attempted suicide, all right-minded persons will agree that guarded windows were among the proper precautions against accidents.

As to "barred doors," there are none at Bellevue Place. Mrs. Lincoln's doors leading to the outer world are never locked during the day time. The outer door only is locked at bed time at night by her private attendant, and the key retained by the attendant, who sleeps in an adjoining room communicating with that of Mrs. Lincoln. This, to my mind, is the proper thing to do.

Mrs. Lincoln has been placed where she is under the forms of law, and, if any have a grievance, the law is open to them. This sad case has commanded the constant endeavors of those who have the care of her unselfishly to do the best for Mrs. Lincoln.

R. J. PATTERSON.

After nine months at the home of her sister in Springfield, Mrs. Lincoln again appeared in court. This time a jury returned a different verdict.[91]

Chicago June 15 1876

State of Illinois }
Cook County } County Court of Cook County

We the undersigned jurors in the case wherein Mary Lincoln who was heretofore found to be insane and who is now alleged to be restored to reason having heard the evidence in said cause, find that the said Mary Lincoln is

[91] From the files of the Probate Court of Cook County.

restored to reason and is capable to manage and control
her estate.

R. M. Paddock M. D.

D. J. Weatherhead

S. F. Knowles

Cyrus Gleason

W. J. Drew

D. Kimball

R. F. Wild

Wm. G. Lyon

C. A. Chapin

H. Dahl

W. S. Dunham

Wm. Roberts

Five years of wandering followed. In 1881 she returned from Europe to Springfield, but in a few months
she was in New York, consulting physicians in an effort to restore her health. It was at this time that newspaper stories about her began again to appear. The occasion was the agitation for an increase in her pension.
The following article from the Illinois *State Journal*,[92]
once her husband's personal organ and still edited by
friends of her closest relatives, needs no further comment. It was headed, "Mrs. Lincoln's Pecuniary Condition."

[92] November 26, 1881.

THE DOCUMENTS

The report printed in a New York Paper, a few days ago, of an alleged interview with Dr. Sayre, the attending physician of Mrs. Abraham Lincoln, while in that city, not only justifies *The Journal* in breaking the silence which, from motives of sympathy and respect for the feelings of the relatives and friends of the Martyred President, it has so long maintained on this subject, but makes it a duty to do so. For some twelve months past, the physical and pecuniary condition of Mrs. Lincoln have been made the subject of frequent reports of a highly sensational character, but having scarcely any foundation in fact. *The Journal* has uniformly refrained from noticing these stories, even for the purpose of correction, for the reasons alluded to.

Dr. Sayre, who appears to have been an early acquaintance of Mrs. Lincoln at Lexington, Ky., and now to be giving her medical treatment in New York, is said to have represented to a reporter of *The New York Times*—ostensibly on the authority of Mrs. Lincoln herself—that she is in a state of virtual poverty, being without means to secure the medical attendance and the aid of nurses of which she greatly stands in need, notwithstanding the pension of $3,000 per annum granted her by Congress. This has been followed by charges reflecting upon Mrs. Lincoln's friends for implied neglect, and especially has it been intimated that this is to be made the ground for an attack upon Secretary Lincoln, whose removal from the position of Secretary of War is to be demanded under certain conditions.

The whole business is a most painful one, but justice to

Secretary Lincoln and other friends of Mrs. Lincoln demands that the truth should now be told. The fact is, that while Mrs. Lincoln is, undoubtedly, physically and mentally ill, she is a hypochondriac as to her health and a monomaniac on the subject of money. It was the latter peculiarity which, some ten years ago, induced her to offer her wardrobe for sale in New York, to the chagrin and mortification of her friends. Each movement for the purpose of honoring some distinguished citizen by raising a fund for his or her benefit, has been the occasion of a new accession of her unfortunate malady. This was the case, a year or so ago, when the movement was on foot for raising a fund of $25,000 for Gen. Grant, and there has been a revival of the feeling, within the past few weeks, in connection with a like movement for the benefit of the late President Garfield. During these periods she has complained of neglect and lack of National appreciation, and has even threatened to go to Washington to make her appeal to Congress for an increased pension.

Those most intimately acquainted with Mrs. Lincoln's pecuniary affairs say that, in addition to her pension of $3,000 a year from the Government, she is in the enjoyment of an annual income of some $2,000 to $2,500 interest from investments in Government bonds, originally made for her by Judge Davis, administrator of President Lincoln's estate —making a total of over $5,000 a year. After her return from Europe, she was, for several months, an inmate of the family of her sister, in this city, where her every want was supplied with the utmost patience, and every whim necessary to her comfort gratified. During this period her personal expenses were reduced to a minimum rate, and there was a considerable increase in her capital. As she has no one to support but herself, it is absurd to say that she is in a state of suffering on an income of over $5,000 per year. While we would not throw a straw in the way of securing an increased allowance from the Government, if Congress should see proper to grant it, her dependence is, today, proportionably larger than that of Mrs. Garfield, with five children and the aged mother of her husband to support.

We have spoken thus at length in justice to relatives of Mrs. L., who have been grossly wronged by the reports which have gone out on this subject through the press, accompanied by insinuations of absolute and wilful neglect. The case is a sad one, but it is so through the unfortunate mental hallucinations of the principal subject of it, rather than from any shortcomings or faults of Mrs. Lincoln's friends.

Mrs. Lincoln's sad mental condition is revealed more clearly in the following letter from her own pen [93] than in anything which has been written about her.

[93] Original in the collection of Wilfred C. Leland, Jr., Detroit.

MARY LINCOLN

Miller's Hotel
Nos. 37, 39 & 41 West Twenty-sixth
Street, New York City.
Turkish, Electric and Roman Baths
Dr. E. P. Miller, Proprietor
New York, Feb. 5th, 1882

MY DEAR MR. MINER:

I write to you *on two* subjects, of the *very* greatest importance to me. I am growing very ill with *anxiety*. Parties coming in tell me that no one knows accurately whether the Bill for $15,000.00 passed the house with the $2,000. a year Pension Bill. Without I see the handwriting of Mr. Springer announcing that the $15,000.00 was passed with the *grand* Pension Bill, may I not implore you, the *hour* you receive this letter tomorrow morning—to write to Mr. Springer and have *him* write to you at once—the truth about it all. Of course (between ourselves) if it passed with the other bill it would be kept from me, and if the $15,000. passed the House of Representatives, they would try to prevent Arthur from *signing* it. I plead with you to write to Mr. Springer about *it all* & please enclose me *his* reply without the least delay. The great anxiety about this business is rendering me very ill. Only a few lines from *Springer* will satisfy me. Many persons are now doubting it greatly. As you were not in Washington at the time of the voting Springer will know best about it. Mrs. Dr. Miller returned from Wash. a few days since accompanied by Susan B. Anthony & other suffrage women who stopped at this house. Through *gossiping* Miller I understand she

had a conference with old Villain Davis. I feel assured Mrs.
M. worked against my Pension. Avoid any conversation
with Dr. Miller save the *mere civilities* of life. He tells
everything. No woman in the drawing room or at table *but*
know everything that is whispered to him. Not a word
from 575 Broadway—moving may be a partial excuse.
Again I implore you, Mr. Miner, to write him again the
hour you receive this letter. This is the only straw left us.
Please write him at once and ask him what contributions
he has received & tell him to send them to me. *This is*
our last week. If you do not write to him *when* you receive
this letter, there will be no success. Your $20. (twenty dol-
lars) on any thousand henceforth received may help you
in your little illness and through 575 & his friends it will
come very easily by a few lines from you.

"Nothing venture, nothing have" and it appears *very,*
very remiss and almost sinful to allow *this* opportunity to
pass. I cannot bring myself to believe that you will neglect
it any longer. The small checque received two weeks since
has proved too much for her, Mrs. Macks, delicate nerves.
As to herself she has not called. Of course she requires no
money. *Please, please Do Not* reply to *one* of her letters.
On Thursday afternoon Dr. Sayre called & said "Did you
receive the letter I sent you." I replied, "No Sir." Then he
fumbled in his coat pockets and drew out a four page
letter, a fresh one from Mrs. Mack. Evidently he wished
to read it to me.

Send me please Springer's letter.

Write Monday morning to 575 requesting to know what. . . .

I said *please* spare me. We began speaking about 575 & as quickly as possible I changed the subject.

Mrs. Mack has acted very ugly. I do entreat you to write Monday morning to Springer.

With best love to your family, I remain

Very truly

Mrs. A. L.

Within six months death came to Mrs. Lincoln. This account of her final illness is taken from the Illinois *State Journal* of July 17, 1882.

The public has known for some time that Mrs. Lincoln was in ill health, but nothing had appeared to indicate that her death at any early day was probable. About the 24th of March last, she returned from New York, where she had been undergoing treatment, and her health was then noticeably improved. Nothing, however, could fully arouse her from the gloomy state of mind which has almost perpetually borne upon her since that terrible night when her husband, "the foremost man of all this world," was shot by her side in Ford's Theatre at Washington. Though her friends had hopes of many happy days for her, she was not able to emancipate herself from the shadow that had clouded her life. After her return, as stated above, she took to her room at the house of her brother-in-law, the Hon. N. W. Edwards, and had since been little seen except by near friends of the family. Instead of gaining in health, she rather declined, and latterly spent much of her time in bed. Within the past few days she has been suffering from an attack of boils, which caused her great pain, and no doubt greatly increased her nervousness. On Friday last she was up and walked across the room. Again on Saturday she walked across the room with a little assistance; but she grew worse later in the day, and about 9 o'clock in the evening experienced a paralysis which seemed to involve her whole system, so that she was unable to articulate, to take food or to move any portion of her body. She soon afterward passed into a comatose state, and so continued, breathing stertorously, up till 8:15 p. m., Sunday, when she died in the same house where, nearly forty years ago, she and Abraham Lincoln were married.

One seldom looks to a funeral sermon for fine appraisal of character. Yet who will say that the biographers of fifty years have approached the essential wisdom and understanding of the Rev. James A. Reed when he spoke the following words?

"For we must needs die, and are as water spilt on the ground, which cannot be gathered up again; neither doth God respect any person, yet doth He devise means that His banished be not expelled from Him." ii Samuel 14:14.

The admonitory words fell from the lips of a princely woman, pleading the common mortality to gain a merciful end with a princely man. They have their fitting repetition now, in the solemnities of this hour, when all that remains of the wife of a princely man lies before us. A poor, desolate, broken-hearted woman, whose sorrows have been too great for utterance even, has at last yielded to the withering hand of death, and entered upon that "silent bourne whence no traveler returns." This is only the climax of the shock of years ago. Death's doings have only now ripened unto maturity.

When among the Alleghany mountains last summer, I saw two tall and stately pines standing on a rocky ledge where they had grown so closely together as to be virtually united at the base, their interlocking roots entering the same rock cavities, and penetrating the same soil. There they had stood for years with intertwining branches and interlocking roots, braving in noble fellowship the mountain storms. But the taller of the two had, years before, been struck by a flash of lightning, that had gone to its very roots, shattering it from top to bottom, and leaving it scarred and dead.

The other apparently uninjured had survived for some years, but it was evident from the appearance of its leaves that it too was now quite dead. It had lingered in fellowship with its dead companion, but the shock was too much for it. In their sympathetic fellowship and union, both trees had suffered from the same calamity. They had virtually both been killed at the same time. With the one that lingered, it was only slow death from the same cause. So it seems to me today, that we are only looking at death placing his seal upon the lingering victim of a past calamity.

Years ago, Abraham Lincoln placed a ring on the finger

of Mary Todd inscribed with these words: "Love is Eternal." Like two stately trees they grew up among us in the nobler, sweeter fellowship of wedded life. They twain became one flesh. Here they planted their home and, in domestic bliss, their olive plants grew up around them. Here they were known and honored, and loved by an appreciative and admiring community, and when perilous times came, and the nation looked forth among the people for a steady hand to guide the ship of state, its heart went out after this tall and stately man that walked like a prince among us. He was their choice, and ascending to the chief place in the nation's gift, he stood like some tall cedar amid the storm of national strife, and with a heroism and a wisdom and a lofty prudence in his administration that won the wonder and respect of the world, he guided the nation through its peril, back again to peace. But when at the height of his fame, when a grateful people were lauding him with just acknowledgment of his great services to the country, and when he was wearily trying to escape from their very adulation into the restful presence and company of his life partner, to be alone awhile in the hour of his triumphant joy, like lightning, the flash of a cruel and cowardly enemy's wrath struck him down by her side. The voice that cheered a nation in its darkest hour is hushed. The beauty of Israel is slain upon the high places. The nation in its grief and consternation, is driven almost to madness. Strong men know not hardly how to assuage their sorrow or control themselves under it. And when the nation so felt the shock what must it have been to the poor woman that stood by his side, who was the sharer of his joys, the partner of his sorrows, whose heart strings were wound about his great heart in that seal of eternal love. What wonder if the shock of that sad hour, that made a nation reel, should leave a tender loving woman, shattered in body and in mind, to walk softly all her days. It is no reflection upon either the strength of her mind or the tenderness of her heart, to say that when Abraham Lincoln died, she died. The lightning that struck down the strong man, unnerved the woman. The sharp iron of this pungent grief went to her soul. The terrible shock, with its quick following griefs in the death of her children, left her mentally and physically a wreck, as it might have left any of us in the same circumstances. I can only think of Mrs. Lincoln as a dying woman through all these sad years of painful sorrow through which she has lingered since the death of her husband. It is not only charitable but just to her native mental qualities and her noble womanly nature, that we think of her and speak of her as the woman she was before the victim of these great sorrows. Drawing the veil over all these years of failing health of body and mind, which have been spent in seeking rest from sorrow in quiet seclusion from the world, I shall speak of her only as the woman she was before her noble husband fell a martyr by her side. . . .

And so, with these words, a brief review of her life and a reminder of the mortality of all flesh, the body of Mary Todd Lincoln was lowered to its grave.

Appendix

THE REMINISCENCES upon which biographers have relied in writing of Lincoln's marriage are in such contradiction that there is no possibility of harmonizing them. Moreover, the accounts of all biographers vary materially from the story of that event as it is revealed in the contemporary letters now available. That being the case, to disregard both reminiscences and biographers' accounts as far as possible, and draw conclusions almost entirely from contemporary material, would seem to be the only course likely to result in a true account of what actually happened. The Mary Todd letters and those which passed between James C. Conkling and Mercy Levering make this approach feasible for the first time.

The first point to be considered is whether or not the story of the wedding at which Lincoln failed to appear, as first related by Lamon and Herndon, is fact or fiction. To this point Mary Todd's letter of December, 1840—which internal evidence shows to have been written between the 13th and 20th of the month—is pertinent. Though written to an intimate friend, and

329

containing one allusion, and possibly two, to her engagement to Lincoln, it gives not the slightest hint that the marriage was to take place in the immediate future.

It is possible, of course, that a wedding was planned for January 1, 1841, after the letter to Mercy Levering was written. However that may be, the Conkling-Levering correspondence proves conclusively that no such episode as Lamon and Herndon describe could have occurred on that day. It is obvious that a break of some sort took place between Lincoln and Mary Todd not long before Conkling wrote to Mercy Levering on January 24, 1841, but it is also obvious that the general impression among friends of the couple was that Lincoln had been jilted. The references to Lincoln in Mercy Levering's letter of February 7 and in Conkling's of March 7 picture him quite clearly as a *rejected lover,* which certainly would not have been the case had he failed to appear at the wedding. Mary Todd's letter of June 18, 1841, furnishes even more conclusive evidence of the unreliability of the Lamon-Herndon wedding story. It is apparent from it that she not only bore Lincoln no resentment, but was anxious that their former relations be resumed. Would this have been the case had he publicly humiliated her six months earlier? The question requires no answer.

APPENDIX

But in spite of the implications of the Conkling-Levering letters, it is certain that the break between Lincoln and Mary Todd came on Lincoln's initiative. His letter of March 27, 1842, to Speed [1] establishes that fact. Upon receiving word from Speed that since his marriage he was happier than he ever thought possible, Lincoln replied: "I am not going beyond the truth when I tell you that the short space it took me to read your last letter gave me more pleasure than the total sum of all I have enjoyed since the fatal first of January, 1841. Since then it seems to me I should have been entirely happy, but for the never-absent idea that there is one still unhappy *whom I have contributed to make so.* That kills my soul. I cannot but *reproach myself* for even wishing to be happy while she is otherwise." [2]

But how can this direct assumption of responsibility be brought into harmony with the Conkling-Levering letters? Only by assuming that friends were permitted to believe that one thing took place, while as a matter of fact something different actually happened. Lincoln must have broken the engagement, but in such a way that it was believed, even among close friends, that Mary Todd had turned him down. It may be objected

[1] *Complete Works,* I., 214-17.
[2] Authors' italics.

that the wedding story can be explained on the same assumption. This is extremely unlikely. Only two people —Mary Todd and Lincoln—were involved in the breaking of the engagement, while several at least would have been concerned in the wedding, and the truth would have leaked out quickly.

In order to discover the exact manner in which the engagement was broken, recourse must be had to the written recollections of friends and relatives. The statements of Speed and Mrs. Edwards,[3] taken together, give a detailed account of just such a situation as that which has been assumed. Lincoln, said Speed,[4] was unhappy about his engagement during the winter of 1840-41: "not being entirely satisfied that his *heart* was going with his hand." While in that frame of mind he wrote Mary Todd a letter in which he told her that he did not love her. "Speed saw the letter to Mary written by Mr. Lincoln. Speed tried to persuade Lincoln to burn it up. Lincoln said—'Speed, I always knew you

---

[3] These statements in their original form were rough but detailed notes in Herndon's handwriting. The Lamon copies, which are in the Henry E. Huntington Library at San Marino, California, have been followed here. The Speed statement, somewhat elaborated, may be found in *Herndon's Life of Lincoln* (Paul M. Angle, Editor), pp. 168-69; the significant part of Mrs. Edwards's statement is quoted in Beveridge, *Abraham Lincoln*, I., 314.

[4] Letter of Nov. 30, 1866; in Lamon, *Life of Abraham Lincoln*, 243-44.

were an obstinate man. If you won't deliver it, I will
get some one to do it.' 'I shall not deliver it now nor
give it to you to be delivered,' (Speed replied), 'words
are forgotten—misunderstood—passed by—not noticed
in a private conversation—but once put your words in
writing and they stand as a living and eternal monu-
ment against you. If you think you have *will* and manhood enough to go and see her and speak to her what
you say in that letter, you may do that.' Lincoln did go
and see her—did tell her &c . . . She rose—and said—
'The deceiver shall be deceived; wo is me'; alluding to
a young man she fooled. Lincoln drew her down on
his knee—kissed her—and parted—she going one way
and he another."

It is evident, however, that the reconciliation was of
short duration. Speed says, "Lincoln did love Miss Edwards—'Mary' saw it—told Lincoln the reason of his
change of mind, heart and soul—released him." Speed's
assertion that Lincoln loved Miss Edwards can be dismissed for a reason to be mentioned later; the essential
part of his statement is Lincoln's release by Miss Todd.
This is confirmed by Mrs. Edwards: "The world had
it that Mr. L. backed out, and this placed Mary in a
peculiar situation and to set herself right and to
free Mr. Lincoln's mind, she wrote a letter to Mr. L.

stating that she would release him from his engagement."

This reconstruction of the episode is corroborated by Lincoln himself. On July 4, 1842, he wrote to Speed: [5] "Yours of the 16th June was received only a day or two since. . . . As to my having been displeased with your advice, surely you know better than that. I know you do, and therefore will not labor to convince you. True, that subject is painful to me; but it is not your silence, or the silence of all the world, that can make me forget it. I acknowledge the correctness of your advice too; but before I resolve to do the one thing or the other, I must gain confidence in my ability to keep my resolves when they are made. In that ability you know I once prided myself as the only or chief gem of my character; that gem I lost—how and where you know too well. I have not regained it; and until I do, I cannot trust myself in any matter of much importance. I believe now that had you understood my case at the time as well as I understood yours afterward, by the aid you would have given me I should have sailed through clear, but that does not now afford me sufficient confidence to begin that or the like of that again."

[5] *Complete Works,* I., 217-19. The original letters from Lincoln to Speed are owned by Oliver R. Barrett.

APPENDIX

Is it far-fetched to assume that Speed had advised Lincoln either to marry Mary Todd or forget her? Lincoln replies that before resolving to do either, he must be confident of his ability to carry out the resolution. How he lost this ability, which he once had, Speed knows too well—the reference must be to Lincoln's decision to break the engagement and his failure, in the crisis, to do so. Speed had advised him to take this course, and Lincoln now realizes that the advice was unsound. Had Speed understood, he would have urged Lincoln to banish his doubts, to look upon them as temporary and certain to yield to ultimate happiness —as Lincoln had done for Speed.

So much for what happened on January 1, 1841. In explanation of why it happened, various biographers have advanced several reasons. All have recognized that Lincoln's state of mind as revealed in the letters to Speed was the fundamental cause, but few have found it the sole explanation. Some have identified the immediate cause in Lincoln's alleged infatuation with Matilda Edwards; others have believed that Mary Todd's flirtation with Stephen A. Douglas—or love for him— precipitated the break.

The evidence now available proves both explanations baseless. The references to Matilda Edwards in the letters of Mary Todd and Conkling are numerous, but every indication points to an intimacy between the two girls which certainly would not have endured had Matilda been the cause of the broken engagement. In this connection Mary Todd's mention of Matilda in her letter of December, 1840—"a lovelier girl I never saw, *Mr. Speed's* ever-changing heart I suspect is about offering *its young* affections at her shrine"—is suggestive. Is it unreasonable to assume that when Speed told Herndon that Lincoln was in love with Matilda Edwards, he was moved more by the recollection of her charms and by a desire to conceal one of his own past loves than by regard for strict truth? And that he disposed of Matilda in the easiest way—that is, by bestowing her on Lincoln?

The absence of all reference to Douglas in the letters of Mary Todd and her friends effectually disposes of the story that a flirtation with him was a factor in the broken engagement. Only one veiled allusion to him can be found. That occurs in the letter of July 23, 1840, where Mary Todd mentions the receipt of various Springfield newspapers, among them the *Hickory Club*. "This latter," she remarked, "rather astonished your friend, *there* I had deemed myself forgotten." In view of the fact that the *Hickory Club* was a Democratic campaign paper, and that Douglas was one of its supervisors, the reference may be to him. If it is, it merely proves that if a flirtation had taken place between him and Mary Todd, it was all over by the summer of 1840.

Nevertheless, another man did figure in the case. He was Edwin B. Webb of Carmi, Illinois; forty years old and a widower with two children. Mary Todd's letters, particularly that of June 18, 1841, show that a real flirtation took place between them during the winter of 1840-41. Seven years later its memory was still fresh: witness her letter of May, 1848, to her husband, with its joking reference to Webb. Yet no known reminiscence even mentions Webb's name as a participant in Lincoln's marital tangle—an omission which strikingly illustrates the weakness of memory as a foundation for history.

The elimination of Matilda Edwards and Douglas as factors in the situation makes the real cause of the broken engagement less difficult to determine. A careful reading of the letters to Speed reveals it as clearly as it is ever likely to be brought out. In 1841 and 1842 Speed was passing through a crisis similar to that which Lincoln had faced, and Lincoln's letters, necessarily based on his own experience, clearly reveal his state of mind at the time he felt a marriage with Mary Todd imminent.

Most explicit in its identification of his own difficulty was Lincoln's letter of February 3, 1842, to Speed,[6] written just before the latter's marriage. "Why, Speed, if you did not love her," he wrote, "although you might not wish her death you would most certainly be resigned to it. Perhaps this point is no longer a question with you, and my pertinacious dwelling upon it is a rude intrusion upon your feelings. If so, you must pardon me. *You know the hell I have suffered on that point, and how tender I am upon it.*"[7]

This admission becomes even more pointed when it is considered in the light of Lincoln's illness of January, 1841. Legislative records show that he attended the House regularly and took an active part in its proceedings until January 2, 1841. Commencing with that day, and continuing until Thursday, January 14, his attendance was irregular and he took little part in legislative business. From Thursday the 14th until Tuesday the 19th he was absent. On the 24th Conkling wrote Mercy Levering that after a week's illness Lincoln was again about, though weak and emaciated.

[6] *Complete Works*, I., 185-87.
[7] Authors' italics.

After the 19th his attendance again became regular, and he soon resumed his customary activity.

It is not the fact of his illness, however, but its nature which is significant. That it was no ordinary indisposition is evident. Men who have merely been in bed a few days do not write, as Lincoln did to John T. Stuart,[8] "I am now the most miserable man living. If what I feel were equally distributed to the whole human family, there would not be one cheerful face on earth."

Three days prior to this Lincoln had written to Stuart urging that he do his utmost to secure the Springfield postmastership for Dr. Anson G. Henry.[9] "You know I desired Dr. Henry to have that place when you left;" he reminded him, "I now desire it more than ever. I have within the last few days, been making a most discreditable exhibition of myself in the way of hypochondriasm and thereby got an impression that Dr. Henry is necessary to my existence. Unless he gets that place he leaves Springfield. You therefore see how much I am interested in the matter."

This letter has more importance than attaches to the further evidence of Lincoln's deep depression which it

[8] January 23, 1841. *Complete Works*, I., 157-59.
[9] Angle, *New Letters and Papers of Lincoln*, 8.

furnishes. Without a doubt it provides the scientific diagnosis of his illness. Hypochondriasm, or hypochondriasis, was what Doctor Henry had concluded was wrong with Lincoln.

Immediately the question of Doctor Henry's professional competence arises. Fortunately, it can readily be answered.

About this time, said Speed,[10] Lincoln wrote a long letter to Dr. Daniel F. Drake of Cincinnati in which he described the symptoms of his illness. Doctor Drake had a wide reputation as a physician and was the author of several treatises on medical subjects. In one of these, "The Principal Diseases of the Mississippi Valley," he repeatedly cited case histories which Doctor Henry had furnished him. Moreover, when he visited Springfield in the autumn of 1844 he spent considerable time with him. It is evident that Doctor Henry was a physician of good standing, and competent to diagnose Lincoln's illness correctly in accordance with the existing state of medical knowledge.

What did the physicians of 1841 mean by hypochondriasis? The "Cyclopaedia of Practical Medicine," published in Philadelphia in 1845, defines it as "a disease in which symptoms of dyspepsia . . . are combined

[10] Lamon, 244.

with a remarkable lowness of spirits or a desponding habit of mind, and a constant disposition to attend to every minute change in the bodily feelings, and to apprehend extreme danger from the most trifling ailments . . ." Excessive morbidity, such as characterized Lincoln's state of mind at this time, was its most marked feature. Other phases of his condition, however, corresponded with the prevalent conception of the disease. When he told Stuart that he lacked sufficient composure to write a longer letter, and that he feared he would be unable to attend to any business in Springfield, he was exemplifying the medical belief that in hypochondriasis "the power of attention is destroyed, at least the patient is persuaded that such is the fact," and that "mental exertion is often the most difficultly endured of all the causes of excitement." When he wrote that a change of scene might help him, he was applying to himself the belief that "change of scene, a removal from customary occupations by traveling, is the best method of ensuring" relief or cure.

The causes of the disease, however, are what concern us particularly. Physicians recognized that it was not of quick inception, and that its manifestations were likely to continue over long periods. "The causes are chiefly of slow and continued influence, and their effect displays itself for the most part gradually and almost imperceptibly. . . . It continues for years, sometimes through the life of the individual, who cannot escape the exciting causes which gave rise to it." These exciting causes were summarily described as "agents which exercise an harmful influence on the mind, and through it on the nervous system; too intent and long-continued application; studies and professions which require great intellectual exertion; anxiety respecting the success of schemes and prospects of worldly advancement; disappointment of various kinds, and consequent dejection; and lastly, though this is by no means the least important article in the catalogue, the indulgence of vicious habits which tend to debilitate the mind and body. . . ."

We know that for many months after the first of January, 1841, Lincoln was in morbid spirits. We know that in his own opinion he was the possessor of a "defective" nervous system. We know that during all of 1840 he exerted himself to the utmost in behalf of Harrison's election, and that he took an active, leading part during the first five weeks of the legislative session. And we know from his own statement—"you know the hell I have suffered on that point"—that intense worry and anxiety over his approaching marriage beset him constantly.

The significance of all this lies in the likelihood that, these other elements being present, that of time was also there. In other words, Lincoln's condition was not the result of some spontaneous occurrence, but was the outcome of causes "of slow and continued influence." Viewed in this light, the "fatal first of January, 1841," becomes merely an aggravated manifestation of his disease rather than the reason for it. On that day his frame of mind was distinctly abnormal. Had this not been the case, the engagement probably would not have been broken.

Only on this assumption can Mary Todd's feeling toward Lincoln, as expressed in her letter of June, 1841, be explained. Had he failed to appear at the wedding, a woman as proud and high-spirited as she would have felt nothing but scorn for him. Had he broken the engagement merely by expressing some such doubts as he wrote to Mary Owens in 1837, she probably would have followed Mary Owens' example in releasing him and forgetting the episode. Only because she recognized that his condition was beyond his own control could she have expressed the wish that "he

343

would once more resume his station in Society, that 'Richard should be himself again.'"

For the eighteen months which followed January 1, 1841, Lincoln's task was to rid himself of his abnormal fears and to recall his nerves and emotions to sound health. Heretofore biographers have complicated the problem by injecting into it, as a new emotional tangle, another unsuccessful courtship.

When Joshua F. Speed turned over to Herndon in 1866 the series of letters which he had received from Lincoln a quarter of a century before, he asked that the name "Sarah" be suppressed wherever it occurred. Herndon complied, but the request aroused his suspicions. He recalled that Lincoln had boarded with William Butler before his marriage, and that Mrs. Butler's sister, who lived with her during part of Lincoln's association with the family, was named Sarah Rickard. Finally he got in touch with the former Miss Rickard herself, who answered his inquiry in a letter signed by her married name of Barrett. "Mr. Lincoln did make a proposal of marriage to me in the summer, or perhaps later, in the year 1840," she wrote. "He brought to my attention the accounts in the Bible of the patriarch Abraham's marriage to Sarah, and used that historical union as an argument in his own behalf. My reason for declining his proposal was the wide difference in our ages. I was then only sixteen, and had given the subject of matrimony but very little, if any, thought. I entertained the highest regard for Mr. Lincoln. He seemed almost like an older brother, being, as it were, one of my sister's family." [11]

The story of the courtship now seemed to rest on a solid foundation, and Herndon printed a paragraph about it in his life of Lincoln. Other writers have generally followed his lead, frequently without the moderation he exercised. Sometimes neat stories of Lincoln's courtship and rejection have been spun out for many pages. On the other hand, the few skeptics who failed to find the proof satisfactory have dismissed the whole affair as one more insoluble problem of Lincoln's career.

Yet, when viewed in the light of the Todd-Levering-Conkling correspondence, the Sarah Rickard episode ceases to be a mystery. Certain salient facts must be kept in mind. To begin with, the three references to Sarah in Lincoln's letters are hardly of a sort which even a lukewarm lover would make. On June 19, 1841, he wrote: "Nothing new here except that I have written. I have not seen Sarah since my last trip, and I am

[11] *Herndon's Life of Lincoln* (Angle edition), 182-83.

going out there as soon as I mail this letter." In the letter of February 3, 1842, he wrote: "I have seen Sarah but once. She seemed very cheerful, and so I said nothing to her about what we spoke of." The last reference occurs in the letter of March 27, 1842: "One thing I can tell you which I know you will be glad to hear, and that is that I have seen Sarah and scrutinized her feelings as well as I could, and am fully convinced she is far happier now than she has been for the last fifteen months past." [12] Infrequent visits and an entire absence of sentiment seem to have characterized their relations.

The second point to be noted is a date which the reference in the letter of March 27 establishes. Sarah was far happier than she had been *"for the last fifteen months past."* What happened about January 1, 1841? Lincoln's break with Mary Todd? Some other answer must be found, for had Sarah been interested in Lincoln, his rupture with Mary Todd would have contributed to her happiness, instead of making her miserable.

However, there were other events which took place about January 1, 1841. Shortly before that date, we

[12] The name "Sarah" has been deleted in the printed version of these letters.

learn from Mary Todd's letter that Speed's "ever-changing heart" was about to offer its affections to Matilda Edwards. Apparently he was rejected, for he sold his business as of January 1, 1841, and soon afterwards left Springfield for Kentucky. If Sarah Rickard had been interested in Speed rather than in Lincoln, either his infatuation with another girl or his departure from Springfield could have given her pain.

Other circumstances fit perfectly into the assumption that whatever intimacy there was existed between Speed and Sarah rather than Lincoln and Sarah. Take the dates and contexts of Lincoln's letters in which allusions to her occur. The first—that of June 19, 1841—was almost entirely devoted to an account of a lawsuit in which all Springfield was interested. The concluding paragraph, however, is significant. "I commenced this letter on yesterday, since which I received yours of the 13th. I stick to my promise to come to Louisville. Nothing new here except what I have written. I have not seen Sarah since my last trip, and I am going out there as soon as I mail this letter." What could be more natural than that Lincoln should be reminded of Sarah by Speed's letter, and that he should scrutinize her feelings so that he could give his friend a first-hand report when he should see him?

Significant happenings had taken place before the next letter containing a reference to Sarah—that of February 3, 1842—was written. Speed had fallen in love with a Lexington girl, Fanny Henning, and had returned to Springfield with Lincoln. He remained until January, 1842, and then departed with the intention of marrying soon after reaching home. It is apparent from Lincoln's letter that Speed had not seen Sarah, but that he had deputed Lincoln to call on her and give her a message of some sort if he thought it advisable. She was so cheerful that Lincoln said nothing.

Speed was married in mid-February. Almost at once he wrote Lincoln that he was happy, but that "something indescribably horrible" still haunted him. Three weeks after his marriage he wrote again. This time there was no reservation to his statement that he was far happier than he had ever expected to be. Although Lincoln received the admission with joy, he included a word of caution in his answer. "I cannot forbear once more to say," he wrote, "that I think it is even yet possible for your spirits to flag down and leave you miserable. If they should, don't fail to remember that they cannot long remain so." It is these sentences, preceding immediately the reference to Sarah, which give it added significance. "One thing I can tell you which I know you will be glad to hear, and that is that I have seen Sarah and scrutinized her feelings as well as I could, and am fully convinced she is far happier now than she has been for the last fifteen months past." In other words, if melancholy should again seize Speed, he could find some consolation in the fact that there was no longer reason for concern about Sarah.

Finally, there is the light shed on the matter by Speed's request that Sarah's name be suppressed. "I have erased a name which I do not wish published," he wrote when he transmitted Lincoln's letters to Herndon. "If I have failed to do it anywhere, strike it out when you come to it. That is the word Sarah." But why, when he was in the very act of revealing all he could about Lincoln's most serious love affair, should he be so careful to suppress the name of the participant in another, especially when he permitted the sentences conveying the hint to stand undeleted? It is difficult to answer this question if he were really making an attempt at suppression. On the other hand, if Speed wished the name deleted for reasons personal to himself, his action is entirely understandable.

But what of Sarah's own account of her relations with Lincoln? Is it strange that after the passage of

forty-seven years—her statement was made in 1888—
she should attach undue significance to her contact
with Lincoln? He had called on her, he had taken her
places, in all probability he had joked about marriage
with her—and now his fame was a household word.
It was no more than natural that she should look back
upon him as a suitor instead of a friend. Even if she
did remember correctly, there was great temptation in
the chance of gaining a measure of immortality by
joining her name with Lincoln rather than with the
now unknown Speed. The plain inferences of contemporary letters are entitled to more consideration than a
reminiscence so likely to be distorted by faulty memory or deliberate intent.

Sarah Rickard has no place in the story of Lincoln's
marriage.

Index

351

353